Local Authority Social Services

Local Authority Social Services

An Introduction

Edited by

Michael Hill

with contributions by
Bob Hudson, Stephen Mitchell,
Ian Shaw, Jane Tunstill

B BLACKWELL
Publishers

Copyright © Blackwell Publishers Ltd 2000
Editorial matter and arrangement copyright © Michael Hill 2000

First published 2000

2 4 6 8 10 9 7 5 3 1

Blackwell Publishers Ltd
108 Cowley Road
Oxford OX4 1JF
UK

Blackwell Publishers Inc.
350 Main Street
Malden, Massachusetts 02148
USA

British Library Cataloguing in Publication Data

A CIP catalogue record for this book is available from the British Library.

Library of Congress Cataloging-in-Publication Data has been applied for

ISBN 0-631-20946-8 (hbk)
ISBN 0-631-20947-6 (pbk)

Typeset in 10.5 on 12 pt Sabon
by Ace Filmsetting Ltd, Frome, Somerset
Printed in Great Britain by T. J. International Ltd, Padstow, Cornwall

This book is printed on acid-free paper

Contents

Figures

Tables

Contributors

Michael Hill is Visiting Professor of Social Policy at Goldsmiths College, University of London and joint editor (with Helen Jones) of the *Journal of Social Policy*. He is Emeritus Professor of Social Policy at the University of Newcastle on Tyne, having left that university in 1997 on taking early retirement. He is author of *Understanding Social Policy* (sixth edition to be published by Blackwell Publishers in 2000), *Social Policy: A Comparative Analysis* (1996), *The Policy Process in the Modern State* and other books.

Bob Hudson is Principal Research Fellow in the Community Care Division of the Nuffield Institute for Health at the University of Leeds. Prior to that he was a Visiting Fellow at the University of Durham, and Senior Lecturer in Social Policy at New College, Durham. He is currently engaged on a number of research and consultancy projects in the field of health and social care, with a particular focus on issues of inter-agency and inter-professional partnership.

Stephen Mitchell is a member of the Senior Civil Service and currently Head of the General Social Services Policy Branch in the Department of Health. He managed the Social Services White Paper team through the preparation and publication of *Modernising Social Services* in 1998, and the team responsible for the resultant Care Standards Bill in 1999/2000.

Ian Shaw is a Lecturer in Social Policy, and the Deputy Director of the Centre for Medical Sociology and Health Policy at the University of Nottingham. At the time of writing, he is involved in four research projects in the area of mental health: evaluating the role of the Mental Health Act Commission, GP referral practices, primary care and management of mental illness, and exploratory work examining associations between different forms of social deprivation and different patterns of 'mental ill health'.

Jane Tunstill is Professor of Social Work at Royal Holloway College, London University, where she has responsibility for qualifying and post qualifying social work education. She has undertaken a range of research studies on children in need/family support for the Department of Health and for child care voluntary organizations. She is a founder member of Making Research Count, a cross-university research dissemination project which aims to make social work research findings more easily accessible to local authorities.

Preface

This work for this book originated from a series of lectures I developed with Frank Tolan for a group of civil servants from Taiwan. We discovered that, while there are many books on social work and on aspects of the local authority social services task, including particularly community care, there was a lack of an up-to-date book which looks at local authority social services as a whole. Frank was at that time just leaving the Social Services Inspectorate and we started work on a book together. In the early stages of work on the book, it became clear that Frank's new career was developing in rather different directions, and he unfortunately decided that he could not continue on the project. This would have left me to cover topics on which I lacked expertise. We suggested that the best way forward would be to recruit a number of contributors to an edited volume. The first acknowledgement here must therefore go to Frank Tolan, for the key role he played in the early work on this volume.

Second, as editor, let me thank my contributors, who all delivered on time and put up with a range of queries and changes, designed to make the book hang together as a whole.

The book has taken rather longer to produce than was originally planned, not only because of the changes outlined above, but also because we became aware at an early stage that there were developments occurring in the Department of Health which ought to be taken into account if the book was not be out of date almost as soon as it was published. In that sense, the book has changed from an account of local authority social services in the wake of the child care legislation of 1989 and the community care legislation of 1990 to an exploration of the many new themes emerging at the end of the century, under challenges to local government from a New Labour leadership unwilling to take older institutional arrangements for granted. In dealing with that change, it has been valuable to have the advice of Stephen

Mitchell on policy developments. Long before he was approached to write a chapter himself, he gave Frank Tolan and myself much wise advice on issues we should take into account. Finally, I am grateful to Jill Landeryou of Blackwell Publishers for commissioning the original book and for the helpful way she dealt with the change of plan. Thanks are also due to other staff at Blackwell Publishers, including Sarah Falkus and Joanna Pyke, who have helped with the development of the manuscript, and to Jenny Lawson at First Class Publishing for her excellent handling of the copy editing and proof stages.

Michael Hill

Acknowledgements

Department of Health
- Table 5.2 Gross personal social services expenditure on older people by type of provision, 1997–98 (£million), *Personal Social Services Current Expenditure in England: 1997–98, Bulletin 1999*, 11, Table 2, p. 6. Copyright © 1999 Department of Health, London.
- Table 5.3 Day and domiciliary provision for older people 1997/8 (£million gross), *Personal Social Services Current Expenditure in England: 1997–98, Bulletin 1999*, 11, Table 4, p. 8. Copyright © 1999 Department of Health, London.
- Table 5.4 People with a physical disability: gross PSS expenditure, 1997–8 (£million), *Personal Social Services Current Expenditure in England: 1997–98, Bulletin 1999*, 11, Table 2, p.6. Copyright © 1999 Department of Health, London.

HMSO
- Table 3.3 Percentages of persons in the UK in various kinds of households by age and gender, 1994–95, *Social Trends*, 26, Office for National Statistics © Crown Copyright 1999.
- Table 3.5 Unemployment rates by gender and age, 1998 (UK), *Social Trends*, 29, Office for National Statistics © Crown Copyright 1999.
- Table 3.7   Percentages with various kinds of 'some' or 'severe' problems by age (sample survey data for Great Britain, 1996), *Living in Britain: Results from the 1996 General Household Survey*, Office for National Statistics © Crown Copyright 1998.
- Table 3.8 Percentages of elderly people unable to manage various activities on their own (sample survey data for Great Britain, 1996), *Living in Britain: Results from the 1996 General Household Survey*, Office for National Statistics © Crown Copyright 1998.
- Table 8.1 Net local authority personal social services expenditure in England relative to education expenditure and total expenditure (figures in £million) with percentages of the totals in brackets, *Annual Abstract of Statistics 1999 Edition*, Office for National Statistics © Crown Copyright 1999.

OECD
- Table 3.1 Actual and estimated percentages of the UK population in various age groups, *Ageing Populations* Copyright © 1988 OECD, Paris.

Part 1

Establishing the Main Concerns
of the Book

Chapter 1

What are Local Authority Social Services?

Michael Hill

Introduction

This chapter introduces this book by defining and describing its topic. It may seem strange that it is thought necessary to devote a whole chapter to this. There are two reasons for this. First, it is considered appropriate to offer a general description of local authority social services right at the beginning of the book so that, as the discussion moves into more detailed issues about policies, activities and organization, readers are quite clear about the basic tasks performed under that heading. Second, the social services responsibilities of local authorities are difficult to define, either in theory or in practice, because there are a range of complicated questions about both where personal responsibilities end and statutory ones begin, and about the relationships between local authority social services and other publicly provided services.

The 1970 Local Authority Social Services Act gives a specified group of local authorities (counties and unitary districts) duties to provide social services. This legislation applies only to England and Wales. Here, at least, it is possible to clear away one basic issue about the concerns of this book. It is a book about services in only two of the

four countries of the UK: England and Wales. There are similar services in Scotland, but they are defined as local authority *social work*
responsibilities, and operate with a slightly different statutory framework (which, of course, the new Scottish Parliament may, in due course,
make more radically different). The same is true of Northern Ireland,
except, there, social services do not even come under local authorities
but under appointed Health and Social Services Boards. Hence, while
much that will be said will apply also to Scotland and Northern Ireland, for the purposes of clarity, this account has been confined to
England and Wales.

Until very recently, one pragmatic way of answering the question
'What are local authority social services?' would have been to say:
'They are what local authority social services departments do.' Nowadays, that would be unhelpful because, in recent years, various local
authorities have decided to integrate social services work with other
activities, and some have distributed that work between more than
one department. It will be seen, later in the book, that a process of
organizational change is developing in this respect, which may well
accelerate in the near future.

An alternative approach to the question is to turn to the key legislation, in place at the time of writing, for help in defining the local authority social services task. The 1970 Local Authority Social Services
Act requires designated local authorities to establish social services
committees, to appoint a director of social services and to carry out a
range of functions specified in that statute. Most people, at that time,
regarded this as creating 'social services departments', as suggested in
the Seebohm Report (1968) but the Act merely talks about 'social
service functions'. Chapter 9 returns to this point, and chapter 10 indicates ways in which this Act may, in due course, be superseded.

A look at the 1970 Act does little to clarify what the social services
functions of a local authority are, since these only appear in the legislation in the rather technical legal form of a schedule of other earlier
Acts which were either partly incorporated in, or partly repealed by,
the Local Authority Social Services Act. Those other Acts, together
with measures passed after 1970, deal with more specific aspects of
social services' responsibilities. It is possible to identify groups of
statutes dealing with child care, care of elderly and disabled people
(including people with learning disabilities) and care of mentally ill
people.

In the case of child care, the 1989 Children Act has almost entirely
swept the previous legislation into a single new codified body. The
only readily apparent exception is in legislation dealing with its role in
adoption – the Adoption Act, 1976 – but already some subsequent

legislation has modified the 1989 Children Act, notably the 1991 Criminal Justice Act.

The statutory position with regard to the care of elderly and disabled people is more complicated. While the community care part of the 1990 National Health Services and Community Care Act radically changed this area of social services policy, it did not entirely sweep away either the sections of the 1948 National Assistance Act dealing with residential care or the earlier law relating to domiciliary care – principally the 1968 Health Services and Public Health Act. A separate Act also deals with social services powers to register and inspect independent sector residential homes. This is the 1984 Registered Homes Act, which rather casually updated earlier legislation and is now of considerable importance because of the growth of this sector and its role as the provider of places for social services departments. Impending legislation is, however, likely to change this; see pages 193–5.

Social services mental health care work, like the children's work, benefits from a single piece of legislation, effectively replacing what went before: the 1983 Mental Health Act.

In many of these Acts, there are clauses which give the Secretary of State the power to issue regulations amplifying or modifying aspects of the basic law. This enables more detailed adjustment without recourse to the elaborate process of passing a new Act. Technically regulations are 'passed' by Parliament, but the reality is that they are merely notified to it. There are many regulations put before Parliament every year. There are powers to scrutinize them, but only a minute fraction receive Parliamentary attention.

While a list of Acts is not sufficient to define what local social services authorities do, it does, however, indicate that the definition of the local authority social services task has been arrived at arbitrarily as a consequence of government decisions about the most appropriate agency for any particular task, bearing in mind the existence of widely canvassed alternatives (the probation service, the health service, sometimes the social security system or the education system and, perhaps, voluntary or for-profit agencies). Many of the implications of this fact are explored in the course of the book. However, the result of the decisions that have been taken is the bringing together of a reasonably coherent bundle of services. The responsibilities of the modern social services authorities can be defined as a general concern for social care or the *personal* social services. Personal is emphasized, both to introduce another common usage to define our concerns and to indicate the way in which the expression 'social services', used in the Act and in many definitions of local authority functions, should *not* be taken to indicate a concern about a wide spectrum of social policy. In various places in the book, it is necessary to insert the word 'personal' for the purposes of clarity. In everyday conversation, the expression social services is both used generically about *all* social policy and, specifically, to refer to social security.

A more concrete approach to the definitional problem can be attempted by

(a)   defining the main areas of concern, and
(b)   specifying some of the things that the authorities might do, but do not.

As far as (a) is concerned, the work of local authority social services can be identified as comprising child protection (services to prevent harm to children and to substitute for family care in the last resort), social care for elderly people no longer able to care for themselves, and care for a range of adults between these two groups who – because of physical disabilities, learning difficulties or mental illness – have difficulties in caring for themselves. As far as (b) is concerned, the statutory responsibilities of local authority social services have been set up in such a way as to try to draw a distinction between *social* care and *health* care. It is also the case (and a special feature of British personal social services by comparison with those of most other countries) that last resort income maintenance – or social assistance – is *not* included in their responsibilities.

Finally, it is important to bear in mind the extent to which statutory personal social services are conceived as 'last resort' services. This is clear enough in the field of child protection, where it is some sense or other 'family failure' that results in intervention by authorities. However, it is equally the case with adults (including elderly people) that a combination of philosophical objections to state intervention and a lack of state resources produces a situation in which strict tests of need are applied (which may include consideration of whether other family members are coping) and means tests are used, which often have the effect of confining much local authority help to those with limited incomes and capital.

The next three sections of this chapter pick up the points raised in the last two paragraphs.

● The first offers a brief concrete account of local authority social services activities, set out to ensure the reader proceeds with a reasonable degree of clarity about its subject matter, but without going deeply into the contemporary policy issues about these activities (which are discussed in the second section of the book).

- The second highlights some of boundary issues, between social services work and other areas of social and public policy.
- The third elaborates the point about 'last resort' services, exploring some of the definitional and philosophical issues that relate to it.

Social Services Work

One county authority offers a 'mission statement' for its social services activities:

> To enable people . . . with social care needs to secure quality services through systematic assessment of those needs and to enhance their choices about how those needs can be addressed through the development of a range of services in the statutory and independent sectors.

It is to be hoped that readers will not progress far into this book before they greet such a statement with 'Well, yes, that sounds very nice but what does it mean in practice?' Another authority, rather more concretely, speaks of its aim 'to provide high quality services to the most vulnerable people . . .[in its area] and to make their protection our highest priority' and then goes on to list who they help:

Vulnerable children, young people and their families
Vulnerable older people
Children with disabilities
People with a physical disability and/or sensory impairment
People with mental health needs
People with a learning difficulty
People affected by HIV/AIDS
People with drug or alcohol problems
Those who care for any of these people

Many authorities take the items in that list and divide them into two broad groups – services for children and services for adults, usually applying the label 'community care' to the latter. This division is influenced by the key roles played in defining the services by the 1989 Children Act and the 1990 National Health Service and Community Care Act. This book inevitably gives much attention to this division of the services into two groups, but, in part 2, it distinguishes mental health services from adult services as a whole. Mental health services are partly regulated by other key legislation and are, to some extent, organized separately from other services for adults.

The 1989 Children Act consolidated previous legislation on the protection of children. The complex legal framework in this Act tries to ensure that children are protected, while at the same time recognizing that public interventions into family life should be kept as low as possible. It carries forward a long-standing concern to minimize the likelihood of the removal of children from their family of origin. The Act identifies a wide range of things authorities can do to try to avoid taking children into direct care.

Most of the staff employed to investigate situations in which children may be at risk – of ill treatment, abuse or neglect – are trained social workers. Their authorities are required to maintain 'child protection registers' of children 'at risk' and to offer appropriate supportive services to these children and their families. In many cases, prevention of child abuse or neglect requires activities other than the institution of legal procedures to transfer formal responsibility for the care of children. Social workers have a number of ways in which they may try to do this; they may try to offer support to families – visiting regularly, making suggestions about how to deal with stresses in the household, listening and counselling, and generally responding to cries for help from families under pressure. In doing this, they may be able to mobilize resources: domestic help, day care for children, grants or loans, help in kind. They may also try to secure help for the family from other statutory organizations: for example, better housing or attention to educational or health problems. There may also be voluntary organizations that they can mobilize to help: support groups, and charitable help in cash or kind. Only a small proportion of children at risk are taken away from their families; see pages 70–1.

The most Draconian powers available to child care workers are those which enable them to activate procedures under which children may be taken into the 'legal' care of a local authority because parents are unable to care for them or are deemed to be unfit to care for them. Care decisions are the responsibility of the courts, but most action to take children into care will have been initiated by social workers in the social services authorities. Once a child has been taken into care, the local authority will seek to ensure a settled future for him or her. In some cases, this will mean return to parental care under supervision, but where this is not possible, foster care is widely used. Hence, institutional care is likely to be regarded as a temporary expedient in many cases, allowing time for the situation to be assessed and longer-term plans to be made. Hence, a large proportion of the children who are in legal terms 'in the care of the local authorities' are not in fact in any kind of institution. Indeed, a significant proportion of them are living in their parents' homes; see the further discussion of this on pages 68–72.

Among the children who may be in need of statutory care is a group of generally older children who are considered to be out of parental control. Under the 1969 Children and Young Persons Act, local authorities acquired increased responsibilities for the care of children brought before the courts for delinquent acts. The object of this legislation was to move away from labelling young offenders as criminals, and to make the issue for decision by the juvenile courts one about responsibility for care rather than punishment for crime. Social services authorities may now have to undertake the 'supervision' of such children, or they may be given legal custody of them under a 'care order'. They may fulfil the parental responsibilities entailed in a care order in a variety of ways, including the supervision of a child within a residential institution.

Where the care responsibilities of local authorities are discharged through the use of foster parents, payment will be made, and the arrangements will be supervised by social workers. Some children in the various forms of care may eventually be legally adopted into another family. Social services authorities have responsibilities to organize and supervise adoption procedures, although, sometimes, these may be subcontracted to private agencies.

Local authorities may provide day care for children, and have responsibilities to supervise that provided by others, including play groups and child minding. Local authority day nursery places are few, and are generally given only to children from deprived backgrounds. This is essentially a resource for efforts to prevent child abuse and neglect. In recent years, there has been a considerable growth of private provision for day care for young children – daily minding, day nurseries and playgroups. Day nurseries should not be confused with nursery schools, provided by education authorities.

Moving now to care services for adults, the White Paper, which preceded the 1990 National Health Service and Community Care Act, started by saying: 'Community care means providing the services and support which people who are affected by problems of ageing, mental illness, mental handicap or physical or sensory disability need to be able to live in their own homes, or in "homely" settings in the community' (Department of Health, 1989a, para 1.1). The fact that the last part of that definition includes 'homely' settings in the community, and that it has long been the aspiration that all social care institutions should be 'homely', means that this definition embraces all care *except* that provided by hospitals and nursing homes. Moreover, social services authorities now also place people in the latter.

It is also reasonable to ask what is implied by 'services and support' in that definition. There are two points about this.

1   First, a distinction is generally drawn between social care and health
    care, in which case the latter (even if given 'in the community') will
    not be included in definitions of community care; this is an import-
    ant and complex issue that arises at various points in this book.
2   Second, it is not clear who is to provide or pay for this. An outsider
    reading that definition may jump to the incorrect conclusion that
    it is the state which is the sole provider and carrier of the costs of
    community care. That is definitely not the case. In reality, anyone
    who seeks any form of community care has to go through rigorous
    tests of need and means before receiving help from the public sec-
    tor. Many who are clearly 'affected by problems of ageing, mental
    illness etc. . . .' (as in the above definition) fail those tests and have
    either to go without services and support, or pay for them or re-
    ceive them from their family and neighbours.

Social services authorities have a wide range of responsibilities for
the social care of adults. The services they may provide, either directly
or through contracts with private and voluntary sector providers, include residential care, home care services (help in the home with domestic tasks or the supply of meals), adaptations to houses and flats to
make it easier for handicapped people to live in them, and advice and
help on how to deal with the practical and emotional problems vulnerable people face. They may provide or support day centres where
elderly and/or handicapped people can go for company, social activities, occupational therapy, perhaps cheap midday meals, and perhaps
some aid or advice. For younger handicapped people, and particularly
for people with learning difficulties, there are centres where company
and therapy may be accompanied by productive activities.

The social services authorities are also, at the time of writing, responsible for the registration and regular inspection of all private and
voluntary care homes. They have powers to cancel a registration. Home-
owners have a right to an appeal to a tribunal against refusal of registration or de-registration. However, the government is, at the time of
writing, introducing legislation to set up an independent Care Commission to take over this inspection task and to regulate all homes
(including those for children) and domiciliary care providers. This is
discussed further in chapter 10.

Before ending this introductory account of the work of social services departments, a comment is appropriate on social work. It is almost as difficult to establish a definition of 'social work' as of 'social
services'. There is a general popular sense of the concept of social work,
as giving help to people with social problems, which would embrace
almost everything social services authorities do, but would also em-

brace a wide range of other public and voluntary care work. An alternative is to confine the use of the term 'social worker' to people who have had a specific professional training leading to a publicly recognized formal qualification; see pages 81–2 for a discussion of some of the controversy about this. The fact is that local authorities use people with a variety of social skills, in a range of situations in which a capacity to assess social needs, recommend measures and use their own interpersonal skills to give help if necessary; by no means all of these people have formal social work qualifications.

Official data on personal social services staff in local authorities in England indicates that there are just over 33,000 'social work staff'. This is just under 15 per cent of total staff. There is no indication as to the proportion of these social work staff that have formal qualifications in social work. Over 40 per cent of them are in work with children and another 27 per cent are in what are described as 'health settings/specialist teams' (Department of Health, 1999j, table 4). Broadly, it will be found that most of the staff engaged in the assessment of children at risk, and the supervision and placement of those children, and in mental health work will be qualified social workers. Outside those areas, the skills of staff will be varied, and much routine service delivery work – in the residential and domiciliary care for elderly people, for example – will be carried out by staff with quite low qualifications. Chapter 9 explores these issues a little further.

Table 1.1 sets out some data on local authority social services expenditure in England, giving an idea of the relative importance of this

Table 1.1 Personal social services expenditure in England, 1997–98, by client group[a] (£ millions)

	Elderly people	Children	Learning Disability	Physical Disability	Mental health	Other[b]
Senior management and purchasing	100	150	30	30	20	130
Care assessment/ Care management	280	350	60	80	90	90
Day care	1,590	1,060	500	400	190	30
Residential care	2,940	2,290	1,320	700	210	20
Totals	4,910	2,260	1,320	700	510	270

[a] Figures calculated from Department of Health (1999i, table 2)
[b] In the 'other' column £90m unattributed expenditure has been put in the 'care management' row.

wide range of work – classified using a matrix that enables work with different groups to be identified on one dimension and different kinds of activities to be shown on the other. It highlights how expenditure on elderly people and on child care dominates.

Social Services and Other Areas of Social Policy

Statements about social services policy indicate, as has been shown, concerns about the protection of the vulnerable, but other services would seem to have similar concerns. This is most obviously true of the National Health Service, but, equally, it can be argued that many other services have some responsibilities in this respect. In particular, it may be pointed out that education services have wide-ranging duties to children. It may also be argued that the police and criminal justice system has responsibilities to the vulnerable, both as victims of others and as the sometimes disturbed and inadequate perpetrators of criminal acts. Public services which offer specific benefits to their 'customers' – pensions, allowances, housing – have some responsibilities to those who have difficulties in obtaining or using these benefits. In other words, it is not self-evident that there is a need for a specific group of public social services – labelled 'personal' – to be delivered through professional or bureaucratic systems, separate from other public policy systems. Additionally, there are related issues about the responsibilities of private organizations, which may be enforced through public law. For example, there are the responsibilities of employers towards vulnerable employees.

One of the reasons that comparative studies of personal social services (Hill, 1996) are much less well developed than comparative studies of health or social security policy is precisely that countries differ in how they draw the lines between personal social services and other services. In chapter 2, it is shown that, even in England and Wales, the boundaries have been drawn differently at different points in time; and, elsewhere in this book, it is suggested that new ideas about how to organize local authority services (including the move away from the idea of a specific social services department already mentioned in this chapter) and new ideas about the health/social services boundary are already having some effect.

In this discussion, the analogy of a large, originally shapeless, river running through a delta is appropriate – like the Rhine as it runs through the Netherlands – which has been channelled and controlled. Over time, the channels were modified, in response to new contingencies or approaches to control emerged. In Britain, state health services, social security services and personal social services, as is shown in chapter 2, all have origins in the Poor Law, but have been separated into separate streams. Moreover, while education and policing have rather different origins, there was much intermingling between these streams of activity in their early days. Modification of the separate streams has occurred, and is still occurring.

In looking at the situation today, it is appropriate to distinguish between those other services that are within local authorities and those that are outside. Education and social services are both located in the same tier of local government, but they are both large and, in most respects, separate activities. Their main area of overlap is the shared concern for child welfare. More specific issues here are the care of the pre-school child and questions that arise when a child has problems that impact on his or her performance or behaviour at school. In the pre-school years, day nurseries and nursery schools operate side by side, but there are, increasingly, shifts towards more integrated services. In fact, at the time this book is going to press, the government has announced proposals to bring the supervision of these pre-school activities under the education inspectorate (Ofsted).

Children with severe learning difficulties were once looked after in personal social services institutions and not sent to school; this is no longer the case. When they leave school, however, liaison between the two services in respects of training and day care is important.

The social welfare issues highlighted by truancy and bad behaviour in schools are mostly still handled by staff attached to education departments; in some authorities, though, such services are linked to the personal social services and, in all authorities, there has to be collaboration in the light of the ultimate child protection responsibilities of social services personnel.

The pioneers of social housing in Britain believed it necessary to have their own welfare services to deal with disruptive tenants and those who had problems in paying rents. The modern view is that practical housing issues and social care issues should as far as possible be kept separate, though that may be difficult where – as in sheltered housing – the tenancy contract is for a combination of rent and social care. Outside the unitary local authorities, housing and personal social services are in different tiers of local government. Within the unitary authorities, there is, despite the relative lack of overlap between services, a number of authorities who have chosen to unify the management of social services and housing; see chapter 9.

Outside local government, there are three areas of overlap to be discussed. One of these, that between social services and health, features considerably in this book. The next section explores the main issues about this. Another – the overlap with social security – is examined in chapter 7. Britain is relatively unusual in having 'nationalized' all social assistance in the 1930s and 1940s. Hence, while in many countries, social assistance is a personal social services function of considerable importance, in Britain, the issues are all about liaison between personal social services and social security, and the implications of social security policies for local authority charging and means-testing practices.

The third area of overlap is between local authority social services and the criminal justice system. Police are obviously brought into involvement with local authorities when abuse or neglect (particularly of children) comes to their attention, and there are then some issues to be resolved about the relationship between the duties and powers of social services staff and the need to prosecute criminal behaviour. The prosecution of crimes committed by children brings social workers into courts as witnesses, and court decisions may include the referral of children to local authority social services care. The position in England and Wales is complicated by the fact that the courts have their own social care service – the probation service – which may become involved in these activities. In Scotland, the role of the probation service is carried out by the social work authorities, and there is a special procedure to deal with juvenile crime, 'children's hearings', at which the evidence and advice coming from social work staff is important. Finally, interventions to deal with mentally ill people who are acting in ways that involve danger to themselves and to others requires close liaison between police and social workers, and the latter are also involved in the care and after-care of mentally ill people who are compulsorily admitted to hospitals after committing serious crimes.

Social Services and Health

There are many ways in which social services and health policy interact or overlap. Picking up again the analogy of an originally shapeless river, the efforts to separate the health and social services streams have been difficult. From time to time, the banks of the neat separate channels have been threatened and, perhaps, breached.

In the case of health and social services, the relationship is between two caring services where there is often no easy way of drawing a distinction. There is a notion that one may distinguish between problems for which medicine may offer a solution and other aspects of human welfare. However, that distinction depends very much on the claims that doctors may make for their skills and our willingness to accept those claims. It is, moreover, perhaps more apparent in efforts to draw a distinction today, than in the past, as scepticism about medicine grows and as the health service tries to reduce the demands on it.

The close links between health and social services has been acknowledged in the decision of central government to put the two services under the same ministry in England, and in the same department in the Scottish Office. In Northern Ireland, when many of the powers of local government were brought under centrally controlled 'boards', the government went even further in creating four combined 'health and social services boards' to deliver services.

The issues about the relationship between local authority social services and health services can best be explored by examining some of the key areas in which services overlap or co-operation is needed between them. Many of these issues are given further attention in part 2, but are introduced briefly here.

Neglect, non-accidental injury to, and abuse of, children is frequently discovered by doctors. General practitioners (GPs), asked to deal with specific maladies may suspect underlying problems. Accident and emergency departments may be called on to deal with child injuries that they suspect were caused by adult maltreatment or neglect. Other health service workers who are particularly likely to come across child neglect and abuse are health visitors, who have a specific statutory responsibility for the care of pre-school children. These workers visit mothers of young children to give advice on child rearing, and run clinics at which the growth of infants is monitored. Health visitors are health service employees, working from local clinics and often attached to GPs' surgeries. GPs are likely to refer issues about children (and sometimes about adults, too) to them, where health and social care issues are evidently closely intertwined.

GPs and hospital doctors clearly have to make diagnostic judgements about the causes of injuries and other abnormalities. There is thus a two-way flow on the issues outlined above. Health practitioners may spot problems where they feel that an investigation by a social worker is necessary, and social workers may encounter issues where they need medical confirmation of their suspicions about the cause of a problem. One particular issue – that was very much brought to attention by a public enquiry in Cleveland (Butler-Sloss, 1988) – concerns evidence of sexual abuse, where diagnosis may be important and (as this case indicated) controversial.

Once child abuse is suspected, continued vigilance is necessary. Sometimes, a health service worker is best placed to maintain a watching brief; sometimes a social worker is better placed. In many cases, both departments accumulate evidence on this problem; it is important that they share that evidence, both formally through case conferences and informally.

All this adds up to a range of situations in which staff from both social services and health services (together with others such as the police and school teachers) may need to collaborate and pool their evidence. Such pooling takes a formal shape where it is deemed necessary to call a case conference, to explore the evidence and make recommendations. Hence, there has been a need for procedures to be developed in the areas covered by local authority social services departments to facilitate this joint work.

Chapter 6 looks at aspects of services for mentally ill people in which social services collaboration with health services is of vital importance. One of those is the particularly fraught circumstances in which compulsory hospitalization and treatment of mentally ill people is required. In these, despite the fact that the diagnostic skills of doctors are required, the legal responsibility for the decision, resting on a determination of the extent to which the ill person may be a danger to others or themselves, falls on social workers.

Where mentally ill people are in hospital, social workers still have important roles in investigating the extent to which appropriate care arrangements can be made back in the community, assessing the risks involved in this and preparing people for return. This extends to a further legal role of giving advice on this topic to their medical colleagues, and to Mental Health Tribunals, where compulsory detention is involved.

In the community itself, care of the mentally ill involves a partnership between psychiatrists, community mental nurses and local authority employed social workers. Actual roles depend on individual needs but may also be influenced by local resources and local service patterns. To put this last remark another way, it may often be difficult to detect a distinction between the roles of community psychiatric nurses and social workers; who does what being determined as much by established sharing patterns as by any self-consciously determined role distinctions.

In relation to the care of people with learning difficulties, there has been a dramatic change. Earlier in the twentieth century, the care of people with severe learning difficulties ('mentally handicapped people' in earlier terminology or, even earlier, 'mental defectives') was principally in large institutions and was the ultimate responsibility of medically trained people. Now, under 'normalization' policies, such people are expected to be cared for in their own homes, with hostels (providing as far as possible a normal environment) for those who cannot be cared for by their own families. There has, thus, been a transfer of care responsibilities to local authority social services. In many respects, the main 'frontier' is now with the education system (which is expected to provide schooling for all children, however handicapped) rather than with the health service.

However, boundary issues with health do remain. While it has been appropriate to see this issue as no longer a 'medical' one, there remain concerns which are within the health service's domain. Some of the conditions that contribute to learning difficulties can benefit from medical attention, and there is a range of borderline issues that arise because of the coexistence of physical with intellectual problems or of mental illness with learning difficulties or because learning difficulties have medically treatable causes.

Before the establishment of unified local authority social services, there had been a quite extensive social work service within hospitals (in addition to the psychiatric social work developed in psychiatric hospitals). This service had its roots in the development, early in the twentieth century, of a distinctive semi-profession of 'almoners' in the hospital system. Almoners were responsible for assessing the capacity of patients to pay fees in the private and voluntary hospitals. With the coming of the National Health Service, almoners shifted much of their attention to issues about the social support available on the discharge of patients from hospital. Some also developed skills in helping individuals and their families to cope – in both a practical and emotional sense – with the implications of terminal illnesses, amputations and other disabilities.

Social work services in hospital were patchy. After the 1970 Local Authority Social Services Act, it seemed logical to take them out of the health service. Local authorities had then to decide to what extent they would move such services out of hospital, in the physical sense, as well as in the hierarchical sense. Clearly, hospital social workers need to work closely with colleagues in the community, inasmuch as they are particularly concerned with provisions for discharged patients.

Regardless of the actual administrative arrangements, liaison between the health service and local authority social services remains important wherever patients are being discharged from hospital in situations in which substantial support services are needed in the community. The whole issue has, in fact, been exacerbated by reductions in the time patients are retained in hospital. Inasmuch as the modern hospital expects to discharge most of its patients as soon as radical medical interventions are completed, this generates a wide range of community care issues. Some of these may be deemed still to be health care concerns. GPs will resume the overall responsibility for their patients, hospital outpatient staff will expect to continue treatment and, in some circumstances, home nursing will be provided. However, none of these services will provide the practical care and support that many still very sick people need. Hence, the point of discharge from hospital is an important one for the mobilization of social services, and, accordingly, liaison and collaboration between the services is important at this time.

The reaction to that last paragraph may well be: so there is a need for close co-operation in relationship to discharge from hospital, but why should there be problems about this boundary? What makes it problematical is that there are very high cost issues for the two authorities in relation to these boundary issues, and, accordingly, some crucial issues about rationing between priorities. On the hospital side, the problem is often rather stridently identified as the phenomena of 'bed blocking'. A patient may be consuming the expensive resources of the hospital system unnecessarily, occupying a bed that is needed for someone more seriously ill. On the social services side, the discharged patient may be competing for scarce resources with others with comparable needs who are not entering 'the system' by way of a hospital. There is resentment that health personnel, or more particularly doctors, may presume to 'prescribe' services without reference to anyone else's priorities. The 1990 National Health Service and Community Care Act makes clear the social services' responsibilities for pre-discharge assessment, but that may still leave the health service with unsatisfactory consequences when little community support is offered or when there are delays in assessment. The whole issue is made more difficult by falling resources and rising political pressures for results on both sides of the boundary. These boundary issues are explored in chapter 5.

At the time of writing, the inspection and registration of care homes is the responsibility of local authority social services departments. Health authorities have the related responsibility for nursing homes. One response to problems about the boundary between the two kinds of homes (desirable as far as the need to minimize disruption for people's lives are concerned but still difficult to deal with in practice for the reasons outlined above) is the 'dual-registered' home, offering nursing care to its most ill residents. Given both the presence of these homes and the desirability of some consistency of response on registration issues between health authorities and social services authorities, in some areas, joint inspection and registration units have been set up involving staff from both authorities, working together on inspection and registration issues. Planned changes to the system, discussed on pages 193–5, deal with some of these issues.

The final issue for consideration in this section concerns the roles of GPs, and to some extent also the roles of other community-based health authority staff – particularly health visitors. Primary health care practitioners (particularly GPs) are people to whom we turn when confronted by medical problems of many kinds. Some people will even see their GP as someone to whom they will take social problems. There is obviously a difficult line to be drawn in many cases between problems for which a health service based solution may be appropriate and ones where it may not. There are debates both within the medical profession and outside, about situations in which the prescription of tranquillizers may or may not be an appropriate response to stress. In any case, there will be many situations in which appropriate remedial action may consist of a combination of medical treatment and other kinds of help or advice. All this puts primary health care practitioners into situations in which, as well as being gatekeepers to health services, they may also be referral agents to other services and, in particular, to personal social services. There are sensitivities here about the relationship between a high paid and high prestige profession and social services staff. An effective relationship between the agencies, of benefit to their clients, requires attention to be given to ways of sharing information and understandings of each other's roles and the development of mechanisms that will facilitate appropriate referrals in both directions. Organizational responses to these issues are discussed in chapter 8.

Social Services as Last Resort Services

As far as some of the activities of local authority social services are concerned, the notion that they are 'services of last resort' seems fairly self-evident. Most work with children – other than handicapped children – only arises when there is child neglect or abuse. The majority of parents and children have no encounters with child protection services. Many of the services for adults are only available to those who are handicapped, mentally ill or have severe learning difficulties, and, even in respect to these services, strict rationing procedures may limit access. However, from their superficial descriptions, most other services would seem to be of more universal availability. Most parents of pre-school children could be interested in a place for a child at a day nursery and, at the other end of life, many old people reach a stage where they need domestic help or even residential care. Yet, in practice, as is shown more explicitly in chapter 3, the supply of these services is far short of the apparent need.

Anyone who seeks any form of social services community care has to face two rigorous tests of need before receiving help from the public sector. Many who would seem to be 'in need' fail those tests; they have either to go without services and support, or pay for them, or receive them from their family and neighbours.

The first test concerns the extent of the problems from which an individual suffers. The scarcity of publicly funded or provided services means that many who may be considered as in need of services cannot receive them. Rationing occurs in terms of severity of need.

The second test concerns capacity to pay for services. Almost all social care services are rationed by means tests, taking into account income and perhaps assets as well. What this implies is (a) the possibility that someone given a publicly provided service will, in fact, be paying all or much of the cost of that service, (b) that, consequently, many people will purchase services on the private market rather than seek an assessment of their needs from the public care provision agency, and (c) many will be deterred by expected costs and will manage without special services, or rely on intensified family care.

Underlying these two approaches to rationing lie important ideological or philosophical questions. In Britain, clearly, there is strong support for the universal availability of free health care or education, but, in the case of the personal social services, the argument for this form of universalism is likely to be opposed by people who argue either that care services should be purchased in the market or that families should care for their disadvantaged members. Obviously, few who take these positions would take an absolute view that under no circumstance should the state offer personal social services. Rather, they would stress the need for the erection of hurdles that limit access to care to situations in which money is unavailable and the family is unable to take on further caring burdens. These people will be joined by many more who, though more sympathetic to the provision of public care, will argue that, in the face of public sector resource constraints, rationing decisions must take into account the other ways in which care may be provided.

Social services authorities face difficult questions about the most appropriate use for scarce resources. These questions are, however, complicated by the inevitable anomalies and inconsistencies which arise when rationing decisions in relation to individual situations are taken by a wide range of decision makers in a diverse selection of local authorities, with responsibilities for only some of the public care services. In the course of this book, these issues are encountered again in various forms. In particular, they emerge in the differences between National Health Service rationing criteria and personal social services rationing criteria (already mentioned above) and in some of the concerns about territorial justice within a locally administered national system.

In evaluating the 'last resort' role played by local authority social services departments, there is a need to take into account philosophical issues about the respective roles of individuals, families, communities and the state. It is important to recognize that the 'last resort' role means that the conditions under which personal social services operate will tend to be determined by other social institutions. Groups who are the victims of discrimination in society – women, ethnic minorities, disabled people – figure significantly among the recipients of social services. Authorities need therefore to be particularly vigilant to combat discrimination within their own services; but those who receive, control, or work within those services will be in a weak position from which to challenge the factors that influence the vulnerability and poverty which determines need.

Conclusions

The object of this chapter is to give the reader a picture of the services that are discussed more fully in the rest of the book. It shows that it is not surprising that many people are far from sure what local authority social services are, since efforts to define this sector of work tend to involve either fine sounding generalizations about care for the vulnerable or a list of groups who may receive help. Furthermore, these definitions do not easily explain why some of the things social services authorities do are not done by other parts of the social policy system, or enable us to establish where the boundaries lie between systems. The concluding discussion also suggests that the matter is further clouded by the way in which strict rationing criteria make publicly provided or funded personal social services very much last resort ones.

The next two chapters in this first part of the book amplify what has been said in this chapter. Chapter 2 looks at the historical process by which the present package of activities emerged. Chapter 3 explores the social context, to give further clues to the extent of the gap between potential need and actual provision, and to highlight the social considerations that influence that gap. These three introductory chapters prepare the reader for the more detailed consideration of local authority social services activities in part 2, and the examination of issues about the structure and the future development of the system in part 3.

Chapter 2

Origins of the Local Authority Social Services

Michael Hill

- ● **Introduction**
- ● **Personal Social Services before 1948**
- ● **Developments in the 1940s**
- ● **1948 to 1971**
- ● **1971 to 1990**
- ● **Conclusions**

Introduction

The modern local authority social services system came into existence in 1971. In some respects, therefore, an historical section for this book could start there, or, it could start just a little further back still, in 1948, when two crucial pieces of legislation – the Children Act and the National Assistance Act – gave local authorities clear responsibilities for some forms of social care. It could go even further, to 1929, when a Local Government Act passed the responsibilities of the Poor Law to local government. In fact, it goes, but only in a brief way, further back. This is because, to understand some of the complexities of statutory personal social services today, it is important to think about why they are such a modern creation. In particular, an examination of the way in which statutory responsibilities for social services emerged helps with the understanding of two things:

1 The limited (and residual) form many contemporary services take
2 The way in which personal social services are intertwined with both social security provisions and with health care

So, the next section of this chapter deals with the way in which relevant services emerged before 1948. It is then followed by a section on the 1948 legislation. Next, there is a section on developments between 1948 and the setting up of local authority social services in 1971. Finally, there is a brief discussion about the evolution of these new authorities between 1971 and two pieces of legislation – the 1989 Children Act and the 1990 National Health Service and Community Care Act – which have significantly reshaped the duties of local authorities.

Personal Social Services before 1948

The best way to approach the issue of antecedents to modern statutory social services is to explore why they are so recent an addition to public sector responsibilities. Perhaps the main answer to this question is that, until very recently, personal care problems have been seen as matters to be handled by individuals and their families. Children have been seen as the responsibility of their parents – one might almost say as the 'property' of their parents. The care of adults with problems has been seen as a matter for the extended family. To this general answer might be added the demographic facts that, until the late nineteenth century, persons with disabilities seldom lived long and the number of people reaching old age was low; however, this would be a little too glib an answer. Earlier generations were not altogether indifferent to exceptional care problems, which families could not or would not handle unaided. Orphans, for example, figure widely in Victorian novels as objects of concern to extended families, to neighbours and to charitable organizations. They also appear in the care of the Poor Law, the most famous example being Dickens' *Oliver Twist*.

Charitable institutions have a long history. The medieval churches played an important role as social care institutions of the last resort. After the Reformation in Britain, individual charities emerged. Some of these still exist (organizations like the Thomas Coram Foundation), while others have left a lasting record in the form of buildings such as almshouses and hospitals.

The second half of the nineteenth century saw an enormous flowering of charitable ventures. Many of these sought to add domiciliary care and social work to the institution-based efforts of earlier organizations. A concern developed about the lack of co-ordination between charities and the Charity Organization Society (COS) was founded in 1869 to tackle this problem. It 'pioneered in England the practice of case-work operating in some German towns' which 'entailed a serious attempt to analyse the nature of the problem confronting the individual or the family and to achieve a lasting solution without removing the clients from their familiar environment' (Thane, 1982, p. 22).

Concerns for the welfare of elderly people tended to take the form of the recognition of the case for income enhancement, leading eventually to demands for state pensions (Gilbert, 1966). By contrast – perhaps because of the dominance of the view that parents should normally work to support their children – charitable concerns about children began to focus on issues of neglect and ill treatment, contesting the view that children were their parents' property. Doctor Barnardo's, founded in 1869 like the COS, together with denomination-based children's societies, pioneered the development of institutional care for children; perhaps more important in the long run was the role the National Society for the Prevention of Cruelty to Children (NSPCC) began to play in 1884 as a pioneer of interventions to prevent the ill-treatment of children. The particular importance of the NSPCC is that it combined efforts to rescue children from ill-treatment and neglect with lobbying to secure more effective child protection legislation. While earlier legislation had been designed to protect children (the 1872 Infant Life Protection Act, for example), it was ineffective in the absence of any enforcement authorities other than the police and the Poor Law boards. The NSPCC secured the passing of legislation in 1889, 1904 and 1908 and played an important role in its enforcement (Hendrick, 1994).

This development of charitable activity ran alongside a statutory response to welfare – the Poor Law. In any account of the Poor Law social care, income maintenance and health care emerge as (by modern standards) very much mixed together. The Poor Law's origins lie in the sixteenth century, but it was legislation in 1834 that established a system that was to survive until the 1940s. The central concern of the 1834 legislation was to try to restore the principle, which had been undermined by extensions of cash relief, that help for the poor should only be given in institutions (workhouses) where all able-bodied persons were required to work for their keep yet not achieve a standard of living superior to that of the poorest class of free labourer. At the same time, it was recognized that both children and disabled elderly people would need to be treated slightly differently to the able-bodied poor. Thus, workhouses provided a form of institutional social care. In some circumstances – in the absence of any other public provisions for the health care of the poor – they also began to develop as hospitals. It is important to remember that the idea of a distinction between social care and health care is a comparatively modern one; indeed, as chapter 1 suggests, it is still not an easy distinction to make.

However, there were also other public policies, in addition to the Poor Law, which began to shape the services we now regard as the personal social services. Legislation was enacted to provide institutional facilities for people who were mentally ill and for the mentally handicapped or, in modern terminology, people with learning difficulties. These were influenced by fear of these two groups: of the mentally-ill as dangerous and of the mentally handicapped as persons who – in an era in which eugenic thinking was dominant – should be prevented from breeding. The essential public response was to provide secure institutions and to see the care of people in those institutions as the responsibility of the health care professions (though profession is much too grand a word to apply to the majority of people who did the everyday work of care within these places!) (Jones, 1972).

These hospitals were made the responsibility of local government. Local authorities also had a range of community health care responsibilities. These came from nineteenth-century public health legislation, which enabled authorities to take preventative responsibilities to deal with infectious diseases and to provide hospitals for mentally ill people. Early twentieth-century legislation creating some community health services – community midwifery and health visiting, in particular – added to the local services set up in the counties and county boroughs under the leadership of 'medical officers of health' (Lewis, 1986). Indeed, a flurry of legislation concerned with the conditions of Britain's children that occurred in the first decade of the twentieth century provided two alternative approaches to replace or supplement the care offered by the Poor Law and by charities. The community health services were one such, working through health clinics and health visitors. The other was the Boards of Education, which had secured powers to provide health care to children and to supply them with meals.

In 1929, the government brought the Poor Law under the control of local government. Local authorities were required to set up 'public assistance committees' to administer the Poor Law. This transfer of powers brought the institutions that had evolved from the old workhouses into the hands of authorities who could more effectively bring them up to date. This was particularly important for the hospitals, since now a unified public service could be provided. It had comparatively little impact on social care.

Clearly, at this point in history, an integrated local government controlled health and social care system could have been created. This seemed a possibility until Aneurin Bevan, in establishing the National Health Service in the 1940s, rejected the case for local government control over hospitals.

Equally, after the 1929 Act, Britain seemed to be travelling along a path followed by other countries, of constructing an integrated social care and social assistance system. However, legislation in 1934, setting up a national body for the administration of social assistance for the unemployed, started a process of separating 'cash' and 'care'. Further legislation in 1940 and 1948 completed that process.

On the other hand, as far as the protection of children was concerned the situation was very confused. As the committee which examined this area of policy after the War observed, 'the problem of providing for children deprived of a normal home life has not hitherto been dealt with as a single one' (Curtis Committee, 1946, para. 423).

Developments in the 1940s

Personal social services was an area of public policy scarcely identified as needing attention in the Labour Party's manifesto for the 1945 election. It was, at that time, an area of public policy that was largely unpoliticized. Yet, some important innovations occurred. These were made necessary by one of Labour's political commitments, to sweep away the last vestiges of the Poor Law. While it saw this as principally a measure to reform social assistance, it had to deal with the fact that the Poor Law authorities had care responsibilities too. The key measures were two pieces of legislation: the Children Act and the National Assistance Act. Both were enacted in 1948.

The 1948 Children Act was a direct consequence of a sequence of events starting from a child care scandal during the war. A child, Denis O'Neill, was killed by his foster father in 1945, and an enquiry into his death (Monckton Enquiry, 1945) found that the existing legislation did not define a clear division of responsibility between the education authorities and the Poor Law. As a response to this, the government set up a wider investigation into the services for deprived and neglected children (Curtis Committee, 1946). This recommended that there should be set up, within each county and county borough, a Children Committee with its own chief officer and trained staff. It should be the duty of this committee and department to investigate cases of child neglect and to take formal steps to bring children in need of protection into the care of the local authority. Then, once children were in its care, the local authority was expected to concern itself with the normal development of the child acting in a realistic sense *in loco parentis* (Packman, 1975, ch. 1).

Here, then, was a proposal to deal with most of the residual parts of the Poor Law concerned with children. The 1948 Children Act enacted these recommendations. In doing so, the government placed central responsibility for children's services with the Home Office. It has been suggested that it did this to try to ensure that this area of policy would be given single-minded attention. It might not have secured this within its obvious alternative bases at that time: the education and health departments. Certainly, the Ministry of Health made a bid for it (Means and Smith, 1985, p. 135).

Within the local authorities, the new children departments were an entirely new concept. Packman (1975, pp. 17–18) reflects interestingly on the early experiences of two such departments, showing how the Home Office took a strong line to influence their work, but also showing what puny organizations they were initially:

> For more than six months it [the Oxfordshire committee] resisted Home Office pressures to unite with Oxford City . . . It also tried to put the new department in the hands of an 'administrative officer' (male) with a Children's Officer (female) as his subordinate. This was vetoed by the Home Office – the intention of the Children Act being clear on this point. Finally, it tried to appoint someone without what the Home Office believed to be 'the qualification for the post'. Central government won that battle, and the first approved Children's Officer took up her duties in October 1948. . . . she was to be assisted by one 'boarding-out officer'.

In Devon, Packman (1975, p. 18) reports a smoother start with a Children's Officer acquiring a staff of nine by the time the Act was implemented, five of whom were transferred from the education and welfare departments. Compare these departments with the modern social services departments as described in chapter 8!

With a set of specific proposals in mind for children, the other welfare service part of the dismantled Poor Law for which a 'home' was needed was services for elderly and handicapped people. This is where the 1948 National Assistance Act was important. It also made the top tier of local government the responsible authorities. However, the specific proposal for children seems to have led the government to rule out the idea of a combined welfare department. In any case, as Means and Smith (1985) show, the government's view of its aim here was the limited one of transferring residential care. It was not recognized, at that time, that there might be other ways of fulfilling these 'welfare' responsibilities without the use of residential care.

1948 to 1971

The 1948 legislation normally led to the setting up of two separate departments in the local authorities: children's and welfare. However, the latter was sometimes linked with a third local government social policy function – the running of community health services – in a joint health and welfare department. Where that linking did not occur, such rudimentary care services for the mentally ill as there were remained separate from the rest of 'welfare' in the health department. This separation of services was to become regarded as a problem.

However, before that issue reached the agenda, another emerged, important for the development of both the children's and the welfare functions of local authorities: the problem arising from the fact that the powers that the key legislation gave were essentially to provide residential care. In the case of the 1948 Children Act, the duties of the new child care officers were to be vigilant for the protection of children, but more or less their only 'weapon' when they discovered abuse or neglect was to take children into care (which, at that time, meant essentially institutional care). The 1948 Children Act, with its demand for trained specialist staff, played an important role in the development of a new public service profession – social work. Packman (1975) has shown how the staff of the children departments soon became important initiators of new approaches to their task, stressing the need for 'preventative' work alongside their powers to take children into care. Hence, subsequent legislation (particularly the Children and Young Persons Acts of 1963 and 1969) gave them a variety of powers to operate to try to extend support and help to families so that they might avoid using the more Draconian power to bring children before the courts with a view to taking them into care. However, even that power to take into care began to evolve as it became recognized that it was possible to care for children without segregating them in special institutions: local authorities sought to create smaller and less institutional homes; they began to exercise their 'care' powers through foster placements in ordinary homes; it also began to be recognized that a care order might involve the supervision of children in their own homes.

There was a contrast at the local level between a rather muddled package of general community health and welfare measures and the new departments set up with a clear 'mission' under the 1948 Children Act. Griffith (1966) has shown how this difference was reinforced by the much clearer central inspection system set up for the latter, pushing standards forward and guaranteeing a dialogue between local and central government. The final advantage for the children's service was that responsibility for it was placed in what was, in those days, definitely a high-prestige ministry (the Home Office) rather than in the Department of Health.

Yet, the health and welfare departments of local authorities also began to evolve domiciliary services to supplement the institutional care they provided. Initially, it was the health service legislation that allowed for the development of a range of domiciliary care services. It is interesting to note here how home help services established in the local authority health departments under this legislation, principally to meet the needs of new mothers in an era when home births were the norm, subsequently became a key element in the provision of home care for elderly people.

The evolution of domiciliary services was slow. There continued to be a high dependence on voluntary organizations to provide services like meals in the home, day centres and sometimes supportive visiting (Means and Smith, 1994, p. 25):

> The belief of the legislators behind the 1948 Act was that domiciliary services were an 'extra frill' and so could be left to voluntary organizations . . . A complex patchwork of visiting services, day centres, meals services and chiropody did emerge but much of this provision was not easily available or was unevenly spread geographically, despite attempts by central government to develop the planning role of local authorities.

Means and Smith go on to point out that the 1962 National Assistance (Amendment) Act gave local authorities the power to be direct providers of meals services and that the 1968 Health Services and Public Health Act gave them the 'general power to promote the welfare of the elderly' but that, in practice, little happened before the formation of social services departments in 1971 and that the 'power' did not become a duty until the 1977 National Health Service Act.

The local authorities were also slow to take on staff for visiting and assessment work, and they were slow to recognize that these staff might – like child care officers – be appropriately given access to social work training. Rodgers and Dixon (1960) sought to identify all staff who might loosely be described as social workers (whether qualified or not) in a local authority serving a Northern industrial town with 100,000 population in 1957; they reported on a welfare department with a chief welfare officer, two welfare officers, two welfare workers, one welfare trainee, one handicraft instructor and one home teacher for blind people. Only one of these had a 'university social science qualification'; none of the others had any significant training. It should perhaps be added that, although the same authority's children's department had trained staff, there were only three of them.

There emerged, after Labour's return to power in 1964, a debate about the need for personal social services reform. Once again, the party politicians were not particularly interested. Both the emergence of ideas about social services reorganization, and the shape those ideas took, depended on determined lobbying by a small group of social workers and academics. This story has been carefully studied by Phoebe Hall (1976). She shows how a small group, with some links with the Labour leaders, reacted against an initial set of ideas for a family service and exploited the concern for new community initiatives to deal with delinquency – see the report of the Ingleby Committee (1960) – to secure the setting up of the Seebohm Committee in 1965 'to review the organization and responsibilities of the local authority personal social services in England and Wales and to consider what changes are desirable to secure an effective family service' (Seebohm Report, 1968, p. 11). Note the use of that word 'personal' again, in the committee's brief.

The Seebohm Committee recommended the setting up of unified local authority social services departments, bringing together the former children and welfare departments. It considered that the existing local authority health services for mentally ill and handicapped people should come into these new departments, as should educational welfare services. The report had an unfavourable reception. Hall, relying on evidence from the Crossman diaries, reports that the initial reception by the Cabinet was hostile. However, it did not reject the report out of hand; rather, it was referred to a subcommittee. The reaction of the local authority associations was ambivalent, they were 'reluctant to react ... before the publication of the Royal Commission on Local Government' (Hall, 1976, p. 87).

Above all, the medical pressure groups were hostile to the report. Arguments for and against the division between health and social services in England had been explored by the committee. Phoebe Hall shows that the British Medical Association (BMA) argued in their evidence to the committee that 'health and social services departments' should be set up to embrace local authority health, welfare and children's departments so that 'the service should be capable of dealing with any social or medico-social problem referred to it and not limited to any specific need' (Hall, 1976 p. 52 quoting evidence from the BMA). The Health Visitors' Association and the Royal College of Nursing took a similar line; other doctors' organizations were not so sure, with representative of the local authority based community doctors, in particular, being mainly concerned to defend the *status quo*. Hall concludes that the quality of the medical evidence to the committee was, by contrast with that from social workers, rather poor.

In fact, any explanation of the outcome of the Seebohm Committee deliberations, and the legislation that followed, needs to take into account the fact that, at the same time, the government was wrestling with the issue, to which it gave much more attention, of how to reorganize the health service. Hence, far from a unification of health with personal social services, there was another issue on the agenda: the taking of community health services into the main body of the health service. However, Webster (1998), in his account of the history of the National Health Service, suggests that the Seebohm recommendation preceded the determination of a clear line on that subject, leaving the community health services in need of a new home. It does not really matter how we explain the events of this period; the point is that no effective case was made at that time (or probably at any time) for the unification of health and social services.

The Seebohm proposals were enacted almost in their entirety (except for some blurring of the take-over of services from education) in 1970. Why did this happen? In essence, Hall's conclusion is that the case for the Seebohm report was advocated effectively by a small group of social work activists operating as 'a coherent political force for the first time' (Webster, 1998, p. 108). By contrast, the medical profession was preoccupied with the health service changes, the main medical group threatened – the local authority Medical Officers of Health – being particularly affected by those (Lewis, 1986). Hall suggests that the responsible minister, Richard Crossman, was similarly preoccupied by the health reforms and, hence, indifferent to issues about the personal social services.

Richard Crossman had, in 1968, been given responsibility for an integrated Department of Health and Social Security. Crossman was one of the most active of the Labour ministers, but this meant he had many preoccupations, including social security issues alongside the health service reforms. It is not surprising that he saw the Seebohm reforms as of fairly minor importance. On the other hand, he was not unsympathetic to social care concerns. He was deeply moved by emergent evidence on problems in long-stay hospitals for mentally ill and handicapped people. Furthermore, the planned health service reform had implications for the personal social services, inasmuch as it was envisaged that the community health services should be taken away from local government. The 1970 Local Authority Social Services Act, implementing Seebohm's proposals, went through with Crossman's reluctant support to be implemented – after the fall of the Labour government – in 1971.

1971 to 1990

As they sought to establish their identity, the new social services departments had to cope with changes to the structure of local government, but they rapidly established themselves as much bigger actors in the local government scene than their predecessor departments. A measure of this can be seen in their growth relative to other local government functions. The examples given on pages 27 and 29 indicate how puny the predecessor departments were. In 1955, their total combined expenditure was only about 0.2 per cent of gross domestic expenditure (GDP). By 1987–88, personal social services expenditure had reached 0.9 per cent (Hills, 1990, pp. 217–18). Its growth was particularly dramatic in the first four years after the establishment of the new departments, about 74 per cent at constant prices (that is, correcting for the effects of inflation) (Ferlie and Judge, 1981). It then continued to grow, albeit more modestly, not significantly increasing its share of GDP, however, in the period following the mid-1970's fiscal crisis and the Thatcherite onslaught on public expenditure in the 1980s (Hills, 1990, pp. 217–18).

Table 2.1 illustrates the social services expenditure trend between the mid-1970s and mid-1990s. It shows a pattern of continued growth, but one only a little above the growth of the prosperity of the nation, as represented by the growth of GDP. A further table in chapter 8 (table 8.1) showing recent figures, offers similar evidence, but readers should be careful about comparing the two tables: table 2.1 deals with *all* government expenditure and calculates this at 1995–96 prices; table 8.1 looks only at *local* government expenditure and does *not* use a common price base.

It may be said that, in the 1970s, the personal social services came out of the shadows they had occupied within much policy debate in the years before. Their activities could not be ignored as they had been by politicians in the 1940s, 1950s and 1960s. They remained linked

Table 2.1   Government expenditure on personal social services (expressed in £million at 1995–96 prices)

Year	Expenditure	As % of GDP	Index of spending[a]
1973–74	3,574	0.8	100
1978–79	4,260	0.8	119
1983–84	4,989	0.9	140
1988–89	5,978	0.9	167
1993–94	7,823	1.2	219
1995–96	8,849	1.2	248

Source: Adapted from Glennerster and Hills (1998, table 6.2, p. 202)
[a] 1973–74 = 100

with health in the ministerial arrangements at central level and, in that sense, they remained 'junior' to health in expenditure terms and in terms of political importance.

In the 1970s, the linkage with health was important as soon as governments began to try to launch budgetary and service planning exercises. What these brought on to the agenda was the close connections between ministerial concerns about 'Cinderella' services in health – mental illness services, provisions for people with learning difficulties, services for elderly or chronically sick people – and the closely related social care services. Much more consideration began to be given to boundary issues between health and the personal social services. When the health service was reorganized in the early 1970s, attention was given to the desirability of coterminous boundaries between health authorities and the local authorities responsible for the personal social services. Two influential documents were published by the Department of Health in the mid-1970s with titles which indicate how health and social services planning issues were seen as related:

- *Priorities for Health and Personal Social Services in England* (Department of Health and Social Security, 1976)
- *Priorities in the Health and Social Services: The Way Forward* (Department of Health and Social Security, 1977)

Circulars were issued requiring attention to be given to joint planning and a 'joint funding' scheme was developed for new projects to further encourage this (Webb and Wistow, 1986). The Central Policy Review Staff (the influential but now long abandoned central government 'think tank') gave particular attention to these issues (Challis et al., 1988).

These issues continued to be on the agenda in the harsher financial climate of the 1980s, though new concerns to control health and local government expenditure led them to be articulated in rather different ways (Webb and Wistow, 1986). Before considering how issues about the relationships between the personal social services and both health and social security were important for further changes to social services in the late 1980s, it is necessary to give attention to another issue that was important for the new post-Seebohm social services departments. Central to the Seebohm committee's arguments for the establishment of the new departments was a concern about service fragmentation. Much was made, in efforts to popularize their ideas, of the image of a number of different officers from different departments queuing up to see the same family. While, in retrospect, this picture may seem to have been rather exaggerated, it did bequeath to the new social services departments – and indeed to the social work profession – a concern about the need for genericism.

Clearly, the idea of genericism embodies different issues. One of these is the idea that social services work draws on a common pool of ideas, skills and talents. There are obviously similarities between assessment, support and counselling tasks regardless of whether the client is young or old. It was a matter of concern to social work that, while child care work had become considerably professionalized (with the expectation that workers should have social work qualifications secured through rigorous training) the same did not apply to case-work with elderly people (Rowlings, 1981). There was a case for a general raising of qualifications, with a common core curriculum for social workers, even if specialized optional or extra courses were needed then for work with specific client groups. There was then a need, within the departments, not to have distinctions between work with different clients groups, which were likely to mean that some had an inferior service.

Evidently, the post-Seebohm departments were designed to be generic departments; indeed, ideas now current – discussed elsewhere in this book – that social services activities might be linked with other local government activities or even fragmented between work groups were decidedly not on the agenda at that time. The thinking of the 1970s, in contrast to that at the present day, lay great stress on the idea of a single department.

At that time, a controversial question about which social services managers were prone to argue was: To what extent should genericism at department level be replicated at field-work team level and even in the work loads of individual staff? (DHSS, 1978, ch. 7). Initially, the thrust towards what might be called 'all-through genericism' was very strong. Then, in the 1980s, a reaction against it occurred. A sequence of inquiries into situations in which social services departments had failed to deal satisfactorily with child-abuse problems came out with recommendations about the need for strong specialization (backed up by good training and well-qualified support) in that area of work.

Then, in addition, the 1983 Mental Health Act required a specialized training for social workers 'approved' to undertake duties prescribed in the Act (broadly, the power to remove people to psychiatric wards). This added a curious division within social work – in that for this work alone, there is a requirement for specialized workers with specific training. It does not altogether make sense that one, relatively small, part of the social work task should be identified in this separate way. In particular, there was an equally good case (now being made) for an approved specialization for those with quasi-legal responsibilities in the field of child care.

Returning to the ferment generated within social services departments by difficulties in acting effectively to deal with child abuse, the debate about this issue contributed – along with concerns to redefine the rights of children and the responsibilities of parents – to the recognition of the need for the updating and consolidation of the law relating to the protection of children. This led up to the 1989 Children Act, one of the two crucial Acts of Parliament for the account of contemporary local authority social services to be provided in the rest of this book.

While reasons were emerging for rethinking the social services role in respect of both child care and the care of the mentally ill, some other developments were leading to a need for new legislation in the fields of the care of elderly and handicapped people. The rapid increase in the numbers of older people, and particularly of the very old – see chapter 3 for relevant data – was increasing the need for both residential and domiciliary care. With that rise, came the use of a variety of private homes by those who (or whose relatives) could afford to pay for them.

The emergence of private care homes obviously reduced the burden on statutory care providers. They made it easier for local authorities to maintain an adequate supply of residential places. Before 1980, the central social assistance authority (the Supplementary Benefits Commission) was, in general, unwilling to help low-income people in such homes. Then, the rules were relaxed and local social security office managers were given considerable discretion to subsidize charges through means-tested benefit payments. The Conservative Secretary of State was placed in a dilemma between the commitment to the development of the private sector and the concern to keep income maintenance expenditure under control. Then, in 1983, national limits were imposed. These were nevertheless much higher than those that had prevailed before 1980 when commercial home charges were rarely met. There followed a dramatic growth of private sector homes. What is more, that growth extended to nursing homes, doing very much what had hitherto been considered to be the work of the National Health Service and charging higher fees than care homes. A special high social assistance rate was allowed for these.

A report on community care by the 'watchdog' body set up by the government to undertake monitoring and 'value for money' studies on local expenditure – the Audit Commission – talked of the 'perverse effects of social security policies' in these areas of private care. It pointed out that anyone entitled to means-tested benefit who chose to live in a residential home was able to obtain support up to the limit imposed by the benefit rules. Some of those people might be better and/or more cheaply cared for through a package of domiciliary services. Yet, these could not be provided by the social assistance system. The Audit Commission went on (1986, p. 44):

> In short, the more residential the care, the easier it is to obtain benefits, and the greater the size of payment. And Supplementary Benefit funding cannot be targeted towards those individuals most in need of residential care. Nor are homes judged on whether they are giving value for money within the category of care for which they are registered.

The Audit Commission team was very concerned about the extent to which this income maintenance subsidy of residential care distorted the pattern of care in the country as a whole. It noted the extent to which private homes were unevenly distributed geographically, commenting on their high incidence in the relatively prosperous southern and south-western parts of England. The consequences of this was, it said, (Audit Commission, 1986, p. 3) that

> while central government attempts to achieve equitable distribution of public funds across the country, through the use of complex formulae within the National Health Service and local government, the effects can be largely offset by Supplementary Benefit payments for board and lodging.

After the Audit Commission report on community care, the government commissioned Sir Roy Griffiths to make recommendations on community care policies as a whole (Griffiths Report, 1988). Griffiths suggested that there should be a system under which local social services authorities decided on social, not income, grounds that care was necessary and then had a responsibility to ensure that individuals obtained that care, either from the public or private sector. If individuals were unable to pay the care costs from the standard social security benefits or from other income, it would then be the responsibility of the local authority to provide a subsidy.

The government accepted these recommendations and embodied them in the 1990 National Health Service and Community Care Act. In doing so, it also incorporated a move towards the partial privatization of all existing local authority services in the area of community care. It aimed to ensure that the relative role of local authorities as the direct providers of care (both in residential homes and community services) would decline in favour of the private sector. Local authorities were to become the 'buyers' of packages of private care for low-income people, while their role as suppliers of such care declined. There was a great deal of talk about the need for a 'level playing field' on

which existing private homes and new private providers of domiciliary care could compete with existing local authority providers.

Hence, by 1990, big changes were occurring to the 'generic' social
services departments set up after Seebohm. This book is concerned
with that new world which emerged in the 1990s.

Conclusions

This chapter provides a brief account of the history of modern local
authority social services. It shows how services were minimal and very
fragmented until the 1940s and indicates the way in which the 1940s
legislation achieved two things:

1 Established a dual framework for the development of the personal
   social services in separate measures dealing with children's services and with adult residential care
2 Separated those services from both the health service and from
   social assistance

The 'Seebohm' legislation of 1970 then eliminated that dual framework, setting up the modern local authority departments and firing
them with the objective of creating a 'generic service'. That genericism,
subsequently, came under attack. Then, the three crucial new pieces of
legislation for mental health services (in 1983), for children (in 1989)
and for community care (in 1990) tended to point towards the need
for separate approaches to the organization of these three activities.
We are now at a point where further separate evolution may occur;
this is a theme that is revisited at various points elsewhere in the book.

Chapter 3

The Contemporary Social Framework

Michael Hill

- Introduction
- The Basic Demographic Picture
- More Complex Demographic Issues
- Ethnicity
- Economic Stresses and Strains
- Ill Health and Disability
- Conclusions: Social Pathology and Social Services

Introduction

Chapter 1 notes that the local authority social services differ from most other areas of social policy in that their effort is concentrated on a relatively small proportion of the population. This chapter reviews available social statistics to illustrate and throw further light on that point. The essential evidence for that proposition can be presented straightforwardly. In England, in 1998, there were just under 54,000 children in the legal care of local authorities and almost a further 32,000 on child protection registers because of concern about their treatment (Department of Health, 1998c tables C1 and C2, pp. 60–1). That represents less than 1 per cent of the child population. At the other end of life, social services involvement is rather higher. There were about 236,000 local authority supported residents in care homes or nursing homes in England in 1997 (Department of Health, 1998c, table C6, p. 65) – about 3 per cent of the over 65 population, and 7 per cent of the over 75 population. Data on numbers receiving various forms of domiciliary and day care is not readily available, but using the estimates made by the Royal Commission on Long-Term Care (1999, pp. 8–9), it can be suggested that the proportions of elderly people receiving any kind of social services support will not be more than four times those percentages.

In other words, direct involvement with social services authorities is comparatively unlikely except for very elderly people. By contrast, almost all people make some use of the health service and nearly all children and young people have some experience of state education (about 6 per cent of children go to private schools but many of these will go on to state provided higher or further education). Even the highly targeted British social security system, nevertheless, provides universal child benefits and near universal contributory pensions.

The difficult task for this chapter is therefore to look at the evidence of (a) the extent of the need for social care services and (b) the changes to that need over the recent past. This leads on to the very difficult questions about the fit, or more realistically the lack of it, between various indices of potential need and the extent of actual provisions. Careful exploration is needed to avoid jumping to inappropriate conclusions which either disregard the extent to which people in so-called vulnerable categories are quite easily able to meet their own needs and solve their own social problems, or the capacity of families and communities to provide social care without recourse to statutory services. The discussion needs to be qualified both by some consideration of definitions of social problems and social pathology, and by some recognition that issues about responses to need have to be seen in the context of philosophical debates about the appropriate roles for the state, the community, the family and the individual.

The Basic Demographic Picture

Most data presented in this chapter is for Britain, since much of the key source data comes for Britain rather than England and Wales, notwithstanding the fact that the services described in this book are those for England and Wales (or sometimes just England). This does not involve much distortion, since the population of England and Wales of 52,211,000 in 1997 was 91 per cent of the population of Britain (Office for National Statistics, 1999b, table 1.2, p. 30). The Welsh element in that total was only 2,927,000 (6 per cent). Some figures are only available as UK wide ones, in that case the percentage for England and Wales in 1997 was 88 per cent of the total.

The concentration of social services activity at each end of the age continuum, and particularly at the elderly end, makes the age distribution of the population important for demand on services. According

Table 3.1 Actual and estimated percentages of the UK population in various age groups

	1950	1980	1990	2000	2010	2020
0 –14	22	21	19	21	20	20
15–64	67	64	66	65	66	64
65–	11	15	15	15	15	16

Source: OECD (1988, table A2, p. 81)

to data for the UK (Office for National Statistics, 1999b, table 1.5, p. 31), in 1997, about 21 per cent of the population were under 16, 74 per cent aged 16–64, 8 per cent were aged 65–74, and 7 per cent were over 75. There has been a fall in the numbers of the children and an increase in older people, but it is appropriate to point out the balance is only changing slowly. Much is made in popular discussion of the growth of the elderly population relative to other groups, but the situation at the time of writing is a relatively stable one (with predicted further change still a quite long way ahead). Table 3.1 illustrates this with a combination of older data and estimates of the future population. The accuracy of the latter depends on the stability of estimates of death and birth rates. Since the former are more likely to be accurate than the latter, we can have more confidence in the estimates of numbers of the old than of the young.

More Complex Demographic Issues

There are a number of other issues, often seen as 'demographic', which have bearing on the need for social services. It is appropriate to start with the issue of the balance between the genders. The proportions of males and females in each age group are similar until late middle age. Then, the higher male death rate means that the proportion of women begins to exceed men. By the age of 85, there are over twice as many women than men (Office for National Statistics, 1999b, table 1.4, p. 31). When linked with the tendency for husbands to be older than their wives this contributes to a situation in which a very high proportion of all elderly people without partners are women; see table 3.2.

That data does not necessarily imply large numbers of elderly women living on their own: however, in practice, composite households in which elderly people live with their offspring are rare in the UK. Table

3.3 provides some data on household composition for middle-aged and elderly people, showing how the likelihood of living alone increases with age. This highlights the significance of widowhood for women.

Table 3.2 Percentages in the UK with various living 'marital statuses' by gender and age 1996–97

	Males			Females		
	Over 16	65–74	75 and over	Over 16	65–74	75 and over
Married or cohabiting	67	75	63	62	54	28
Single	23	6	5	18	6	7
Separated or divorced	5	6	3	8	6	3
Widowed	4	13	29	12	35	62

Source: Adapted from Office for National Statistics (1999b, table 1.9, p. 33)

There are two opposite ways in which this data has implications for social services:

- Given the income differences between men and women and the fact that many of the pensions of men are not inherited on death, widows tend to be poorer than widowers. This can have implications for needs in general (see pages 48–52) and does have quite explicit implications for all the social services that are rationed by means tests.
- An examination of the last column in table 3.3 suggests that while living with other adults (including offspring and siblings) is rare, it is less uncommon for women than for men. That may reduce need for social services for elderly women. More controversially, it should also be pointed out that women on their own are more likely to be able, or to be deemed to be able, to care for themselves adequately than men on their own. The author reports this as a 'social' fact, neither a biological one nor as one that (as a male) he can justify as a reason for differential service provision.

The discussion so far has focused on issues about bereavement. Some comment is necessary on issues about marriage and divorce. Over 90 per cent of the population marry at some time in their life. Until recently, there has been a steady rise in the percentage marrying, but

Table 3.3 Percentages of persons in the UK in various kinds of households by age and gender 1994–95

	One person	Couple	Single parent	With others[a]
Males				
45–59	13	83	1	4
60–74	20	78	–	2
75–	35	63	–	2
Females				
45–59	13	77	3	7
60–74	35	60	–	5
75–	68	27	–	5

[a] 'With others' means with other adults including adult relatives other than spouses, but the table does not include those in institutional living arrangements
Source: Central Statistical Office (1996, table 2.8, p. 53)

there are signs that this may now be beginning to fall. There has been a distinct rise in the average age of marriage in the UK. In 1996, it was 28 for males and 26 for females (Office for National Statistics, 1999b, table 2.13, p. 48). It had risen to this from a figure of 25 for both sexes in 1961. Yet, in the face of such a change, it is difficult to estimate whether this will lead to a fall in the proportion which ultimately marry. Prediction of this kind is made particularly difficult by the extent to which heterosexual cohabitation, often on a very stable basis, is replacing formal marriage. *Social Trends* reports that 'the proportion of all non-married women aged 18 to 49 who were cohabiting in Great Britain has doubled since 1981, to 25 per cent in 1996–7' (Office for National Statistics, 1999b, p. 46).

Alongside these complicated trends in respect of marriage has been a rise in divorce. There were 147,000 divorces in England and Wales in 1997, affecting 150,000 children (Office for National Statistics, 1999b, p. 49). The number of divorces rose from a very low level before World War II to a peak of around 175,000 per year in the early 1990s, and has fallen away a little since (Office for National Statistics, 1999b, p. 49; Halsey, 1988, p. 80). 'Almost one in four children born in 1979 is estimated to have been affected by divorce before reaching the age of 16' (Office for National Statistics, 1999b, p. 50). However, a large proportion of divorced people remarry. Two-fifths of all marriages in 1996 were re-marriages (Office for National Statistics, 1999b, p. 47).

The other phenomena on which it is appropriate to report data at this stage is the birth of children to unmarried parents and the incidence of single-parent households. *Social Trends* reports that 'over a third of live births in Great Britain in 1997 occurred outside of marriage, more than four times the proportion in 1974' (Office for National Statistics, 1999b, p. 50) and that 'about a fifth of all children live in single-parent families' (Office for National Statistics, 1999b, p. 43). Again, it is important not to rush to simplistic conclusions. We are in an era of considerable change, with its manifestations a variety of different kinds of family relationships and extensive movements by individuals over time between different household arrangements. Children born to unmarried parents very often have two active and effective parents. About four-fifths of all the births outside marriage were registered by both parents (Office for National Statistics, 1999b, p. 50). Single-parent households arise more from the break up of marriages and cohabitations than from births to women already on their own. Many, moreover, will be temporary, before the resumption of an old relationship or the start of a new one. According to *Social Trends* 'over the period 1991 to 1997, on average, around one in six lone parents with dependent children each year ceased to be lone parents. Of all those leaving lone parenthood, seven in ten got married or formed a new partnership' (Office for National Statistics, 1999b, p. 45).

Simpson (1994) acknowledges, after quoting some of the kinds of statistics reported above, that what they represent:

is nothing less than the fundamental transformation of one of the key institutions of western society and the emergence of families which are re-constituted, blended, recombinant, step- or otherwise 'unclear' when measured against the former certainties of the nuclear family.

Later, Simpson (1999, pp. 121–2) says: 'The implications of these new arrangements for the way that men, women and children might look to one another for care and support in the longer term are profound.' However, there is a need for caution in interpreting this change. Simpson (1999, pp. 133–4) acknowledges that:

[i]t is readily apparent that old securities centred on the traditional models of family life are eclipsed and with this process new insecurities arise . . . Nowadays, it is divorce and not death which brings long-term conjugality to an end. Those who exit from marriage are likely to be faced with an arduous struggle to carve out new securities and to address the crises and anxieties which arise from these distinctive shifts in the organization of personal and domestic life . . .
In recent times, exiting with dignity is as much about preserving relationships between men, women and their children as it is about ending

them. The imperatives of kinship and the quest for security in a world where change and insecurity [are] all too evident, are not totally undermined by divorce. Indeed, one should not under-estimate the commitment and sense of responsibility that many divorced couples develop towards one another and towards their children. Theirs is the task of making new networks and carving out new securities from the networks of potentiality which remain when long term conjugality fails. . . .

Understanding the impact of relationship breakdown on individuals is well advanced. However, understanding the wider social implications of large-scale relationship breakdown is still at an early stage.

In looking at the implications of all this for the local authority social services, a similar caution is needed. These changes in family structure need to be examined in terms of two issues: their direct impact on individual need for social care and their indirect impact on need through their impact on the caring capacity of families. These two issues need then to be related to the main areas of social services work (as identified in chapter 1): with elderly people, with other handicapped adults, with people suffering from mental illness, and with children.

As far as elderly people are concerned, clearly divorce, when not followed by remarriage, is likely to increase the numbers living alone. Otherwise, the issues for this group are all about the caring capacity of other family members, assuming (see page 20) that it is regarded as appropriate that they should be involved in the caring process. The most fundamental influence on the availability of carers is the number of surviving offspring. In that sense, the number of available carers has been reduced by lower birth rates. Absolute family size has fallen and is probably still falling, though a tendency to have children later makes the data about today's potential mothers difficult to assess. Clearly, we have a situation in which few older people have more than two adult children and many have fewer, but then there is much uninformed speculation about the implications of the family status of those children, and particularly about the impact of high divorce. The crucial point here is that the ratio of offspring to parents is not changed by the former's divorces. The difference between the caring capacity of a married or a divorced daughter or son is not readily predictable from that fact alone. Divorce may have an impact on income, or on where people live, or on their own nuclear family obligations. These may then have their own effects on caring capacity, in either a positive or negative direction. It is futile to try to predict these effects from the fact of divorce alone.

As far as disabilities among adults are concerned, the arguments must surely be similar. There are no simple causal links between family status and the experience of particular disabilities. As far as caring capacities are concerned, family break-up may reduce the extent of care available for younger adults with disabilities or learning difficulties. Similarly, as will be further explored in relation to children, single parents may have greater difficulties caring for handicapped adult offspring than do couples. It also needs to be recognized that heavy caring responsibilities may be a cause of stress in a family, contributing to divorce. In that sense, there is a role for social services to try to reduce family stress arising from exceptional caring responsibilities.

Some very similar points can be made about carers for those with mental illness but, in this case, it must be recognized that there are suggestions being made, far beyond the concerns of the present book, about the extent to which the family changes of the kind outlined above may themselves contribute to the incidence of mental illness. Should that be the case, it raises questions both about the capacity of the care services to deal with new demands, and about problems which must face them if their assumptions about 'normal' family life are out of line with patterns of behaviour which are becoming widespread.

Finally, the issues about the implications of family changes for child care are probably the most controversial of all. Simpson has been quoted at some length because of the balanced way he weighs against each other the inevitable insecurities that arise with changing family life and the evidence that people rise to the challenge of new relationships in flexible ways. Single parents have pressures on their capacities as child carers that are bound to exceed those on couples. On the other hand, stressful relationships among couples may undermine the quality of child care. There are inevitably many anxieties about what we may call 'second families', reinforced by the number of child-abuse cases in which stepfathers have figured, but it is both unhelpful, and flying in the face of the large number of 'second families' which never reach the attention of social services authorities, to stereotype stepparents in Grimms' fairy-tale fashion.

To sum up this section, some of the data on family change does suggest that need for the work of social services authorities will be on the increase, both because of direct effects on individuals and because of their impact on the caring capacity of the community. Yet, at the same time, direct arguments from the data should be treated with great caution. It is much more important to give attention to the interactions between the phenomena discussed here and economic difficulties, as the next section does, or to go more directly to other evidence on the incidence of need as embodied in data on disabilities and illness in the final section of this chapter (pages 52–4).

Ethnicity

The caution about the implications of the data just expressed is equally necessary in looking at data on ethnicity. The ethnic diversity of the population served by social services authorities needs to be noted, not as evidence on need *per se* but as evidence that responses to need must be framed in ways which avoid discrimination; social services authorities need to be sensitive to the effects of discrimination, and responsive to differences in culture and language.

The composition of the population of Britain has been influenced by immigration and emigration throughout its history. Without going back to the population movements of pre-medieval history, we can note, before the twentieth century, the migration of Huguenots escaping persecution in France at the end of the seventeenth century, settlements of sailors and liberated slaves in the major seaports in the eighteenth and nineteenth centuries and, above all, massive migration from Ireland during the middle and late nineteenth century (extending well into the twentieth century). The first laws enacted by the government to try to impose formal limits on the inflow of people, the Alien Acts of 1904 and 1905, were directed against the first of the twentieth century's many waves of refugees, Jews fleeing the pogroms of north-eastern Europe. Nevertheless, there has continued to be movements into Britain of European refugees – Jews fleeing Nazism in the 1930s and 1940s, Polish and other East European people displaced during World War II and, of course, other more recent refugees from the still 'unstable' countries of south-east Europe.

Clearly, the most significant recent immigrants – in terms of numbers, visibility (particularly in terms of skin colour) and the extent to which they have been subjected to hostility and discrimination – are those who came to Britain from the countries of the Commonwealth or former British Empire – in a period roughly extending between the early 1950s and the mid-1970s. This immigration was stimulated by the British need for labour in the 'long boom' that followed the economic recovery after World War II. It was brought to an end by a combination of restrictive legislation and the fall in the demand for labour. Migration of people who hitherto had rights of entry as Commonwealth citizens was initially restricted in 1962. Those restrictions have been progressively tightened so that there are now very few new migrants from the Commonwealth. The contemporary 'politics of immigration control' focuses on issues about the reception of refugees. Despite the fact that Britain receives, relative to other European countries, proportionately few refugees, the two major parties have engaged in a 'Dutch auction' as to who can make Britain most unattractive to them.

Hence, while there are some important issues about the support social services authorities can give to refugees, the main issues about Britain's ethnic minority population are those outlined above concerning sensitivity to problems arising from discrimination and cultural differences.

Just under 6 per cent of the British population belong to non-white ethnic groups. These are almost equally divided between people of Caribbean and African origin, people of Indian origin, people whose families originate from Pakistan or Bangladesh and 'others' (including Chinese people and people of mixed origin) (Central Statistical Office, 1996, p. 40). There are some definitional problems here, which we will not explore; on the whole, the main approach to these issues is to accept individuals' self-definitions of 'origin' or 'ethnic group'. What is important to bear in mind about these people is that many of them were born in Britain. This is particularly true of children – 94 per cent of under 16s in the 'black Caribbean' group were born in Britain, as were 96 per cent of 'Indians' and 93 per cent of 'Pakistanis' (Office for National Statistics, 1999b, p. 33). The inverted commas in that sentence are to denote an essential 'shorthand' – these are British citizens of various ethnic 'origins'. Even among adults, many are now British born – for example, 86 per cent of those between 25 and 34 in the 'Black Caribbean' group.

It is inevitable that, with an inflow of prime-age adults between the late 1950s and 1970s, many of whom settled and produced offspring in Britain, the ethnic minority population in the late 1990s is young, relative to the population as a whole. In 1995, about a third of the ethnic minority population, as opposed to a fifth of white people, was under 16. At the other end of life, less than 6 per cent, as opposed to 20 per cent were over 60 (Central Statistical Office, 1996, p. 40).

We have already identified the significance of the two ends of the age spectrum for social services work. Clearly, the incidence of a high child population among minority ethnic groups means that social workers working with children have had to give attention to the extent to which particular needs require attention. A controversial issue has been the extent to which placements of children outside their original families (including adoption) should or can be with ethnically compatible adults. This issue is discussed a little more in chapter 4.

In addition, needs for support for ethnic minority families have been affected by the extent to which bread-winners experience discrimination, and have higher rates of unemployment and lower incomes than others (Office for National Statistics, 1999b, pp. 75 and 109).

Notwithstanding the relatively low numbers of ethnic minority people among the elderly, there are particularly important issues for social services authorities stemming from (a) the extent to which, in the process of establishing themselves in Britain, they have experienced considerable economic difficulties and are likely to have low pensions and assets, (b) the fact that almost all of them grew up in rather different cultures, and many do not have English as their first language, which means that satisfactory care arrangements will need to pay particular attention to communication issues, special dietary needs and so on. Some of these people will face particularly severe problems of isolation.

Clearly, the age structure of the ethnic minority population is changing rapidly towards one more like that of the population as a whole. Needs for care arrangements that take into account minority requirements will grow. There is some evidence that there is a return flow back to the country of origin on retirement. This may have an impact on demand for services for the elderly, but it also has the effect of reducing the availability of young elderly people to play grand-parenting caring roles.

This short section has sought to highlight the main implications for social services authorities of the presence of ethnic minorities. Clearly, inasmuch as there is an expectation that social services authorities will be in the forefront of struggles against disadvantage, issues about racial discrimination pose particular challenges to them. In any case, as agencies offering personal services to vulnerable people, there is a need for authorities to be vigilant to prevent individual discrimination and to ensure that they are not allowing forms of institutional racism to develop. In this context, a concern about the ethnic composition of their own staffs must be important.

Economic Stresses and Strains

Data on incomes, and particularly on the incidence of low income or poverty, is pertinent to a discussion of needs for local authority social services for three interconnected reasons:

- Poverty is likely to be, in itself, a cause of, or contributing factor to, need. There is now a substantial literature on the impact of poverty and inequality on health; see Acheson (1998) for the most recent authoritative examination of this. While the evidence of the association between poverty and need for social services has not been assembled, in the same way, much of the evidence on need for health care (particularly on disability and chronic illness) has similar implications for social care. In addition, in the area of social services where health problems are not the only reason for a need for social care – that is, child care – the unsurprising connections between poverty and child neglect and abuse have long been recognized; see chapter 4.

- Poverty has an impact on caring capacity. In this sense, there is a possibility that conditions that would secure attention among the poor will go unrecognized among the better off. Inasmuch as this may mean that the better off deal with problems of disability, learning difficulties and mental illness without involving publicly provided social services, this may not be a matter for concern. On the other hand, it is possible that certain phenomena which should come to the attention of social services authorities – notably child abuse or neglect – will sometimes be effectively hidden among the better off. This phenomenon also contributes to the stereotyping of poor people as less than adequate parents.
- As indicated in chapter 1, many local authority social services are, in fact, rationed by the use of means tests. This fact alone means that the work of social services authorities will mainly come from those with lower incomes, in itself obscuring the actual relationship between specific problem incidence and actual demand for social services, and increasing the pressure on the better off to 'absorb' their own social problems.

These connections are explored further elsewhere in this book, particularly in chapters 4, 5 and 7. Here, attention is confined to relevant evidence on poverty and inequality. The British government has been unwilling to give recognition to an official definition of poverty; however, it does publish evidence on the incidence of incomes at various levels and has been prepared to highlight some of the evidence on low-income families. Pulling together this evidence, Oppenheim and Harker report that, in 1992, in the UK, 13.7 million people (24 per cent of the population) were living at or below the level of income prescribed for those on income support, the main means-tested social security benefit. At the same time, using an alternative measure, 14.1 million people (25 per cent) were living below 50 per cent of average income after housing costs (Oppenheim and Harker, 1996, p. 24). The 1992 figures are a little dated, but later figures show little change from the picture in that year (MacDermott, 1999).

These are substantial proportions of the total population, with considerable implications for pressure on social services authorities. Moreover, there was a substantial rise in the figures in these two categories between 1979 and 1992. In 1979, only 14 per cent were below income support level (then called supplementary benefit level) and only 9 per cent had incomes more than 50 per cent below the average (Oppenheim and Harker, 1996, p. 24).

However, to move from general figures into the implications of low income for the personal social services, there is a need to look more specifically at who are the poor. Table 3.4 sets out data on specific households where low income is concentrated (after the application of a statistical technique to adjust for the impact of differences in family size). It highlights the incidence of poverty within single-parent families. Earlier, it was cautiously suggested that family stresses might be greater in single-parent families than in two-parent families. This dramatic evidence on poverty among this group surely offers a more cogent reason why children in single-parent families may be 'at risk'. The data on couples with children suggests, not surprisingly, that they will be likely to be less well off than couples without, but obviously any analysis of poverty among these families would need to give attention to the incidence of unemployment, low wages and sickness.

Acheson (1998, p. 45), in his report on inequalities in health has little doubt that 'unemployment and stressful or hazardous working environments are potentially major risks to health'. However, certainly as far as social problems are concerned, there are difficulties in separating those problems that arise from unemployment and those that arise from insecure, unsatisfactory and poorly remunerated employment. In addition, disentangling the impact of these issues from the issues about poverty is very difficult. However, it is pertinent to refer here to the fact that, in the UK, during most of the 1990s, over 2 million people have been unemployed. At the time of writing, the fig-

Table 3.4 Income levels by family types, data for Great Britain in 1996.

	Bottom fifth	Middle three-fifths	Top fifth	Numbers in group (millions)
Pensioner couple	23	65	12	5.1
Single pensioner	25	67	7	4.1
Couple with children	19	63	17	17.2
Couple without children	10	53	38	10.5
One adult with children	42	55	3	4.6
One adult without children	18	58	24	8.2

Source: Calculated from Central Statistical Office (1996, table 5.17, p. 95)

ures are looking rather better, with unemployment falling towards 1.5 million, but there are doubts about the security and quality of employment for many.

Unemployment, as officially defined, is higher among males and the young, as table 3.5 indicates, but there is a need for caution about this, because the definition of unemployment rests essentially on active job seeking. Women (particularly married women) and older people are less likely than men and younger people to continue to seek work once discouraged by their prospects. Married women often cannot obtain social security benefits. Older people may take out pensions prematurely, and may find it easier to obtain benefits for sick and disabled people when they are less than fully fit for work.

The previous two paragraphs suggest a variety of qualifications against jumping to conclusions from unemployment statistics. The most important of these is that it seems particularly necessary to recognize that the major effect of unemployment on social disadvantage may well be that it is a cause of poverty. There is no clear evidence that unemployed poor people are more vulnerable to other social problems than other poor people. Indeed, it may be that a relatively secure state-provided benefit income offers a better foundation for family life, and for attention to family care problems, than long hours of work for a low return or stressful regularly changing insecure work.

Table 3.4 also provides evidence on the extent to which pensioner incomes fall short of the national average, particularly the incomes of single pensioners. With respect to the latter, it is important to bear in mind the extent to which this group is female. What, of course, is crucial about low income among older people is the extent to which, when they need social care, they are unable to pay charges. In the application of means tests, attention is given to assets as well as income. There have been suggestions that the economic situation of elderly people is more favourable when viewed in terms of assets rather

Table 3.5 Unemployment rates by gender and age 1998 (UK)

Age group	Males	Females
18–24	13.0	9.3
25–44	5.8	5.2
45–54	4.8	3.1
55–59	6.7	3.5

Source: Office for National Statistics (1999b, table 4.20, p. 81); figures derived from a Labour Force Survey using ILO definitions

than income. Available data on savings does not support this (Royal Commission on Long-Term Care, 1999, p. 12). However, it is true to say that the economic position of older people is improving, and that, in particular, there is a significant group moving into old age who are owners of their own houses; see table 3.6. What is controversial is the extent to which housing assets should be taken into account when assessing charges for care; at present, houses are only taken into account in residential care means tests when there is no surviving relative with a clear claim to reside in the home that has been left behind.

Table 3.6   Percentages of owners and renters in various age groups in the UK

	Owners			Renters
Age	Owning outright	With a mortgage	All owners	
45–54	16	62	78	22
55–64	42	31	73	26
65–74	58	8	66	33
75–	54	4	58	42

Source: Calculated from Central Statistical Office (1996, table 10.4, p. 169)

III Health and Disability

It is perhaps better to look at social services need in terms of explicit problems of disadvantage rather than in terms of some combination of demographic and income data. With respect to many aspects of adult care, including that for elderly people, it is pertinent to look at evidence on sickness and disability. There are some difficulties in finding figures on these phenomena that are independent of the services offered by the caring agencies. It is not satisfactory to define those in need of care in terms of data on those who receive care. On the other hand, the alternative tends to be self-ascribed sickness and disability rates, in which case it is fair to recognize that some who claim to be in need would not be so regarded by those who offer care. Nevertheless, some of these alternative statistics will be quoted, and related to official definitions where possible.

The 1996 Health Survey for England (Prescott-Clarke and Primatesta, 1998, p. 183) reported just under a quarter of all adults not assessing their health as 'good' or 'very good' but 43 per cent reporting a long-standing illness. Corresponding figures for children were about one tenth who said their health was not good and 23 per cent who reported a long-standing illness. Figures like these, which indicate large numbers with some health care needs, do not help much to identify social care needs.

A sample survey of the British population identified percentages in various adult age groups who had various kinds of general health problems in 1996. Table 3.7 reports some of the findings from that study. It should be noted, in interpreting the figures in tables 3.7 and 3.8, that the survey did not include persons living in care homes and other institutions.

In England, in 1993, the percentage of the population registered with local authorities as 'handicapped' was 1 per cent; the corresponding percentage aged over 65 was only 6 per cent. So there is quite a big gap, assuming we can roughly compare English and British data, between those figures and the much larger self-reported incidence of either problems of self care or problems of mobility, as set out in table 3.7.

Yet, evidence that the data in table 3.7 does not exaggerate the extent of problems with various activities comes from some more detailed evidence on problems among elderly people derived from the same survey. Table 3.8 reports percentages unable to manage various activities on their own.

The data on anxiety or depression in table 3.7 can be supplemented by data from a study of the prevalence of psychiatric morbidity (Metzer et al., 1995) which indicates that around 16 per cent of the population had suffered from a neurotic disorder of some kind in the 'past weeks' before the survey (a figure reasonably close to the 19 per cent reporting anxiety or depression indicated in table 3.7). This study's figures for psychosis are then very much lower – a rate of 0.04 per cent over

Table 3.7   Percentages with various kinds of 'some' or 'severe' problems by age (sample survey data for Great Britain, 1996)

	16–44	45–64	65–74	75–	All adults
Pain or discomfort	19	39	52	61	33
Mobility	6	21	36	55	19
Anxiety or depression	16	21	22	25	19
Self care	2	5	8	16	5

Source: Office for National Statistics (1998, table 8.35, p. 134)

Table 3.8 Percentages of elderly people unable to manage various activities on their own (sample survey data for Great Britain, 1996)

Activity cannot manage	65–74	75–	Total over 65
Washing all over	5	13	9
Dressing and undressing	3	5	4
Feeding	0	1	0

Source: Office for National Statistics (1998, table 8.50, p. 144)

the past 12 months. However, the study reports rates of alcoholism of 4.7 per cent and of drug dependence of 2.2 per cent over the previous 12 months (Metzer et al., 1995, table 6.1 p. 76).

The data on mental illness might lead the reader to expect high levels of social services work in this field. While it does not seem possible to identify the extent of such activities, the evidence on expenditure – see page 11 – and on staffing levels does not indicate extensive work. As chapter 6 shows, it is difficult, in practice, to disentangle social services work and health services work in relation to the care of mentally ill people.

The statistics in this section offer a range of evidence on the extent of need arising from health problems and from disabilities. They support a general contention, hard to quantify more precisely, that there is extensive unmet need in the community.

Conclusions: Social Pathology and Social Services

This chapter examines a range of data that may help towards the identification of needs for social services. It could have gone further into the examination of crime rates and evidence of anti-social behaviour. However, doing so raises a series of very difficult problems of interpretation. Social statistics are largely the products of either official or subjective definitions. Official definitions are highly influenced by the particular requirements that services have to identify needs and measure activities. Political considerations may influence what is recorded and what is reported. In some circumstances, authorities may have an interest in magnifying issues and problems, to support their needs for more resources; in other circumstances, they may want to minimize, so as to prove that they are doing a good job. In either case, they will be affected by the public's willingness to bring issues and problems, including (particularly in the case of social services) personal problems, to the attention of officials.

Surveys avoid some of these difficulties by seeking information on problems and needs directly from the public, in confidence and without any direct implications for services, but the issue of subjectivity emerges here, about the ways individuals conceptualize and are prepared to talk about their problems.

There seems to be some more straightforward data around – more objective and less the product of administrative needs – such as demographic data and data on the economic circumstances of households. However, other difficulties emerge with the use of this, as shown in this chapter. There are many efforts made, in popular and political discourse, to infer needs and problems from such data – about ageing or divorce or poverty, for example – although much is left to inference about the impact of these phenomena on individuals.

This all leads up to perhaps little more than the rather limited conclusion that there is evidence that inasmuch as social services authorities set up their stalls, as quoted in chapter 1, as concerned to 'provide high quality services to the most vulnerable people', there is little doubt that there is plenty of work to be done. Beyond that clearly the issues about the age structure of British society are relevant, though there is a need to avoid an alarmist position either about the rate of demographic change or about the inevitability of dependency among the old. The data about the increased incidence of poverty is also important, because of various aspects of the work of social services authorities. As suggested, social services authorities can well align themselves with those who have emphasized the significance of social inequalities for ill health (Townsend et al., 1992; Wilkinson, 1996; Acheson, 1998) to say 'this is important for our work too'. The issues about changing family structures need approaching more cautiously, as has been indicated.

Part 2

The Local Authority Social Services Task

Chapter 4

Child Care

Jane Tunstill

Introduction

The evolution of statutory responsibility for children and their families at local level between the Elizabethan Poor Law and the Sure Start Programme of 1999 is a long and continuing story which can be taken as a case study of the highs and lows of the history of child and family welfare at both national as well as local level. The parameters and definition of *the task* – that is what social services authorities *do* in respect of children and families – are dependent on the period under examination, being subject to a diverse range of pressures and influences. These include the influence of ideology, both political and professional, and the implications of empirical investigation. In practice, it is difficult to separate these two, given, for example, the political role in commissioning research and implementing the results. Often, of course, research, government commissioned or not, will be ignored. Some elements remain the same; others change. In addition to agreed legal (or otherwise) definitions of *what* the task is, there is the linked policy question as to *who* should undertake it. A historical list might start with Poor Law Relieving Officers, work through child care officers, and would currently need, as a minimum, to include health visitors, family centre workers, voluntary befrienders and day care staff.

While child care tasks undertaken by social service authorities may appear to change profoundly over time, in fact, such change merely reflects the current political and/or professional ethos of any specific era. At heart, the task remains essentially the same, that is to say the resolution of conflict between the needs of children, their families and the wider society. Acknowledging this fact helps to make sense of the present, as well as minimizing the danger that what is written on the topic at the end of any one year will be irrelevant half-way through the next.

For the most part, since the post-war welfare reforms and, in particular, the 1948 Children Act, local authority child care work has been prescribed by specific child care legislation. However, this is only part of the story. Other legislative frameworks also have a bearing on the way the task is conceptualized and on the particular personnel who will carry it out. (These include aspects of universal provision such as health and education, as well as criminal justice legislation.) The extent to which these impact on the child care task is itself a mercury level of the current dominant social philosophy in relation to children and the family.

So, a description of the local authority child care task written in 1999 will already need to differ from one written in 1989. The intervening decade has seen the passing of not only the 1998 Crime and Disorder Act, but also the introduction, since 1997, by New Labour of a swathe of government initiatives, some of which create new links between social services, health and education, and economic regeneration. However, at the same time, both the 1989 and 1999 accounts would manifest echoes of major child care legislation in 1933, 1948, 1963 or 1975. This apparent riddle merely expresses the way in which each successive era produces different social constructions of state, family and child. Changing combinations of the three ultimately lead to different policy responses.

One phenomenon, above all others, makes the characteristics of locally provided child care policy particularly difficult to pin down: its intended recipients, unlike other areas of welfare provision, can be *families and children*, whereas, in other personal social services contexts, a single person is likely to be the primary focus of service provision or professional intervention. In the context of provision for children, it is almost impossible to disaggregate the single child from the wider family unit. In other words, by definition, where there is a child there must be, or, at least have once been, a parent. Therefore, any discussion of state responsibility at the local level for children must start with an

acknowledgement of prevailing assumptions about the *family*. Fluc-
tuations in the relationship between family and state (along with the
level of financial resources available) will have enormous influence on
the nature of child care policy; conversely, changing historical concep-
tions of the role of 'child' eventually feed through to the nature of
family and social policy (Pascall, 1986; Quortrup, 1994).

This chapter therefore, while picking up from the broader historical
account of chapter 2, begins with brief reference to an historical perspective on the relationship between state, family and child. It goes on
to provide an overview of the legal and administrative responsibilities
of local authorities for children and their families as laid down in the
1989 Children Act, which takes account of both the framework as
laid down in statute, as well as the additional implications of recent or
current policy initiatives. It then provides an overview: (a) of the settings within which services for children and families are provided, and
(b) the nature of the main services provided.

It closes by drawing some conclusions as to the key issues (including
both problems and successes), which can be currently identified and
points to likely future trends and prospects.

A Brief Historical Perspective on Social Services Provision for Children

There are obvious and uncontested signposts towards the general intentions and scope of current social services provision for children
such as the Seebohm Report and the 1989 Children Act, but the reality is that, in common with the other tasks of social services authorities, its detailed nature has emerged over a very long period (Heywood,
1978; Hendrick, 1997; Denney, 1998). As indicated in chapter 2, for
several centuries, British social policy, inasmuch as one can call it this,
was indistinguishable from the Poor Law. Provision for children within
the latter reflected all the horrors and advances of each successive era.
For example, outdoor relief administered to families in the nineteenth
century, which meant that children could stay with their families, as
opposed to being separated within the workhouse, might be seen as an
early version of the notions of prevention and family support which
underpin the 1963 Children and Young Persons Act and the 1989
Children Act. Throughout this period, the roles of the local state en-
compassed a range of tasks including moral rescue, the reduction of
crime, poor relief, the prevention of child abuse, and the improvement
of the working classes.

Historical examination reveals the significance of individual developments, which remain clearly discernible in the framework of current policy and practice – for example, many, if not most of the voluntary child care organizations such as Barnardo's and the NSPCC play key roles – but its real value lies in identifying the way in which social policy concepts change over time (Fox Harding, 1991; Pilcher and Wagg, 1996; Daniel and Ivatts, 1998).

Fox Harding categorizes the socio-legal characteristics of different child care policy periods. She has identified a fourfold typology which embraces the four perspectives: '*laissez faire* and patriarchy'; 'state paternalism and child protection'; 'the modern defence of the birth family and parents' rights'; and 'children's rights and liberation'. The emergence of each of these is, broadly, associated with different chronological eras, but their boundaries overlap and they can be seen to re-emerge in various guises at different periods. Indeed, she concludes (Fox Harding, 1991, p. 229) that the 1989 Children Act, while containing both state paternalist and pro-birth family provisions, leans more heavily to the latter, though only time will tell whether this is borne out in practice. She argues that, indeed, it is reasonable for the Act 'to proceed in two directions at once, adding to the power of parents here, strengthening the courts and the local authorities there' (Fox Harding, 1991, p. 231). Other writers have taken a variety of views as to its nature and intentions, ranging from the essentially conservative (Daniel and Ivatts, 1998, p. 205) 'anti-collectivist' (Denney, 1998, p. 153) to 'harking back to the pre-Thatcherite era' (Packman and Jordan, 1991). However, these views illustrate the fact that the one perennial theme which dominates the framing of all child care policy is a tension between the needs/rights of children and the needs/rights of parents. A closely related subtheme is the relationship between these needs/rights and the needs/rights of the providers of services, and especially of adopters or foster carers who wish to adopt. In many ways, the 1989 Children Act, can be said to face these tensions head-on.

The Legal and Administrative Framework

The 1989 Children Act

Lord Mackay, the then Lord Chancellor, declared, when he opened the House of Lords debate on the second reading of the 1989 Children Act:

> The Bill in my view represents the most comprehensive and far-reaching reform of child care law which has come before parliament in living memory. It brings together the public and private law concerning the

care, protection and upbringing of children and the provision of services to them and their families.

The Act is an unusually 'rational' piece of social policy legislation. The raft of child care scandals and reports between the death of Maria Colwell and the Cleveland Enquiry produced an unusually explicit debate about the role of the social worker in relation to children and families. This prompted considerable consultation and research, much of the latter commissioned by the Department of Health (DHSS, 1985b; Department of Health, 1991b). These research studies informed a detailed review process undertaken by the Social Service Select Committee which set out to recommend how to modernize and rationalize child care and family law (DHSS, 1985a). The publication of the Act itself was accompanied by a set of principles for practice and several volumes of official guidance (Department of Health, 1990).

The overall conclusions drawn from the research findings and the more general philosophical debate have been covered extensively from a range of perspectives (Packman and Jordan, 1991; Parton, 1991; Thoburn, 1994; Aldgate and Hill, 1996; Pilcher and Wagg, 1996; Denney, 1998). However, most commentators agree that, in essence, the problems before the Act centred on the following failures within the child care system:

- Inadequate protection of children by social workers who failed to act quickly enough to investigate possible abuse
- Over heavy interventions when they did
- Failure to offer help/support to parents who needed it
- Stigmatization of those who might receive support
- Tendency for parents to lose contact with children who were placed in care, either deliberately (through permanence policies such as adoption) or unintentionally through bad practice, even though contact is associated with early return home

The Act constitutes the central foundation of local authority responsibilities in respect of children and families. It repeals 55 earlier Acts, either partially or entirely. Its 108 sections and 16 schedules govern the configuration, design, and implementation of the majority of the elements which characterize any western child welfare system. These elements include:

- family support (including day care services) services
- child protection services
- substitute family services (including respite care)

- residential care
- checks on children living away from home
- basic standards of provision in the statutory, voluntary and private sectors.

The Act also alludes, in passing, to provision in the areas of adoption and juvenile justice. The last two are, however, the major focus of separate legislation, although they both have considerable implications for the work of local authorities.

The central and most widely publicized concept in the new Act, and that which most clearly illustrates the political and professional philosophy which underpins it, is almost certainly the concept of *children in need*. Needless to say, it has also been the most complex and contested element (Tunstill, 1996). Section 17 of the Act states:

A child is in need if:
(a)   he is unlikely to achieve or maintain, or have the opportunity of achieving or maintaining, a reasonable standard of health or development without the provision for him of services by a local authority
(b)   his health or development is likely to be significantly impaired or further impaired without the provision for him of such services
(c)   he is disabled.

It is left to individual authorities to define which children in their area are in need, and to make appropriate provision for them. However, there is clear direction in the Act, and in the accompanying guidance, that services should not be restricted to those children who are only seen as being at risk of abuse and maltreatment. In addition, services can/should be made available to any member of the family of a child in need if it will benefit that child.

However, perhaps its greatest legal innovation is that, in addition to these 'traditional' components, it has brought together, for the first time, public and private law in respect of children and their families. The scope of the Act and its potential significance in middle class, as well as working class, lives is therefore extensive.

In essence, its main purpose is to 'forge a new set of balances between parents, children and the state' (Daniel and Ivatts, 1998, p. 205). The Act according to the Department of Health is based on the following principles (Ryan, 1994):

- The primary responsibility for the upbringing of children rests with families and, for most children, their interests will be served best by enabling them to grow up within their own families; family means the extended family. Where children are separated, they should be enabled to maintain contact with them.

- Race, culture, language and religion are crucially important in the context of services and/or courts.
- The relationship between local authorities, children and their families should be based, wherever possible, on partnership and participation.
- Children should be involved as fully as possible in actions and decisions about themselves.
- The provision of substitute care should be seen as a service.
- Local authorities should adopt a corporate approach in providing for children and families.
- There should only be one route for the state to intervene in families, that is, through the courts and on the basis that the child is suffering or likely to suffer significant harm.

Children's services plans

In addition to the legal requirements laid down in the Act itself, a new mandatory requirement was established in March 1996 for local authorities to prepare Children's Services Plans to promote the 'kind of holistic, multi-agency strategies that are increasingly recognized as necessary to enhance the well-being of children' (Utting, 1998, p. 32) They are intended to result in greater integration between agencies in respect of their provision for children, and they emerged from the overview undertaken by Sir William Utting of *Children in the Public Care* (Utting, 1991). This report drew attention to the many gaps in coordination between social services and other agencies such as health and education which could threaten the health and welfare of children. They were originally introduced by government on a voluntary basis but following the critical comments of the Audit Commission in its review of health and local authority provision for children (Audit Commission, 1994b), they were made a mandatory requirement, and their status considerably raised. They may be thought of as putting policy flesh on the legal bones of Section 27 of the Act.

The introduction of this new legal requirement was accompanied by guidance, which attempted to broaden the concern of social service planners beyond the population of 'children in need' as defined by the 1989 Act to a wider concern with all potentially vulnerable children in the locality. It indicated that strategic approaches to planning children's services should be based on the following principles:

- A reliable and updated knowledge base
- An analysis of need and supply
- The views of users and the local community
- Consultation with other agencies
- Monitoring and feedback

In addition, according to the Department of Health (1998h, p. 55), to work effectively with other organizations, social services authorities need to:

- establish a joint planning process supported by good understandings of roles and responsibilities, shared values and a commitment to long-term goals
- develop protocols, and commit budgets to achieve agreed priorities and establish problem-solving arrangements
- develop joint assessment, care management, commissioning and training arrangements.

The Department of Health has responsibility for monitoring the plans. Hearn and Sinclair (1998) undertook a study to ascertain how far the planning process has led to changes in the pattern of services to children and families, with particular reference to the relationship between the assessment of local needs and the planned allocation of resources. Their study of 15 authorities concludes that considerable progress had been made in multi-agency planning to meet the needs of children, with greater effort being made to analyse the needs of children and their families, and consultations taking place with service user and members of the wider community, but that, so far, there is little evidence of significant shifts in resources or fundamental changes in service provision.

Post-1997 Government initiatives of key relevance to local authority children's services

The 1998 White Paper (Department of Health, 1998e) – discussed further in chapter 10 – underlines the importance of a corporate approach to children's services. Chapter 3 of that document makes it clear that the welfare of children must be seen as a corporate responsibility of the entire local authority, and that social services for children must be seen as an element of that wider responsibility; see also, para. 6.26. The White Paper (para. 6.27) proposes that corporate responsibility is reinforced by 'redefining the requirements for children's services planning' by, for example, placing a duty on the local authority as a whole to:

- improve the health and education of looked-after children
- determine priorities for improving support for children in need, including disabled children and those with emotional and behavioural difficulties
- address housing needs of families with children in need
- summarize the outcomes intended in youth justice, behaviour support, and early years' plans, and thus bring together action on behalf of the main groups of children at risk of exclusion.

An earlier source of the contemporary expectations of central government was embodied in *Quality Protects*, a document from the Department of Health's Social Care Group, which establishes the following major objectives for children's services, along with associated sub-objectives:

- To ensure children are securely attached to carers capable of providing safe and effective care for the duration of their childhood
- To ensure that children are protected from emotional, physical and sexual abuse and neglect
- To ensure children in need gain maximum life chance benefits from educational opportunities, health care and social care
- To ensure young people leaving care as they enter adulthood are not isolated, and that they participate socially and economically as citizens
- To ensure that referral and assessment processes discriminate effectively between different types and levels of need, and produce a timely service response
- To ensure that resources are planned and provided, represent best value for money, allow for choice and allow for different responses for different needs and circumstances

All local authorities are required to demonstrate that they are achieving these objectives, and are required to submit management action plans which set a baseline for the authority in relation to each of the objectives. Failure to achieve these plans may result in additional grants being withheld.

Services and Settings

This section describes the day-to-day activity of social services authorities as they try to apply the basic 'framework' just set out. This account is organized under two groups of headings:

1   The main settings within which services are provided
2   Current issues in service provision

This division involves distinguishing *settings*, the organizational
framework within which a service is provided, and *service*, what is
actually done. Given the necessary brevity, this selection is intended to
be indicative rather than comprehensive.

Community care teams

The major access route to children's services is the community child
care team, although its members will work in conjunction with a con-
stellation of other specialist teams within the local authority, including family placement teams, family support teams and youth offender
teams. The community child care teams, which vary in the size of their
catchment areas and geographical location, will undertake the core
tasks as described below, but this will be in conjunction with the work
of the other specialist teams, who may in the context of the previous
purchaser–provider split described in chapter 1, be seen as *providers*
of resources such as day care, foster care placements, and adoption
services. Some of the issues about how these fit with other social services activities are explored further in chapter 9.

Community child care teams constitute the central planks of local
authority provision for children and families, and are to be found in
almost every local authority, although, as can be seen from job advert-
isements, the actual name may vary; these teams may, for example, be
called 'children and families teams'. Indeed, the child and family social workers in the community child care teams have been described
by Thoburn (1996, p. 292) as the '"general practitioners" of the child
welfare system, whose daily activities will comprise a mix of assessment, social care planning, and the direct provision of therapeutic service to children and families.' Teams will incorporate intake systems
for referrals, the detailed organization of which can vary from one
social services department to another. The teams are responsible for
the provision of a flexible case-work service. There is a long-standing

tendency for this term to be (wrongly) equated with a psychoanalytical approach, a perception which might be thought to underline the traditional superior ascribed status of medical rather than social approaches to service provision. However, this is not the case and, as Thoburn (1994, pp. 24–5) states, 'the knowledge required by the area child and family social worker in order to put together the most appropriate package of support, therapy and services is extensive'. Alternative theoretical frameworks for practice by social workers may well include learning theory (Lishman, 1991), systemic theory (Gorrell Barnes, 1994) and ecological theory (Maluccio, 1981; Garbarino, 1982).

The methods which social workers use to put these theories into practice may include any of the following:

- Psychodynamic social work, including crisis intervention and brief focused therapy
- Behavioural social work
- Work with individuals and families based on systemic theory
- Group work with children and adults
- Community work
- Direct work with children

The route into accessing any of these or other services is via a 'referral'. This may be made by a parent, carer or child, as well as by a member of staff in another agency, such as a health visitor. The referral may be made in person or by phone or post, and, once contacted, a social worker must assess whether any child in the household is 'in need' under the terms of the legislation. This will be achieved by consulting with family members to work out how best the needs in question may be met. As the account of the 1989 Children Act philosophy has stressed, research indicates there are many factors which threaten the welfare of children, including the risk of maltreatment. Typologies vary but work for the Department of Health (Grimshaw and Sinclair, 1997) led to the following summary, and reflects current thinking:

- Intrinsic need: relating to children's own physical condition, developmental delay or difficulties such as behavioural problems at home or school; learning problems at school
- Children at risk of abuse or neglect
- Need because of parental mental and physical illness, addiction, depression or severe stress
- Need because of family stress, as a result of living within an unstable, conflictual, emotionally or developmentally damaging family

- Need because of offending behaviour – breaking the law
- Need because of social deprivation, poverty or social disadvantage

The characteristics of the children and families in the population most likely to be the actual or would-be recipients of help from the community child care team, are not, of course, representative of the population as a whole. As Schorr (1995, p. 8) has put it:

> The most striking characteristics that clients of the personal social services have in common are poverty and deprivation. Often this is not mentioned, possibly because the social services are said to be based on universalistic principles. Still, everyone in the business knows it.

It is certainly not an obscure fact 'to know' given that almost every study of children's services has underlined the low socio-economic status of the clients. Bebbington and Miles (1989) conclude that of the population of 5–9-year-olds whose families are on income support, live in poor housing and may be other than white, one in ten is admitted to care. Of the same age group, not dependent on income support, white and in 'decent' housing, the chances of being admitted to care rise to one in 7000.

The reality is that admission to care – or 'starting to be looked after' to use the new legal terminology of the 1989 Children Act – is rare across the child population as a whole, and that children admitted are more likely to have complex problems than children supported at home. In fact, exploring the characteristics of children in care through an analysis of the data on children's services, residential or otherwise, is a complex task, given the current scarcity of centrally held statistical information. However, it is known (Department of Health, 1997d) that, as at 31 March 1996, there were 51,200 children looked after by social services authorities in England.

Of the 11 million children in England, it is estimated that there are 600,000 children in need, as defined by section 17 of the 1989 Children Act; see page 64 for a further discussion of this. In any one year, somewhere around 160,000 will be referred to the child protection process. For about 40,000 children, there will be no further investigation. A family visit will be made to 120,000, resulting in the further investigation of about 80,000. There will be child protection conferences held on 40,000 cases, resulting ultimately in approximately 24,500 additions to the child protection register. The majority of these children will remain in their own homes; only about 6000 will not do so (Department of Health, 1995a).

Data on the age, ethnicity and gender of looked-after children (Department of Health, 1997d) shows that the average age of these children in 1996 was 10 years 11 months with 61 per cent of children being over 10. About one in ten were from a minority ethnic group. There was a slightly higher proportion of boys than girls.

The most commonly cited reasons for a child starting to be looked after were to give relief to parents (29 per cent), abuse or neglect (20 per cent), parents' health (14 per cent) and concern for the child's welfare (8 per cent).

However, being in care, or looked after, as mentioned in chapter 1, does not necessarily mean being in an institution. The proportion of children in foster placements as opposed to residential settings has risen steadily since 1989. By 1996, it had reached 65 per cent. There are differences between children admitted to residential settings and those admitted to foster settings (Department of Health, 1998b, p. 20):

> Children in residence are a small unusual group of all children. On the whole children who spend periods in residence have more complex and demanding problems.

The potential for an insatiable level of demand for services, posed by the children and families just described is almost certainly a key determinant of the 'gatekeeping mechanisms' which have been built into the Act, such as the definition of a *child in need*. As shown in the discussion of family support services (pages 69–70), the allocation by social services of the *need label* is alternately a truncated/short or long/complex process. While the majority of referrals will have been assessed as to whether the child is in need under the terms of the legislation, and their needs met or not, a second, smaller group will, in reality, make the greatest demands on social services time. These are the group who are suspected of being in need of protective services because of maltreatment by a parent or carer, or because the parent is unable to protect the child from accidental or deliberate harm.

The child welfare system in England is intended since the 1989 Children Act to constitute a seamless entity, with no structural chasm allowed to develop between family support and child protection. The basis of the system is the expectation that, initially, the social worker would offer family support services to the family, but where concerns are not met by services alone, then a second formal complex administrative 'child protection' part of the system (described more fully in the next section on services) can come into play. This system is intended to produce a co-ordinated multi-disciplinary response, and is laid out in a document called *Working Together to Safeguard*

Children (Department of Health, 1998k) currently in the process of being rewritten. In the last analysis, if it becomes clear that compulsion is required to protect the child, a social worker can apply to the Family Proceedings Court for either a Supervision Order or a Care Order and, in some cases, this move will result in subsequent prosecution of a person alleged to have maltreated a child.

Family placement teams

The second element in the organization of children's services is family placement teams. These teams, sometimes known as fostering and adoption teams, have the linked tasks of recruiting, assessing and supporting the individuals or families who offer short- or long-term placements in their own homes for those children *provided with accommodation* or *looked after* by the local authority. In some ways, the tasks they undertake constitute a microcosm of the challenges which confront local authorities in successfully implementing the 1989 Children Act. In the course of strengthening the emphasis on early services to support families, the Act requires 'provision of accommodation' to be offered as part of the menu of family support services, that is as a way of supplementing and supporting parental care rather than as a substitute for it. This provision of 'respite care' (Aldgate and Bradley, 1999) applies to children in need across the board, not just to children with disabilities.

In addition to work with short- and long-term foster carers, these family placement teams are responsible for the recruitment, assessment and post-adoption support of adoptive parents. Overall, there has been a considerable increase in the potential demand for the placements which the teams find and support. As pointed out above, the proportion of children in foster care placements represents about 65 per cent of children in care, although there are variations between children in different age groups; for example, approximately 90 per cent of children in care under ten, are fostered. However, the converse is that breakdown rates are also high, in the region of 20 per cent for short term and 30–40 per cent for long term. However, the challenge for the family placement teams is that the overall number of foster carers stays very much the same. Social services authorities routinely report great difficulty in making and sustaining placements, and that they are only able to make long-term placements from their existing carer pool. Johnstone (1999, pp. 8–9) points out: 'Agencies battle to retain carers against the pull of employment, the rise in the number of allegations against carers, growing dissatisfaction with organizational changes and low status.' All these problems are compounded by the changing profile of the children cared for, whose needs have become more complex and whose behaviour is often more challenging. In these circumstances, training and support for the foster carers is essential, but often scarce.

One frequently reported problem is the relative clarity of role of those social workers who support the foster carer and those who support the child. The 1994 Social Services Inspection of local authority fostering services reported that different expectations of foster carers in respect of their link worker and the child's social worker were particularly marked (Department of Health, 1994). However, researchers are agreed that support and training for foster parents are crucial for the needs of the child (Sellick, 1996, p. 167):

> [W]ell supported foster carers are more likely to weather the storms of fostering and to experience fewer placement breakdowns with the associated human and financial costs involved.

Or, as Triseliotis et al. (1995) conclude, 'support keeps carers, cuts costs and prevents placement breakdown'.

Indeed, the work of child placement teams is crucial to the implementation of current policy, and is not overlooked by *Quality Protects*, which includes a commitment to increase both the volume and quality of foster care to ensure more choice of placement and to minimize the number of moves in care for children.

Youth offender teams

Then there will also be youth justice or youth offender teams within social services authorities. These teams are in a state of major change at the time of writing, and, indeed, the transition of structure and role which is in progress represents a clear example of the powerful influence on local children and family social services provision of new political ideologies at central government level. In this case, the ideology is a New Labour prioritization of law and order issues, and, in particular, the need for a team approach to combat youth crime. The earlier youth justice teams, composed solely of social workers and education welfare officers, had a brief to work with children and young people between the ages of 10 and 18 who were known to be, or are at risk of, offending. However, new youth offender teams, the provision for which is laid down in the 1998 Crime and Disorder Act, have, at the time of writing, begun to replace them. The idea for these teams has its origins in the 1991 Home Office White Paper, *Safer Communities*, which enshrined the idea that, as a provider of a range of services which directly impact on the causes of crime, the local authority should have a co-ordinating function in respect of community safety initiatives. They are currently being piloted, but each local authority must have one in place by April 2000. Their role is a much broader one than their youth justice predecessors, and, most importantly, their membership is multi-disciplinary and includes police and probation officers. In addition to direct case-work with young people and their families (which can be contracted out), they have important strategic planning and service development roles.

Family centres

Local authorities also provide family centres. These are highlighted in the 1989 Children Act, schedules to the Act actually require that every local authority is required to 'provide such family centres as it considers appropriate in relation to children within its area'. In addition, the Audit Commission (1994b) singled them out as the most promising way forward for configuring services for children in need. This newly increased profile stems from the importance of family support within the overall structure of the Act, and the widespread view that the purpose and range of family centres are particularly well suited to the intentions of the Act in respect of family support. There is no absolute way of knowing how many family centres run either by both local authorities or voluntary organizations are in existence, but the relevant umbrella group, the Family Centre Network currently has 550 centres in membership.

The definition of family centre in the 1989 Act (Department of Health, 1991a) is 'a centre at which the child, his parents and any other person who has parental responsibility for him or who is looking after him, may (a) attend for occupational, social, cultural or recreational activities; (b) attend for advice, guidance or counselling; or (c) be provided with accommodation while he is receiving advice, guidance or counselling'.

However, this apparently straightforward definition obscures the variation in types of family centre, a degree of variation so considerable it might be thought that one term will not suffice to describe them all. There have been several approaches to categorization, of which Holmans' (1988) classification is probably the best known:

- Client focused
- Neighbourhood focused
- Community development model

More recently, Vallender and Warren (1997) list and define seven models for family centres:

1   *The mixed model*
    Most centres are likely to fall into this category, and may be run by local authorities or voluntary agencies with a local authority contract. They mainly work with referred families, using a mix of methods.
2   *The referral only model*
    These centres work closely with the child protection staff in area teams, and manifest two dominant models; the family therapy model and the parent training model.
3   *Family resource centre*
    These are a second-tier service working with area teams to organize direct work with children, support for carers and specific packages of support.
4   *Adolescent resource centre*
    These are less numerous and involve the use of residential and day care programmes
5   *Adult education/community development*
    These are mostly run by voluntary organizations, using collective practices based on neighbourhood issues, group work, and a focus on opportunities for education and work.
6   *Day care/early education*
    These centres work from a universalist base of full-day care and tend to work under the auspices of education departments or combined education/social services.
7   *Without walls*
    These are centre-less organizations based on work in people's homes and are particularly relevant in rural areas.

However, despite the variety of approaches, common themes emerge from the literature as important issues for the work of family centres:

- An emphasis on notions of *prevention* in respect of child abuse, reception into care and family breakdown
- The importance of *community work*
- A *health perspective* on problems
- Dealing with the problem of *stigma*
- The principle of *working in partnership* with parents and children

Key Services Issues

The previous section describes some of the most important settings within which social service authorities meet their statutory responsibilities to provide for the needs of children; young people and families. This section highlights the two key issues which have arisen within services across the continuum of social services child-related activity and demonstrates the perennial nature of these two sets of tensions within statutory child welfare policy:

- Family support versus child protection
- Can the local authority be an adequate corporate parent?

Family support versus child protection

There are really two elements in this policy/practice dynamic embodied in the conflict between *family support* and *child protection*. The first concerns the efficacy of the family support service, and the second, the tendency of the child protection service to intervene overzealously and/or inappropriately.

Section 17 of the 1989 Act gives local authorities a general duty to 'safeguard and promote the welfare of children in need by providing a range and level of services appropriate to their needs' which, the Guidance makes clear, may include day care services, befriending services, parent toddler groups, toy libraries, drop-in centres, playbuses, family centres, accommodation, and social work support. The emphasis of the Act is on supporting, wherever possible the child in her/his own home, and on social services attempting to meet *need* rather than only intervene in cases of *risk* or *abuse*.

However, the picture which has emerged since 1990 is a mixed one. The first national studies of Section 17 – Aldgate and Tunstill (1995) in England, Colton et al. (1995) in Wales – found that local authorities had established a hierarchy of access to services, and were concentrating their provision of family support on children seen to be at risk of significant harm or neglect rather than those seen as in need in the community. This second group would include, for example, children living in homes where the gas, water or electricity was disconnected, children in substandard housing, children with special health needs and refugee children. On the other hand, even where the question of risk had precipitated social services action, research (Gibbons et al., 1995) had shown that, in about 75 per cent of cases where there were suspicions of child abuse, preliminary investigations indicated no need for a case conference; and in most instances, the family received no further help and the case was closed. Yet, most were living in situations of extreme poverty and deprivation, which were not addressed. The overzealous nature of the child protection system, characterized by legalism and inspectorial practice by social workers has been under review since the publication of *Messages from Research* (Department of Health, 1995a). The 1993 Children Act Report concluded on these issues (Department of Health, 1993a, para. 239):

[A] broadly consistent and somewhat worrying picture is emerging. . . . Further work is still needed to provide across the country a range of family services aimed at preventing families reaching the point of breakdown. Some authorities are finding it difficult to move from a reactive social policing role to a more proactive partnership with families.

This issue was picked up by the Audit Commission (1994b) who stated that 'prevention is better than cure', and was still reflected three years later in negative findings by the Social Services Inspectorate (Department of Health, 1997f).

This picture has recently been seen to be changing. Tunstill and Aldgate (1999), in a later study of children in need in seven local authorities, identified examples of proactive policy and practice, appropriate provision of family support services and a high level of satisfaction on the part of families receiving them. A recent Social Services Inspectorate inspection (Department of Health, 1998h) similarly found that:

80% of the families contacted expressed satisfaction with family support services . . . family centre users were particularly appreciative . . .

Such initial shortcomings in the application of the original philosophy of the Act have led to a range of criticisms of social services, although Utting (1998, p. 7) concludes that:

notwithstanding the very serious concerns that have been raised there is a presumption that it would make better sense to apply the existing Children Act in the spirit intended, rather than return to the legislative drawing board with a blank sheet of paper.

However, he warns that:

a shift towards preventive services holds out the long term prospect of savings on expensive crisis intervention in children's lives, but in the short term it requires resources as well as the political will to change.

Four linked questions can be seen to arise from this (albeit improving) state of affairs:

1   Is the slowness to maximize family support services due solely to lack of financial resources, or do professional attitudes also play a part?
2   Should/will the new initiatives (within departments other than the Department of Health) which have come on stream under the present government – such as Sure Start, Health Action Zones and Education Action Zones – replace the role of social services in respect of early intervention to promote children's welfare?
3   Will there be moves to redefine the role of the social services authority into a purely child protection agency?
4   Finally, and most importantly, would such developments be good for children and their families?

Can the local authority be an adequate corporate parent?

The second question highlighted at the beginning of this section was: *Can the local authority be an adequate corporate parent?* The 1989 Act set out implicitly to modify negative views of the care system on the part of children, their parents, professionals and the public. It intended that the provision of accommodation (which effectively replaces voluntary reception into care) should be seen as a service, and that both children in this category, and children looked after following a care order, should be free of stigma and provided with a high-quality experience, whether for a longer or shorter period of time, and whether in foster care or, more unusually, in a residential setting.

However, in the last ten years, a consistent pattern has emerged from research studies, inspections by the Social Services Inspectorate, and individual high-profile enquiries into abuse: all is far from satisfactory for children and young people either *within*, or indeed, *after* the care system. A summary of key data about children in and following care (Hill and Tisdall, 1997) highlights serious failures:

•   Unplanned and ill-prepared admissions
•   Several moves of home
•   Infrequent or no parental contact
•   Reduced contact with other significant family members
•   Changes in household composition which make it harder for chil-

dren to fit in with other children coming and going during the placement
- Staff changes in residential care
- In excess of 75 per cent of care leavers have no educational qualifications
- Between 50 and 80 per cent of care leavers are unemployed
- 23 per cent of adult and 38 per cent of young prisoners have been in care

Taken together, the data reveals a devastating catalogue of deficits in provision. These have had serious effects for the day-to-day life experiences for children. They will have been a source of major abusive threats/damage to their health and welfare and serious problems in their post-care lives. The Department of Health has set in train an ambitious programme of assessment and policy initiatives (Parker et al., 1991; Ward, 1995; Department of Health, 1997e, 1998h). *Quality Protects* (Department of Health, 1998i), the key current initiative for local authority children's services, lays down specific and detailed targets for local authorities. However, while there are tangible policy initiatives, which, if robustly implemented, may have a good chance of impacting on these problems, other more profound questions have been debated, and new policy developments may yet be floated from what, critics would argue, is the wreckage of local authority failure in this area. Currently, the government's preferred lifeboat appears to be the reintroduction of a more proactive, and some may argue, aggressive policy of adoption. This hardly constitutes a new idea. The permanent removal of children from their birth families has been a feature of child care policy since the Poor Law. Such a strategy, however, raises fundamental issues about the scope and purpose of social services work with children and families (Ryburn, 1996, p. 196):

[I]t challenges us to consider both whether nurture and environment can supplant nature, and whether it is desirable that they seek to do so. It calls into question the extent to which the State should act as an arbiter and regulator of family life, and in seeking to build permanent new families raises vital questions about the status to be accorded to original families ... More than anything else, perhaps, adoption has reflected in microcosmic form key social issues of the times and it continues today to operate as a barometer of public attitudes to families, child care and parenting.

Indeed, the reasons for its political popularity are not hard to fathom; it sits easily with a rediscovery of the value of family which has been a consistent theme in New Labour rhetoric. In addition, as Kirk and

McDaniel (1984) point out, the use of adoption is a cheap option since, in essence, it transfers the cost of care from the public to the private purse.

Government commitment to the increase in adoption is unambiguous; it is incorporated as one of the eight *Quality Protects* objectives for children, within the requirement for local authorities to ensure that children are securely attached to carers capable of providing safe and effective care for the duration of childhood. The target is to reduce to no more than 16 per cent in all authorities, by 2001, the number of children who have three or more placements in one year. There is a performance indicator in the Performance Assessment Framework (Department of Health, 1999n, indicator C23, p. 52):

> Definition = the number of looked after children adopted during the year ended 31st March. Purpose/rationale = to encourage the use of adoption. Action required = to make additional efforts to increase the proportion of looked after children who are adopted.

However, the data on adoption is incompatible with a policy which its critics have suggested errs on the side of treating children as commodities to be made available to meet the needs of childless couples. The social context of adoption has changed massively since the days when to produce a child out of wedlock resulted in massive stigma. Few mother now give up their babies for adoption. Only 4 per cent of adoptions involve babies. It is, however, the image of unproblematic and needy babies which dominates the public mind. The reality is that children who may be candidates for adoption are likely to be of school age and have experienced a range of adversity which may militate against their settling easily with new parents. One of the reasons for the more challenging histories which lie behind such children is that more effort is likely to have been made to enable them to stay at home with their birth families. Only a small proportion of children entering care are available for, or in need of, adoption, given that about 90 per cent go home to their parents within six months. As has been shown above, more than a quarter are temporarily in care to give their families respite from looking after them, including reasons associated with disability. Fortunately, or otherwise, the myth of uncomplicated tiny babies needing care is exactly that.

The Role of Training

A new Post Qualifying Award in Child Care Social Work will come on stream in 2000. This new award is only the latest development in a long-running sub-plot, and can only be understood in this longitudinal context. The tensions and debates which characterize the evolution of training provision mirror many of the perennial conflicts within service provision for children. That is to say, the structure and design of training for child care social work has tended to veer between voluntarism and professionalism; specialism and genericism; psychodynamic and systemic approaches; a singular focus on child protection and an holistic approach to the needs of children; and political as opposed to professional or academic regulation. The 1948 Children Act had led to the first system of professional training for the new children's officers, as one of the ways in which the welfare of children would be safeguarded. Subsequently, the first generic social work course was introduced at the London School of Economics in 1954, developed by Eileen Younghusband, one of the doyennes of social work training. The really major changes to the ethos of social work training followed the publication of the Seebohm Report in 1968 and the 1970 Local Authority Social Services Act. The Seebohm report also recommended that generic social work training be developed. The Central Council for Education and Training in Social Work (CCETSW) was set up to regulate the first unified social work training qualification, the Certificate of Qualification in Social Work (CQSW). As Denney (1998, p. 13) explains, this 'led to the establishment of numerous social work departments within institutions of higher education and the general academization of social work education'.

The 1970s were characterized by robust, and sometimes aggressive, debate as to the ends and means of social work between commentators: Corrigan and Leonard (1978) viewed it from a Marxist perspective, as yet one more form of social control; others such as Brewer and Lait (1980) castigated it as irresponsible left-wing indulgence which failed both society and the clients it set out to help. However, throughout this rather stereotyped exchange of views, the reality was that approaches to training increasingly incorporated rather more pragmatic and eclectic approaches to the social work task such as task-centred case-work (Reid and Epstein, 1977).

However, the status of social work failed to attain a perceived level of unqualified professionalism. It could be argued that, in any particular era, criticism of either the task or the training merely serve as examples of its tentative professional status, albeit in the context of varying ideological agendas and rhetoric. So, for example, in the 1980s and 1990s, the training debate moved to the desirability of anti-oppressive approaches, where the hierarchy of oppression often seemed to be dominated by race, over and above class, gender, disability and sexuality. Interwoven with this critique has been a debate about effectiveness (Sheldon, 1986) and, in particular, given the deficits in care provision highlighted above, about the outcomes for those children received into the care of a local authority. It is this more recent focus on the outcomes for children, dominated by the Department of Health (Ward, 1995), which has had a direct impact on the introduction of the new Post Qualifying Award in Child Care Social Work. Here the Department of Health's declared intention is to improve standards of child care practice as part of its new initiatives such as 'Modernising Social Services' and 'Care Protects'. Extensive funding has been made available by the Department of Health for a 'training support programme' sub-programme of £1 million in 1999 rising to £6 million in 2001–2, to enable local authorities to train a projected number of 7,000 workers in child care and child protection over the next six or seven years. Eight pilot programmes have been selected, whose work will be evaluated to identify the effectiveness of this new approach to training.

As was stated above, however, it would be wrong to see this new award as an isolated phenomenon. Definitive judgement can only be made in the future, but given other developments such as the review of social services training and the establishment of a new General Social Care Council – see pages 195–6 – the end of the century would seem to herald a new approach to social work and the training for it. Specifically, the new award probably heralds the beginning of a return to specialism from the now discredited generalism – see chapter 10 for some of the organizational aspects of this development – as well as an emerging centralization and consolidation of government and inevitable political party control. It is also intended that the existing mental health award – see page 196 – involving the identification of 'approved social workers' will be extended. This, and the new child care award, will form the building blocks for 'new' social work specialisms; in other words, a retreat from the ambitious ideas of the post-Seebohm era.

Conclusions

The picture just described raises the spectre of four underlying questions which current policy and practice seem far from answering, and which, it could be argued, have in one form or another characterized child welfare history from the Poor Law onwards:

1 Is it possible to eradicate stigma from the care system?
2 Can paid, even professionally qualified, staff provide for the day-to-day development of children, or is this a task which can only be delivered on a purely affective and/or altruistic basis?
3 If care is so precarious, why are greater efforts not made to prevent it happening in the first place?
4 Can adoption ever co-exist with supporting birth families and the consistent allocation of resources for high-quality foster and residential care?

The problems which have been identified in the last decade are only the latest in a long list which reflects society's failure to meet all or even most of the needs of children who are its most vulnerable members, and, indeed, the problems themselves underlie the necessity to explore child welfare within a structural and political context. It is here that questions may be raised about the basic assumptions which underpin the social policies introduced by New Labour, and, in particular, the extent to which they have or, indeed, can benefit the population of children and families who form the constituency of social services authorities.

The greatest effort and publicity has clearly been focused on the creation of an inclusive society. Policies have been introduced to reduce social exclusion, whether in the form of poverty, crime, ill health or poor education. Data suggests some progress in these fields. For example, as Piachaud (1999) has shown, it is likely that anti-poverty measures taken up to the time of writing should, by 2002, reduce the numbers of children in poverty by around 800,000 (with about 555,000 parents raised out of poverty). However, the greatest number of these will be in low-income working families, and the lot of children in lone-parent workless households may still be one of poverty. The danger would seem to be that the rhetoric of social inclusion/exclusion can all too easily run into the rhetoric of the underclass, a concept seen on the left to be largely unacceptable. If this happens, those who remain on the excluded side of the social divide may all too soon find themselves the objects of benign social engineering, or of the more oppressive aspects of social services functions such as compulsory removal of children and/or adoption orders sought against the wishes of parents.

Where universal approaches founder or fail, the possibility exists that the selective policies which fall within the remit of social services might increase in importance and, indeed, in punitiveness. The emphasis which New Labour has put on child protection and looked after children, including adoption targets, far outweighs the emphasis it has attached to family support and preventative work. The thrust of *Quality Protects* has been seen to put at risk some of the emerging progress in the area of the implementation of Part 111 of the 1989 Children Act. Some of the statements emerging, in particular from the Home Office, about inadequate or anti-social parenting seem to have their roots in a crude authoritarian populism rather than an empirical grasp of the link between social deprivation and parenting difficulties.

It would be a supreme irony if the impact of a left of centre government were to reduce the progressive nature of the best of social services work with children and families. A cynic might wish to recall that the last child care act which prioritized the needs of substitute carers over the needs of the birth family, and made it easier to remove children from their parents with no compensatory requirement to provide preventative services was the 1975 Children Act. This Act, originally a private member's bill introduced by David Owen, was the product of a Labour government.

This account has attempted to locate local authority children's services within a broader social policy framework, and to provide a necessarily selective overview of their key responsibilities. It serves to underline the impossibility of understanding child welfare outside of a structural and organizational context. The problems, which have surfaced in the 1990s, are only the latest in a long list which reflects society's failure to meet all or even most of the needs of the children who are its most vulnerable members. To a very real extent, the degree to which social services authorities succeed in achieving the targets set for them in this area, will determine their survival and/or future development as welfare organizations within the local authority. If the score goes against them then the victims will be not merely the organizations themselves, but quite possibly the credibility of child care social work and, most importantly, the children of the poor.

Chapter 5

Adult Care

Bob Hudson

- Introduction
- Services for Older People
- Services for People with a Learning Disability
- Services for Physically Disabled People
- Conclusions

Introduction

The remit of this chapter is to examine the role of local authority social services agencies in relation to three client groups: older people, people with a learning disability and physically disabled people. As shown on page 11, these groups account for around 70 per cent of gross personal social services expenditure, the bulk of which (50 per cent) is accounted for by older people, followed by learning disability services (13 per cent) and physical disability (7 per cent).

Over the past two decades, services for these groups have been shaped by exposure to a common range of factors: the shift towards a mixed economy of care; the attempt to move people and support from institutional to community settings; the move from a medical towards a more social model of care; and the uncertainty as to whether support and funding should come from the National Health Service or from local authorities. However, the impact of these factors has been variable across the different groups.

Services for Older People

The delivery of local authority social services to support older people has undergone a transformation in the past twenty years or so. The main change has been that of the relative 'market position' of the statutory, private and voluntary sectors of care and, associated with this, the issues of targeting of care and of funding responsibility.

Trends in institutional care

Until 1980, private provision in residential and nursing homes was very small. Social services departments had come into existence in 1971 based on an implicit understanding that the personal social services would be both state funded and state provided – the profit motive was felt to be incompatible with the provision of care for vulnerable people (Hardy and Wistow, 1999). Table 5.1 shows how this position has been transformed over the past three decades.

The same time series data does not exist for private nursing home places, but this also shows a pattern of remarkable growth from the mid-1980s onwards, with places rising from around 20,000 in 1970 to 205,000 in 1998, almost all of them in the private sector. This increase in private provision, in part, reflects a decrease in long-stay care funded and provided by the National Health Service. Over the period 1970–93, the number of long-stay hospitals fell by 18 per cent, and again by a further 36 per cent between 1993 and 1998 – a shift from publicly funded care, free at the point of delivery, to private sector care funded by user payments or means-tested local authority support.

The main explanation for these dramatic changes is to be found in the changing policies on public funding, for the decline in public provision was not associated with reductions in public sector expenditure *per se* but rather with the terms and conditions of this expenditure.

Table 5.1 Residential home care places for elderly, chronically ill and physically disabled people; market share by sector, UK 1970–98 (%)

Date	Local Authority	Private	Voluntary
1970	63	14	23
1980	63	17	20
1985	51	32	17
1990	39	48	13
1995	26	55	19
1998	22	61	17

Source: Adapted from Hardy and Wistow (1999)

These are described in chapter 2; see pages 35–7. Between 1982 and 1993, the number of residents in private and voluntary residential and nursing homes supported by the Department of Social Security rose from 16,000 to 281,000, and the cost of supporting them grew from £39m to £2.57 billion. As shown in chapter 2, the 1990 National Health Service and Community Care Act phased out the subsidy of institutional care through the social security system. Some of the savings from this change were redistributed to local authorities, who were given the freedom to spend this on either institutional or non-institutional care. To safeguard the position of the independent sector, however, local authorities were required to spend 85 per cent of the sums transferred on the services of independent sector providers. Since the independent sector has been initially slow to develop domiciliary services, the '85 per cent rule' tended simply to bolster the growth of independent institutional provision – gross expenditure on independent residential and nursing homes for older people more than doubled between 1994/5 and 1996/7 (Department of Health, 1999i). The current distribution of expenditure by type of provision for older people is shown in Table 5.2.

Table 5.2 Gross personal social services expenditure on older people by type of provision 1997–98 (£million)

Residential care	*2940*
Day care	1590
Care management	280
Management	100
Total	4910

Source: Department of Health (1999i, table 2, p. 6)

Trends in non-institutional care

As has already been noted, the ready availability of demand-led payments for institutional care between 1980 and 1993 contrasted strongly with the tight cash limits on local authority mainstream expenditure for, among other things, non-institutional provision for older people. As a result, while the number of residential and nursing home places grew more rapidly than the population of older people, the reverse was the case for domiciliary services. By 1984/5, for example, the number of home help hours and meals had fallen by 14 per cent and 15 per cent respectively from their 1977/8 levels per head of population aged 75 and over (Wistow, 1987). Similar reductions took place between 1986/7 and 1992/3 with 10 per cent and 13 per cent reductions respectively taking place for the same services. The changes in the funding arrangements since 1993 have seen some reversal of this trend. Since 1994/5, gross expenditure on home care has increased by over 20 per cent from around £800 million to £1 billion (Department of Health, 1999i), and as table 5.3 indicates, this accounts for the bulk of non-institutional provision.

Table 5.3 Day and domiciliary provision for older people 1997/8 (£ million gross)

Home care/Help	1020
Day centres	170
Meals at home/Lunch clubs	90
Field social work	50
Admin./miscellaneous	260
Total	1590

Source: Department of Health (1999i, table 4, p. 8)

However, unlike earlier patterns of activity, this shift towards domiciliary and day care has been accompanied by what is being described as 'higher service intensity', or targeting of those in the greatest need. The view that community care services should be allocated in this way was one of the six key principles in the 1989 White Paper, *Caring for People* (Department of Health, 1989a), and was reiterated in the criticisms by the Audit Commission of those local authorities held to be failing to do so (Audit Commission, 1997). Since 1993, this has generally meant an increase in the number of households provided with five hours or more home care services at the expense of those receiving what is termed 'low-level care' of two hours or less per week. Since 1992, there has been a 9 per cent drop in the number of households receiving home care services and a 56 per cent increase in the contact hours provided. As Age Concern has noted in evidence to the Health Select Committee (House of Commons Health Committee, 1998b):

> Rather than social services departments being the first port of call for older people needing services, they appear to be considered the last resort.

The existence of a national strategy on targeting has not thus far been matched by any national strategy on preventive services, and resources remain scarce for investment in pilot projects which could test the cost-effectiveness and viability of low-intensity support services. Research into such schemes suggests that occasional, but regular, contact with staff or volunteers enables people to better care for themselves, maintain their homes and reduce the need for costly institutional care. The research message is that while means testing and service rationing may make short-term sense to agencies with tight budgets, it will often prove a false economy.

Fragmentation of service responsibility: the inter-agency level

As has already been seen, agency responsibility for services for older people has become increasingly fragmented and confused, and this has had a direct effect on service users who are finding themselves having to pay for 'social care' support which, in the past, had been seen as a 'free' health service good. In 1948, local authorities were not expected to provide personal and nursing care in their residential homes, but rather to support those pensioners who were unable to live independently but needed mainly board and lodging and some supervision. The Health Minister, Aneurin Bevan, was also anxious to end the stigma attached to the former Poor Law institutions, and envisaged local authority homes being more like hotels for poor pensioners for which there would be a nationally regulated charge. This was seen as a way of avoiding the claim that pensioners were receiving 'charity', but the realization of that ideal depended on a substantial supply of good quality accommodation for all who wanted it. It has been shown above that, while what actually happened has been complicated, the long-run outcome has been – and is likely to remain – the rationing of places to those in severe need of care.

Much of the current difficulty with inter-agency fragmentation results from the fact that the boundaries between the National Health Service and local authority responsibilities for services have shifted and become unclear over time (House of Commons Health Committee, 1998a). In particular, health service agencies took full advantage of the social security funded growth of private nursing homes from 1980 onwards to withdraw from such provision themselves and pass the responsibility on to the nursing homes and the cost to local authorities, who had been given the nursing home budget under the 1990 National Health Service and Community Care Act. Local authorities became increasingly agitated about what they saw as a transfer of responsibility without corresponding funding, and, in 1995, the Department of Health issued guidance on continuing health care responsibilities in response to 'a number of concerns' raised in a report by the Health Service Commissioner. This report had investigated the failure of Leeds Health Authority to make available long-term care for a seriously incapacitated patient deemed to no longer require health care (Health Services Commissioner, 1994). Its publication had reflected the widespread concern that the boundary between health and social care had shifted too far in the direction of means-tested local authority provision – a conclusion which had also been reached by the Health Select Committee (House of Commons Health Committee, 1995).

A related issue concerns the fact that social care homes are run by home owners and managers who do not have to be medically qualified. The expectation is that their residents will not need continuous nursing care. This assumes that residents will have entitlements to health service care just like anyone else living in the community – they will be visited by their GPs when necessary, they may be referred for hospital treatment and they may have attention from community based nursing services. Since many of the residents of care homes are very frail, many of them will have health problems and will make heavy demands on those services. Those demands may rise – in some cases – to the point where the needs for health-care may be so high that it may be deemed more appropriate or cost-effective to move them to an institution offering more intensive care. Until the early 1980s, the debate about this 'boundary' issue was about the arrangements which might be made for hospitals (meaning National Health Service funded institutions) to take over the very sick residents of local authority homes. The changes described above have altered the issues. Consider the case of an ailing resident of a care home. The input of services from GP and district nurse is rising steadily. There may be increasing concern that the staff of the home, who will generally not have nursing qualifications, will be encountering situations, particularly at night, which they are not necessarily qualified to deal with. The cost of care for the home will be rising. Therefore, both the medical authorities and the care home managers may argue that nursing home care would be more appropriate. However, quite apart from the fact that a move would be unsettling for the person concerned, it would also sharply raise the costs for the social services department (or the person and/or his or her family). Not surprisingly, social services departments, on their side, are urging homes to keep sick residents as long as possible while, in some cases, health authorities are raising difficulties about expensive inputs of health care services into residential homes.

Politically, the more important consequence of the shifts in responsibility described above was the resentment felt by older people who
were being asked to pay for their long-term care (often by selling their
property) when they had assumed their national insurance contributions and taxes had guaranteed them 'cradle-to-grave' support as envisaged in the 1942 Beveridge Report. The Conservative government
tried to defuse the issue by increasing the amounts of capital that
people could retain before becoming liable for charges, but the Labour
Party made a manifesto commitment to set up a Royal Commission to
investigate the issue more fully. The Commission reported in 1999
(Royal Commission on Long-Term Care, 1999), recommending that
personal care, including nursing care, should be free of charge following an assessment of need, but that those who receive care should still
pay towards housing and living costs – a recommendation which had
been also made some years earlier by a Joseph Rowntree inquiry (Joseph
Rowntree Foundation, 1996). At the time of writing, the Labour government has not felt able to respond to this recommendation. Clearly,
it does not want to rush a decision on a matter that has substantial
public expenditure implications. Nevertheless, rumours suggest that it
is not happy with this suggestion, and would prefer to adopt a more
modest proposal from two dissident members of the Commission who
suggested that they should liberalize the existing means tests.

Fragmentation of service responsibility: the inter-professional level

The fragmentation at inter-agency level is both reflected in, and further shaped by, differences between the key professionals involved with
older people. The introduction of assessment and care management
processes under the 1990 National Health Service and Community
Care Act, and the assignment of lead responsibility for this task to
social services, was both an acknowledgement of professional fragmentation and a response to it. Much of the evidence on implementation points to continuing difficulties. In a review of 11 social services
authorities, the Audit Commission (1997) found that eight had no
checks on the quality of assessments prior to admission to institutional care – and the three using multidisciplinary panels were less
likely to use such provision. A Social Services Inspectorate inspection
of care planning for older people put some of the problem down to the
inability of social services care managers to act in a sufficiently authoritative way so as to co-ordinate the services identified to meet
assessed needs, though there were also concerns that the assessment

process itself was insufficiently comprehensive (Department of Health, 1997b). The Health Advisory Service similarly reported social services care managers to be too often unaware of the medical illness that can be behind functional failure, while members of Primary Health Care Teams could be slow to accept that some disability in older people can be improved by multi-disciplinary packages of therapy (Health Advisory Service, 1997).

The impact of the fragmentation of service responsibility in respect of continuing health care is perhaps most starkly seen where *no* professional or agency accepts responsibility for assessing, monitoring and reviewing the needs of vulnerable older people. The reality for many older people is that it is enormously difficult to access a health care assessment from the National Health Service or continuing health care services if the individual is in any other setting than in hospital. Further, it does not seem that many older patients' needs are assessed while in hospital to confirm that the home in which they are currently resident continues to be appropriate, other than when staff at the home have suggested that they will not re-accept the resident after hospital care has finished (House of Commons Health Committee, 1998b). Similarly, social services authorities may not see it as their task to assess or reassess those older people in residential or nursing homes who pay entirely for themselves (some 91,000 in 1997) or those who continue to have their 'preserved rights' to Income Support paid directly by the Department of Social Security (a further 108,000 in 1997).

Overall, developments in the personal social services for older people have therefore been characterized by issues of process, structure and market sector. Much less emphasis has been placed on developing innovative approaches to care, on involving older people themselves in the determination of these approaches or on articulating a user-led model of care. The position on services for people with a learning or physical disability is rather different. Although not immune from sectoral shift and service fragmentation, there has also been a sharper focus on developing innovative 'service philosophies' and seeking to reshape services in line with these.

Services for People with a Learning Disability

In broad terms, three factors have shaped personal social services for people with a learning disability: the gradual acceptance of a social (rather than a medical) model of care; the run-down and closure of long-stay hospitals; and the search for a new paradigm of community services. As in the case of older people, it is not possible to describe the role of social services without also exploring the changing role of the National Health Service.

Models of care: social versus medical

Alternatives to institutional care began to be considered seriously in the 1950s when the Royal Commission on Mental Illness and Mental Deficiency (1957) recommended that more provision should be made for people with mild intellectual disabilities in hostels in the community, partly to relieve pressure on hospital places. Little progress was made until the mid-1960s when a series of public scandals in institutions revealed extensive ill-treatment and neglect in overcrowded surroundings (Martin, 1984). In response to this, a government White Paper reinforced the goal of providing community services and set targets for the growth of local authority residential places and adult training centre places (Department of Health and Social Security, 1971).

Alongside these early indications of a policy shift, interest developed in an alternative 'model' of learning disability. At the beginning of the 1970s, a new lobby developed, focusing on a group called Campaign for the Mentally Handicapped (now known as Values into Action), which for the first time called for the complete abandonment of hospital care and its replacement by support in the community. This lobby drew its inspiration from the first community services in the USA and Scandinavia, and from ideas about 'normalization' (Brown and Smith, 1992). In Britain, the interpretation of this term by O'Brien and Tyne (1981) became particularly influential. This identifies five major service accomplishments:

1 ensuring that service users are *present* in the community
2 ensuring that service users are supported in *making choices* about their lives
3 developing the *competence* of service users
4 enhancing the *respect* afforded to service users; and
5 ensuring that service users *participate* in the life of the community.

These developments were given added impetus following the publication of the Jay Report (1979) which also recommended an end to long-stay care in hospitals and the development of housing-based services.

Although relatively slow to begin with, these factors did herald a major shift in the nature and scale of personal social services support for people with a learning disability. The most obvious impact has arisen from the decline of long-stay institutions provided by the National Health Service and their replacement with community housing and support from social services and housing agencies. The first large-scale institutional closures took place in the mid-1980s (Korman and Glennerster, 1985; 1990) and as the process gathered momentum, 'deinstitutionalization' became tacitly accepted as a general policy goal (Mansell and Ericsson, 1996). Between 1980 and 1991, the numbers of people with learning disabilities living in long-stay National Health Service institutions in Britain fell from 56,000 to 30,000, and, by 1997/ 8, this had been further reduced to around 12,000 (Department of Health, 1999i).

Social services authorities were initially given encouragement (through the national demonstration 'care-in-the-community' initiative) and funding (through more flexible joint finance and voluntary budgetary transfers from the National Health Service) to develop their own community provision but, as with older people, this became complicated in the 1980s when the National Health Service found it easier and cheaper to use the social security funding route. This began to give rise to concerns about the direction and quality of care. In 1985, an investigation by the Social Services Select Committee concluded that there were problems, deficiencies and anxieties that needed to be addressed (House of Commons Social Services Committee, 1985), and this was followed up by a review from the Audit Commission (1986) which identified a number of underlying problems:

- A mismatch of resources to meet the requirements of community care policies
- The need for short-term bridging finance to fund the transition to community care
- Social security policies which provided a perverse incentive for residential rather than domiciliary based care
- Fragmented organization and a lack of effective joint working and planning

The recommendation of the Audit Commission that local authorities be made responsible for the long-term care of people with a learning disability in the community was not accepted by the government, but social services *were* given a strong financial and professional lead under the 1990 National Health Service and Community Care Act. To some extent, the 1990s *has* seen a significant improvement in service standards. For example, a recent investigation into services for adults by the Social Services Inspectorate (Department of Health, 1998f) praised the improvements which had taken place over the previous decade and noted that sound principles (along 'normalization' lines) had been developed which emphasized independence, respect for users and community presence.

The critique of community provision

Just as the dominance of the institutional paradigm was accompanied by an institutional critique, so the now dominant community paradigm has found itself the subject of criticism. Some of these criticisms have been of a general nature, speculating on whether there is any such thing as 'community' (Willmott, 1986), noting the slow and piece-meal nature of change (Collins, 1992) and pointing to the transfer into community facilities of institutional practices (Sinson, 1992). Critiques of normalization have pointed out that some interpretations have not empowered service users and have failed to incorporate equal opportunities and anti-discriminatory principles (Brown and Smith, 1992), and in general the self-advocacy movement has only slowly and partially succeeded in giving a voice to people with learning disabilities. Other concerns relate more specifically to the nature of community support organized or provided by social services authorities. Four broad problem areas can be identified: services for older people and their carers; short-term care; supported living; and support in community activity.

Services for older people and their carers

The number of people with learning disabilities living into old age is increasing, but relatively little is known about how they view their changing needs or how services respond. Fitzgerald (1998) talked to 31 older (aged 55 or over) people living in a variety of settings, as well as to members of their social and support networks, to discover what they wanted from services. Although her work was not intended as a critique of services or as a comparison with services for younger people, it did identify several areas of difficulty. First, there were concerns about service organization and delivery: there was wide variation in the provision of services, confusion surrounding who was responsible for providing support, and, in some cases, there was no real impetus to resettle older people from long-stay institutions. The second set of concerns were around the failure to apply normalization principles to this group. Fitzgerald noted the wide lack of respect for the future of older people in terms of expectations and potential for independence, as well as a marked lack of opportunity to develop networks with others of similar ages or interests.

Complementary studies by Walker and Ryan (1995) and Walker and Walker (1998) examined the situation and service needs of older family carers supporting relatives with learning disabilities at home. Much of the policy discussion and research of the past decade has concentrated on resettlement from long-stay institutions, with a relative neglect of those who continue to live with their families. The study by Walker and Ryan, for example, found that people living with their families received different levels and types of provision from those living in group homes or resettled from long-stay hospitals, and family carers reported needing higher levels and more flexible forms of support. Those continuing to live at home were described as the Cinderellas of the service, whose pattern of care had changed little and was confined to traditional day centre and respite care. Walker and Walker focus more directly on older family carers themselves, noting that they are more likely to be sole carers, have smaller support networks, have negative experiences of the paid sector of care, and are especially reluctant to seek help. Although they wanted to be able to support their relative for as long as possible, they lived in fear of the future and felt undervalued and unsupported by the paid care system.

Short-term care

Short-term care has long been recognized as a useful way in which to support families who care for someone with a learning disability, but concerns have been expressed about both the nature and extent of the support. Hubert (1991), for example, found considerable dissatisfaction among families of adults receiving short-term care to the extent that many parents had been put off any prospect of care outside the family and expressed a hope that their son or daughter would not outlive them. A more recent national survey of respite services by Flynn et al. (1996) found the most common type of care to be provided was in residential units, and also discovered that service providers and service users had quite different views about what constituted a valued service. While social services authorities typically referred to the benefits of short-term care for parents and carers, service users emphasized other requirements such as exercising a measure of control, offering good experiences, the promotion of individual planning and sustaining people's significant relationships.

Staffed accommodation or supported living?

Although most people with learning disabilities will need some form of support to live outside of staffed accommodation, this will vary in nature and degree. Some local authorities still have a legacy of provision, established in the 1960s and 1970s, of large hostels accommodating between 12 to 30 people, but in general these are now being closed down in much the same way as their predecessors, the long-stay hospitals. Although smaller staffed houses have been shown to be a successful way of accommodating people with profound or multiple disabilities (Mansell and Ericsson 1996), many small staffed homes have retained institutional characteristics. The last few years has seen an increasing interest in the idea of 'supported living': enabling people with learning difficulties to live in their *own* homes as an alternative to shared residential care, and providing flexible, individualized support to people wherever that might be. In a review of the way this idea has developed in the UK, Simons and Ward (1997) report on successful support in people's own homes using detailed 'personal futures' planning and focused personal assistance, and drawing on a much wider range of housing options. As well as accessing more mainstream housing tenures, there has been interest in service users gaining more control over their own lives by accessing cash payments rather than directly receiving services. The Community Care (Direct Payments) Act 1996 came into force on 1 April 1997 and enables social services authorities to make such payments, but does not require them to do so. Ryan (1999) reports some reluctance to implement the legislation, particularly for people with learning difficulties.

Support in daily activity

The main form of day provision has been the traditional Adult Training Centre typically catering for around a hundred or so people, many of them built to a factory-type design and located in industrial areas at a time when they were oriented towards sheltered work rather than the broader educational aims which are now articulated. Barnes (1990), identified three models for such centres:

1 'warehousing' or containment-oriented
2 'horticultural' or training-oriented; and
3 'enlightened guardian' or advice and activity-oriented.

He argues for a fourth model – 'disabled action' – in which day services offer support and give control to people pursuing their own interests, choices and definitions of need.

Williams (1995) suggests that these models have coalesced into two broad types of day care provision. In the 'choice' model, a menu of opportunities is provided from which each person can have an individual programme reflecting their choices; in the 'community dispersal' model, day care is dispersed into small local enclaves from which use can be made of a wide range of community facilities. Whichever model is followed, there is now a general consensus that traditional adult training centres are as outmoded as long-stay hospitals and staffed hostels, and there is a further argument that the preferred strategy should be simply to incorporate people with learning disabilities into mainstream education and employment activities beyond the remit of the personal social services.

Services for Physically Disabled People

Developments in services for physically disabled people have shared some of the characteristics of those for people with learning disabilities. In particular, there has been an ideological struggle over models of disability and the patterns of care associated with each – a feature which resembles, but is not identical to, the role of 'normalization' in the case of learning disability. On the other hand, there has been no strong policy strategy such as that associated with 'deinstitutionalization', although elements of this approach and the shift from the statutory to the independent sector are both evident.

Services, models and strategies

There has been a long-running difference of opinion about the very nature of physical disability and its relationship to service provision. Official definitions and perceptions tend to draw on the terms developed by the World Health Organization and its *International Classification of Impairment, Disability and Handicap* (Wood, 1980). An impairment refers to 'any loss or abnormality of psychological, physiological or anatomical structure or function'. 'Disability' denotes 'any restriction or lack (resulting from an impairment) of ability to perform an activity in the manner or within the range considered normal for a human being'. 'Handicap' is defined as 'a disadvantage for a given individual resulting from an impairment or disability that limits or prevents the fulfilment of a role that is normal (depending on age, sex and social and cultural factors) for that individual'.

This approach has been strongly challenged on the grounds that it assumes the existence and nature of intellectual and physical 'normality' and presents impairments as the cause of disability and handicap. People accordingly become objects to be treated, changed, improved and made 'normal', while the physical and social environment is inferred to be inflexible and unadaptable (Oliver and Barnes, 1998). However, although a social/political model of disability now has widespread academic backing, it is not evident that it has made the sort of impact on local authority social services that has been secured by normalization principles in the case of learning disability.

In general, local authority social services for physically disabled people have received low priority in comparison with other user groups (Beardshaw, 1988; Department of Health, 1993b). Nocon and Qureshi (1996) note that, in contrast to other users, this area has not been the subject of major policy changes such as the closure of long-stay institutions, and that the majority of people with physical impairments are older people for whom disability is frequently seen as one aspect of ageing. A concern with community care for older people has resulted from projected increases in the numbers of frail older people along with a need to develop less expensive non-residential support, but there has been no comparable policy imperative for the much smaller number of people with physical impairments who are under retirement age.

Again, unlike services for older people and those with a learning disability, there has been a lesser degree of inter-agency conflict over responsibility for support and funding for physically disabled people. In part, this simply reflects the low level of long-stay provision within the National Health Service as compared with the other groups, but there are still areas of conflict over such services as aids and equipment, occupational therapy and residential and respite care. A particularly unhelpful distinction has been made between 'aids to daily living' (a social services responsibility) and 'nursing aids' (a National Health Service task), and this is now often seen as the sort of service which can benefit from a joint commissioning approach.

Gross local authority social services expenditure broken down by type of provision is shown in table 5.4.

In contrast with older people and people with a learning disability, expenditure on services for physically disabled people is weighted towards day care rather than residential care. This reflects the trend to move services outside of institutions, but, more importantly, reflects attempts to maintain younger disabled people at home. The Royal Commission on Long-Term Care (1999), for example, notes that, in

Table 5.4   People with a physical disability: Gross PSS expenditure 1997–98 (£million)

Day care	400
Residential care	200
Care management	80
Senior management	30
Total	710

Source: Department of Health (1999i, table 2, p. 6)

England, for every one younger disabled person in a care home, there are 14 households with a younger disabled person receiving home care, whereas the comparable ratio for older people is nearer to two in a care home for every five households with home care. There is also a greater willingness on the part of social services to use higher upper limits for meeting the costs of home care packages between the two groups. Again, the Royal Commission notes limits of between £100–£200 per week for older people compared with between £300–£400 for younger disabled people. This is partly explained by the way in which the latter have access to the resources of the Independent Living Fund which provides an extra £50 million across the UK to supplement the cost of home care packages – on average the Independent Living Fund pays a supplement of around £190 per week on top of a minimum local authority contribution of £200 per week.

Problems in meeting need

Given the low priority accorded to services for physically disabled people, it is inevitable that a range of problems has been identified. These partly relate to general issues affecting a range of groups, and also to matters concerning specific types of physical disability.

At their inception in 1971, social services authorities were handed the task of assessing the needs of physically disabled people under the provisions of the 1970 Chronically Sick and Disabled Persons Act. Section 1 of the Act required local authorities to inform themselves of the numbers and needs of disabled people in their area and to publish information about services, while Section 2 listed a range of services which were to be provided to meet need where appropriate. Although widely dubbed 'The Disabled Persons Charter', almost from the outset the legislation was bedevilled by arguments about resources and legal interpretation, and the outcome has generally been seen as disappointing (Topliss and Gould, 1981). Two decades later, and with new requirements to assess need arising from the 1990 National Health Service and Community Care Act, a Social Services Inspectorate/National Health Service Management Executive monitoring exercise was still describing problems in needs assessment. It found that information from different sources was not shared across agencies and that there was little involvement of disabled people themselves or their carers (Department of Health, 1993b). The position in the National Health Service seems no better. Health authorities have a duty to assess the health care needs of their populations, but an investigation by the National Audit Office (1992) found that only 10 per cent of them maintained registers of disabled people.

Disabled young adults

Considerable numbers of young people aged 16–25 have discernible disabilities. The OPCS (Office of Population, Censuses and Surveys) suggest that around one in 40 have one or more functional impairments, the most common concerning intellectual functioning, behaviour and mobility (OPCS, 1988). These young people do not constitute a discrete and readily identifiable group, but research has highlighted a number of common elements in their circumstances including extended dependence on parents, more limited social and leisure opportunities, and higher rates of unemployment (Hirst, 1991; Hirst and Baldwin, 1994). An investigation by the Social Services Inspectorate (Department of Health, 1995c) revealed a catalogue of shortcomings in social services support:

- The absence of a discrete policy framework
- Little involvement of young adults themselves or their representatives
- Poor collection and use of information for service planning
- A generally low level of co-ordination with other agencies from health, education and training

People with a visual impairment

The 1990 National Health Service and Community Care Act accords visually impaired people a right to an assessment of their social needs and gives social services authorities the lead role in undertaking this, but typically this group has been given a low priority (Shore, 1985; Department of Health, 1988; Bruce et al., 1991). Registration is the most common route to information, assessment and help, but has been a particular target of criticism, characterized by poor practice and weak inter-agency collaboration. Reports and guidance appear to have had little effect on performance (Department of Health, 1989b). Research by Lovelock and Powell (1995) explored the extent to which the new arrangements arising from the 1990 Act were helping visually impaired people to gain a proper assessment of their needs and reported continuing difficulties at both a strategic and operational level. Community care plans were found to contain little discussion of their needs or of the services to meet them, and the whole area was acknowledged by those involved to be badly under-resourced.

At the operational level, visually impaired people may come into contact with social services by two routes – either through 'certification' of eligibility to be registered following an ophthalmology assessment, or by referral in the same way as other people seeking, or seen as needing, social care. The majority of visually impaired people are elderly, have some limited vision and may have other needs which they share in common with other disabled and older people. However, registration – which is the key source of information for users and carers – has tended to be viewed by social services authorities as an administrative task rather than an opportunity for a proper assessment of social needs. Lovelock and Powell also raise other concerns:

- The wide variations in local assessment practice
- The rigid application of assessment guidelines which can deny help to people not in a high-risk category
- The difficulty of separating assessment from the provision of services by specialist voluntary sector organizations
- The poor levels of information available to service users

People with a hearing impairment

A somewhat similar situation to that of visual impairment can be found in the case of hearing impairment. While the numbers of deaf people are small (around one per 1000 population), an estimated one in seven has some degree of hearing impairment. The 1995 Disability Discrimination Act requires all parts of a social services authority – not just specialist teams – to take reasonable steps to ensure their services are accessible to people with a hearing impairment, but there is little evidence to suggest that this is happening. An investigation into the practices of eight authorities by the Social Services Inspectorate (Department of Health, 1997a) found only one of them to be providing adequate support.

As with visual impairment, the registration system was neglected. From as far back as the 1948 National Assistance Act, there has been a duty on local authorities to keep a register of deaf and hard of hearing people, but of the authorities visited under the inspection described above only one claimed to have an up-to-date register and two simply did not keep a register at all. Following on from registration, assessments were found to be poorly developed or did not happen at all, and service levels varied across the country with little apparent relationship to likely needs and demands. As seen already with younger disabled people, deaf people under 21 were found to be receiving a particularly poor service, with not one of the departments inspected contributing effectively to assessments of 14-year-olds as required under the 1986 Disabled Persons Act. Particular difficulties were also experienced in communicating and consulting with deaf people, who need a different approach to those who have residual hearing. Only 18 per cent of social workers with deaf people are qualified in British Sign Language up to the minimum standard for fluency and the rest can, therefore, be expected to have difficulty communicating with their clients. Voluntary organizations for deaf people have more developed systems for consultation and involvement than social services, but their role in service planning and delivery is unclear (British Deaf Association, 1996).

People with complex and multiple disabilities

The emphasis which is being placed on targeting services on those with the greatest need and on working in partnership across agency boundaries might be expected to work to the benefit of people with complex and multiple disabilities. Again, reports from the Social Services Inspectorate paint a disappointing picture. An inspection of the ways in which eight authorities provided support for adults with progressively disabling conditions was undertaken to gauge the extent to which assessment, care planning and resource allocation was responsive to changing physical conditions and needs (Department of Health, 1996a). Some positive findings were reported, such as a greater focus than in the past on users' needs and an increase in the number of independent living schemes. However, the bulk of the evidence points to the sorts of problems which have typified social services involvement with physically disabled people:

- Physical disability did not have a high profile, with little strategic inter-agency work in terms of planning, information and assessments.
- Service users were not regularly and actively involved in planning services strategically for the community or for themselves as individual users.
- Equal opportunities policies and equality of access were not consistently translated into information in appropriate formats so that people knew about processes and procedures.
- Care plans were not consistently and regularly completed, often did not include reference to carers, and a copy was not routinely given to users.

Conclusions

This chapter examines the role of social services and related agencies in the cases of three key client groups: older people, people with a learning disability and physically disabled people. All have been, to some degree, affected by the major factors which have shaped the local authority social services over the past two decades, most notably: the shift from institutional towards community-based care; the privatization of provision and, to a lesser degree, of funding; the introduction of quasi-market principles; the emphasis on needs-led services and individual care planning; and the growing complexity of the boundaries between local authority social services and other agencies. However, each has a distinctive experience in terms of being shaped by and adapting to these factors.

Services for older people have had the highest profile because of the scale, cost and complexity of the problem, those for people with a learning disability have had an importance in the context of closure of long-stay hospitals, while those for physically disabled people have generally been seen as a lower priority. There is now, generally, an acceptance of the permanence of the mixed economy of care, and much positive support for ideas around care management, user and carer involvement, and more flexible forms of partnership between related agencies and professionals. However, the record of achievement in relation to these ideas remains patchy.

Chapter 6

Mental Health

Ian Shaw

Introduction

Mental health is a state characterized by psychological well-being and self-acceptance. The term 'mental health' usually implies the capacity to love and relate to others, and the willingness to behave in ways that bring personal satisfaction without encroaching on the rights of others. In short, this means to be well adapted and emotionally well adjusted. However, texts about positive mental health are scarce in both the policy and the medical literature, and the term is more commonly associated with social problems and the 'mentally ill'.

The meaning and status of mental illness is subject to some dispute. Within the medical model, it is an illness that, like any other illness, can be diagnosed and classified according to objective symptoms and measurable criteria. It is, consequently, best treated by a medical approach in which pharmacology plays a key role. Opposed to this is an alternative interpretation that stresses the subjective and meaningful nature of mental health problems, which are seen as the result of interpersonal, social, and environmental pressures, and as a part of the ordinary difficulties of life. The medical model is commonly applied to psychotic conditions such as schizophrenia or severe depression; the social model is most commonly applied to neurotic disorders such as depression or obsessional behaviour. Some analysts espousing the social model go beyond the search for social factors in the causation of mental illness to deny the existence of mental illness itself, regarding it as a social construct (Szasz, 1971).

Historically, people with a mental illness had been treated within asylums, segregated from the community physically as well as socially. Moving the locus of treatment away from the asylums by developing broad systems of community care was one of the objectives of the 1930 Mental Treatment Act. This Act had given the local authorities permissive responsibilities for the aftercare of those discharged from hospital, though Jones (1975) argues that it was not until the 'three revolutions' of the 1950s that a significant move towards community care occurred.

- The first 'revolution' was the introduction of new drugs. Chlorpromazine (largactil), although sedative in effect, enables patients to continue daily activities while being relieved of the more disturbing symptoms of their illness.
- The second 'revolution' was an administrative one which involved the modernization of hospitals to utilize a wide range of services, such as in-patient, outpatient units, day care, hostels, etc. which facilitated the development of community care.
- The third 'revolution' involved legal reforms brought about by the 1959 Mental Health Act. This abolished compulsory admission as the regular means of admission and aimed to reorient the mental health service away from institutional care towards community care.

The reason for these changes in policy away from hospital provision has been the subject of vigorous debate – a debate that echoes wider contemporary discussions about how and why welfare systems have developed and changed since the nineteenth century. In this case, the notion that first medical, and then social, enlightenment have resulted in policy change, has been strongly challenged by Andrew Scull. Although Scull recognizes the contribution of these developments to the moves towards community care, he does not consider it a sufficient explanation for policy development. Scull also questions the positive interpretation given to the shift towards community care, and suggests that economic policies underlined the process. In the early to mid-nineteenth century, the institutionalization of those who were unable to survive the rigours of wage labour that had spread across the country was the most effective means for governments to cope with them. The building and staffing of asylums was the cheapest solution. Later, the establishment of welfare states with national income support systems meant that support in the community could replace more expensive institutionalization, and the hospitals began to empty well before the 'revolutions' described by Jones. Thereafter, Scull suggests that mental health policy has been driven by the relative costs of alternative technologies of social control, since the medical profession had, and still has, relatively little treatment available. 'Segregative modes of social control became, in relative terms, far more costly and difficult to justify' (Scull, 1979, ch. 5).

Current research, however, suggests that community care has not had the cost advantages that Scull assumes (Knapp et al., 1999). If the quality of care is taken into account, it appears that community care is not cheaper than hospital care; rather, it has been cheaper because the quality of care has been lower. In addition, the control function of community care has had some spectacular failures, discussed later, which have now stimulated a major policy review in the UK.

However, it is certainly the case that one of the central difficulties of community care has been related to money. The full gains of hospital closure come only at the final stage and, until then, there is the cost of running a parallel community service. Also, new community services have rarely made up for the lost hospital provision. Money that should have been available to build up services in the community has been allowed to drift across into the acute sector. Moreover, a lack of co-ordination between health and social services has led to overlaps and gaps in service provision.

Mental Illness and the New Community Care

As chapter 2 notes (and also the discussion in chapter 5), the 1990 National Health Service and Community Care Act clarified the care responsibilities of local authorities. In boundary areas like mental health, where both health and social services were involved, there was a need to identify 'lead' authorities. The Griffiths Report (1988) recommended that local authorities should take this role. However, in the case of mental health, the government was reluctant to do this because local authorities had a limited care tradition in this field. Moreover, psychiatrists were fighting hard to retain their clinical responsibility for patients in the community. Another key issue was that the patients who were the central focus of planning were those with severe mental illness, particularly those with schizophrenia. This group were perceived to need care and control by the medical professions for their illness, but, at the same time, many of the problems they would face living in the community would be social: the need for housing, social networks, purposeful activity, etc. This suggested the importance of a joint approach between health and social care.

The Care Programme Approach (CPA) was introduced in 1991 requiring social services authorities to collaborate with the District Health Authorities (DHAs) in developing a co-ordinated framework of care. Multidisciplinary teams, including professionals from both health and social services, provide care. CPA involves four key stages: assessment, care plan, appointment of key workers and reviews of the care plan. The government also introduced a new funding arrangement to support CPA: the 'ring-fenced' Mental Illness Specific Grant. This grant is paid by central government to local authorities on a 'matched basis'. Local authorities put one-third and the government two-thirds of the funding into a ring-fenced budget for the provision of mental illness services; table 8.2 gives information on the central government contribution.

Consequently, the mental health task for local authorities is to collaborate closely with the health services in the implementation of mental health policy so as to produce a 'seamless service' which overrides the division between primary and secondary care. This task is based on communication and effective liaison. The encouragement of multidisciplinary working was designed to ensure this. However, the shifting location of mental health services has had a significant impact on the ways in which professionals organize their work and the ways in which they relate to patients and to each other. The shift to community care can be viewed as giving patients more autonomy and the power to set the agenda for their relationship with professional workers. Professionals have no automatic right of access to patients in their own homes and, often, cannot monitor their medication and other treatments. This shifting of power towards patients has posed problems for professionals, and, indirectly, for the state, in the management of patients who are perceived to be a threat to themselves or others. The relocation of care into the community also provides more chances for patient needs to be hidden until a crisis appears. This is a particular concern when resources are limited, and community care is seen by many as a 'cheap option'.

Intuitively, one would also expect social services to be interested in addressing the well-established 'class bias' one finds within mental health services, particularly with respect to functional psychosis. There is also an established relationship between housing tenure (high prevalence among those in rented accommodation), family type (high prevalence among single parents), marital status (higher prevalence among the widowed, divorced or separated) and neurotic disorder (Middleton and Shaw, 1999). These are all indicators of social isolation and should fall more within the remit of social than health services. However, there is little funding available to make any real impact on the isolation of these sections of the community other than referral to self-help groups if they come into contact with the statutory services.

Mental Health and Social Work

Social workers have a varied and established role in mental health. This was formalized in 1983 with the introduction of Approved Social Workers (ASWs) under the Mental Health Act, which specified duties and responsibilities in relation to the compulsory admission of patients to hospitals. The minimum requirement of two years' post-qualification relevant experience and completion of specialist training for the ASW indicated the importance of this particular role. However, the increasing specialization of mental health within social work does not mean that social work's role is unique. Pilgrim and Rogers (1993, p. 87) have argued that 'competition between mental health workers is evident in relation to occupational territory'.

The overall aim of social work, as prescribed by the Seebohm Report, was to provide a universally available community-based and family-oriented service. Traditionally, social work has utilized case-work, working with families and individuals, as its primary model of service delivery (Davies, 1986). Applied to health settings, the Otten Report (DHSS, 1974) identified a variety of social work tasks, including: the assessment of psychosocial factors relevant, or contributing, to the health problems of the client; providing advice and input in relation to the case management of social factors; provision of appropriate support for clients in the face of health difficulties; and contributing to an adequate care plan for those discharged from hospital. Within these tasks, social workers were perceived to use skills in social assessment, social 'treatment' methods, resources and educational work. The Barclay report (National Institute for Social Work, 1982) extended the social work role by emphasizing the development of social care networks – developing networks of support in the community for those with emotional and/or practical problems – and this marked a shift towards the form of 'community' social work in practice today.

However, there are clear similarities in the tasks undertaken by social workers and those undertaken by Community Psychiatric Nurses (CPNs) – both would lay claim to having similar roles with similar client groups – in particular, in relation to the assessment therapist and educator roles. Perhaps the only noticeable difference is the clinical role adopted by CPNs (providing injections, etc.) and the community social work role identified in the Barclay report. The specialized ASW role also provides a distinction, particularly in relation to assessment for compulsory admission. On the face of things, the knowledge base and interventions with clients of the two professional groups differs only in emphasis. Social work draws on a psychosocial model whereas CPNs tend to adopt eclectic psychiatric ideologies, with perhaps less attention given to conceptual issues. There have been suggestions that, because the two professions share similar skills, they are interchangeable. For example, Goldberg and Huxley (1980) claim that 'the community psychiatric nurse shares many skills with the social worker'. However, differences have tended to emerge when longer-term contact with clients is considered. Sheppard (1990, p. 83) argued:

> The differences conform, to a considerable degree, expectations arising from the examination of occupational socialisation and discourse. Social workers define their clients primarily in terms of social problems, whereas mental health case definitions received a higher profile amongst CPNs. Social workers operated in a wider community context than CPNs. Social workers acted as advocate or resource mobilizers, worked with outside agencies and professionals, and tackled more practical, emotional and relationship problems indirectly to a far greater extent than CPNs. Indeed, in terms of active use of community resources and agencies, CPN work appears to have been negligible.

The difference is less marked now than it was in 1990, and the role of CPNs in engaging and developing community resources is increasing (Todd, 1999). Also, nursing remains a profession that medicine is comfortable with, as there is more of a tradition of accepting the authority of psychiatrists than there is with social work. CPNs are also more likely to respond readily to mental health crises in the community than social workers (Rogers and Pilgrim, 1998). As health service employees, funding for psychiatric nurses comes from the main mental health budget, whereas social workers are funded out of the smaller allocated resources of social service authorities. Moreover, much of community care policy for people with long-term mental health problems still relies on continued compliance with, and uptake of, maintenance doses of neuroleptics.

The relative scale of activities for social and health services in mental health is difficult to establish, in part due to the way in which the mental illness specific grant operates. National statistics are sketchy. For example, the Department of Health (1999i) indicates that the gross expenditure by social services in England on people with mental health needs is £510 million. This is around 5 per cent of total expenditure on mental illness. Of this figure, £190 million is spent on day care services, £210 million on residential care, £90 million on care assessment/care management. This leaves only £20 million available for 'field social work' – which would include preventative services. However, the distinction made in these figures between care assessment/management and field social work may be more an accounting device than an indication of the reality on the ground. This is because some local authorities, such as Nottingham, do not have a clear purchaser–provider split, preferring a more integrated purchasing arrangement. As many social workers are also care managers, it will be difficult to distinguish between time spent on care management activities and fieldwork. Even so, it is clear that the resources available for preventative mental health work by social services are limited.

Problems with Community Care

As the 1990s progressed, it became clear that mental illness services were in trouble. In the USA, community mental health facilities have not been able to compensate for the poverty that all marginalized groups suffer in a mean-spirited income support system, and face hostility from suburban dwellers who support community services in principle, but 'not on our street' (Dear and Taylor, 1982). As a result, mentally ill people have become concentrated in inner city areas, living in very poor circumstances, and are often homeless, in what, in effect, are 'asylums without walls'. The situation in the UK is not as dire as in the USA but rates of mental illness are significantly higher in inner cities and the problems encountered are not dissimilar. A series of critical reports by the Audit Commission (1994a), the Mental Health Foundation (1996), the House of Commons Select Committee (Department of Health, 1994) and others detailed failings of the system.

Lack of joint working between health and social services is identified as a recurring problem. One recent suggestion was that a new and separate commissioning body for mental illness, a 'mental health care authority' should be formed (Department of Health, 1997c). Although this idea is currently not on the political agenda, the problem with such responses is that the difficulties not only arise at the commissioning level but out of long-established barriers to collaboration and effective joint working at the coal-face. It is here that the differing professional cultures of social work and psychiatry clash. This is not inevitable; various forms of joint working have been in place for almost twenty years now and some examples of good practice are beginning to emerge. However, problems over the different interpretation and meaning of mental health and illness, and the necessary treatment persist. The extent to which this could be addressed by structural changes at the level of service commissioning is questionable.

Difficulties in ensuring multidisciplinary co-operation stem from the differing socialization and training of mental health workers (Murphy, 1993, p. 20):

> Professionals in both health and social services are taught almost exclusively in isolation from each other. Doctors, nurses, therapists, psychologists and social workers plough their own educational furrows, their courses focused almost exclusively on their own professional contribution to the care of individual patients. They are rarely taught about service development during their basic training years, and multidisciplinary team working is supposed to come naturally after graduation and with experience ... it is not surprising then to find that community teams, primary health care teams and hospital based community outreach teams and social work teams rarely develop a good overview of the total service or appreciate its broader objectives.

Onyett (Onyett et al., 1994, p. 2) points to the particular problem of professional identity in multidisciplinary teams:

> The concentration of practitioners into teams places professional workers in a special dilemma. They become members of two groups: their profession and the team. As a result they may find themselves torn between the aims of a community mental health movement that explicitly values egalitarianism, role blurring and a surrender of power to lower status workers and service users on the one hand, and a desire to hold on to traditionally, socially valued role definitions and practices on the other.

As a consequence, multidisciplinary success is rarely achieved. Nor are professionals wholly to blame for a lack of co-operation. This exists at every level of community care policy, from government departments to the agencies implementing the service. There is also the problem of the changing focus of mental health services as a result of limited resources and shifting government priorities in the face of public opinion.

Managing Dangerousness

One consequence of the policy of reducing the numbers of psychiatric inpatients in the name of community care has been that the issue of dangerousness has become an increasing focus of mental health policy and legislative endeavour. Large-scale public asylums may not have been therapeutic for many who ended up in them, and almost certainly also confined some who were not disturbed, yet along with prisons they contributed to the containment of dangerousness, which provided the dominant rationale for compulsory powers. The sharp reduction in the levels of service provision and the discharge of patients into the community has meant that the issues of dangerousness and risk have now come to dominate policy concerns in the public mind. This is despite a lack of any real evidence that there has been any increases in the number of homicides committed by people with mental illness over the years since community care policies were introduced. In part, this concern is because of the media attention to cases where psychiatric patients discharged into the community kill or injure someone. This leads to calls to halt the policy of closing down mental hospitals and to increase secure accommodation. The provision of an extra 221 secure places in mental health services was announced in July of 1999 (Department of Health, 1999l). Such concerns have also led to the development of a new category of supervision orders and supervision registers that introduce an element of compulsion into the supervision and treatment of disturbed individuals in the community (usually following a period as an in-patient). This has been done on the grounds that, as long as those discharged continue with their medication, their dangerousness will be kept under control.

However, while policy issues surrounding dangerousness are important, they also tend to give emphasis to treatment by health services rather than social work services. Managing dangerousness is associated with secure accommodation and medication regimes that are the realm of health services. With such an emphasis also, regrettably, they often take attention and resources away from other areas of mental health work where social work plays a more prominent role, particularly in relation to people suffering from depression or anxiety, often referred to as 'the walking worried'. A recent example of this was the National Audit Office's criticism of Derby Social Services for developing its depression and anxiety services instead of focusing these resources on patients with schizophrenia (Todd, 1999).

This would indicate support for the views of Kelman (1975) who argued those countries with western capitalist economies adopt a functionalist definition of health and illness because of the priority assigned to the overriding needs of the economic system. He points out that maintaining a work-force which is healthy enough to perform essential roles does not necessitate an approach to health which is more than mechanistic (Kelman, 1975, p. 43):

> A population is said to be optimally functionally healthy if the last in-
> crement of resources directed towards health contributes as much to
> overall productivity and accumulations as it would if directed towards
> capital investment (accumulation).

Accordingly, the focus is on 'disruptive illness' in mental health,
such as schizophrenia, rather than on people who may be psycholo-
gically distressed but who do not pose a threat either to themselves or
the wider community and who may be able to maintain some, or all,
of their social roles.

Certainly, the release of large numbers of patients from mental hospitals has caused significant problems both for patients and for the
communities that become their new homes. Adequate community services often are unavailable to former mental patients, a large percentage of whom do not receive services to meet their needs, or lose contact
with services altogether. This was particularly highlighted by the case
of Ben Silcock, who climbed into the lions' den at London Zoo, and
Graham Clunis, who stabbed to death Jonathan Zito in the London
Underground. Such incidents have been well publicized and have placed
a great deal of pressure on the government to ensure that public safety
is not compromised by care in the community programmes. This has
led to further changes in policy designed to reassert control over people
with severe mental illness. There has been a general concern, backed by
research (Kagan, 1984) about maintaining quality through a time of
organizational change. Supervision registers were introduced early in
1994 for clients who were deemed to be at risk of harming themselves
or others, and the well-being of patients on these lists were monitored
regularly by care staff. It seemed to the public and government that the
registers alone were insufficient.

The Mental Health (Patients in the Community) Act was implemented
in the UK on 1 April 1996. Under this legislation, a patient subject to
supervised discharge is required to abide by the terms of a care plan.
The appointed key workers, who may be social workers, have powers
to: require the patient to reside in a particular place; require the patient
to attend for medical treatment and rehabilitation; and convey a patient
to a place where he or she is to attend for treatment. If a patient does
not comply with the conditions, the individual's case would be reviewed,
including the possible need for compulsory admission to hospital. However, key workers have been reluctant to exercise such powers as it threat-
ens the relationships that professionals have built up with clients and
the therapeutic benefits gained.

The politics of violence reminds us of the dangers of mental health
policy becoming shaped by immediate concerns. Fear of violence can

lead to alarmist or reactive policy making where it becomes linked to a wider modern fear of 'risks' in the context of current economic and social change. Beck (1992) has argued that modern societies are 'risk' societies. Certainly, there is widespread fear of crime, for example, often among those for whom it is actually the least likely (Hale, 1992). The media presentation of mental health issues has not helped in this respect (Philo et al., 1997), with a less than accurate presentation of the realities of mental illness. Sensational news about occasional violence committed by patients in the community may become the natural successor to the earlier series of sensational revelations about mental hospital malpractice reviewed by Martin (1984), driving policy on the basis of short-term concerns. In January of 1999, the Health Minister, John Hutton made no apologies over the governments stress on the safety of the community. Referring to a review of national research and independent enquiries which highlighted numerous failings of community care support systems, he said (Department of Health, 1999k):

> No wonder that service users, carers, professionals and the wider public have lost confidence in mental health services. That is not to say that we do not recognize that care in the community benefited some people. But we are also in doubt that it failed too many vulnerable people who found it difficult to cope.

The failure of community care policies for those people with severe mental illness has recently been officially recognized by the government (Dobson, 1998):

> Care in the community has failed. Discharging people from institutions has brought benefits to some. But it has left many vulnerable patients trying to cope on their own. Others have been left to become a danger to themselves and a nuisance to others. Too many confused and sick people have been left wandering the streets and sleeping rough. A small but significant minority has become a danger to the public as well as themselves.

The government is now fundamentally reviewing the Mental Health Acts to include possible measures such as compliance orders and community treatment orders to provide effective and prompt supervised care if patients do not take medication or if their condition deteriorates. Promised enhanced services are to include an increase in the number of acute mental health beds. There is also to be an emphasis on improving the mental health training for GPs and others in primary health care, which may serve to provide an added awareness to health professionals of the role of social workers. This is to be backed by extra funds for mental health services. This seems to indicate a reassertion of the medical model of care.

The government also recently announced a new mental health strategy entitled *Modernising Mental Health Services: Safe, Sound and Supportive* (Department of Health, 1998d). This is an important new strategy which was a very long time in gestation, and which provides the basis for the 'national service framework' on mental health that was published in the autumn of 1999. This new strategy includes the provision of an extra £700 million over the next three years, and it sets out clear proposals to modernize both the National Health Service and the personal social services. Proposals for the National Health Service are concerned with the need for health services to tackle the root causes of ill health, and ensure high standards of care and quicker treatment. Proposals for social services highlight three priorities – promoting independence, improving protection and raising standards – and it is worth examining these in more detail.

To support policies that promote independence and give people more say over how their service is delivered, the government will ensure that more local authorities will offer direct payment schemes to users in their area. The 'social services modernization fund' – see also pages 147 and 186 – will also deliver substantial extra funding to assist services that promote independence, such as rehabilitation services. The White Paper, *Better Services for Vulnerable People* (Department of Health, 1997b), already sets out the requirement for health and local authorities to implement jointly agreed plans for improvement in this area. Policies to improve protection will be linked to proposals for a Care Standards Commission together with a General Social Care Council contained in the White Paper *Modernising Social Services* (Department of Health, 1998e); see chapter 10. The Commission will regulate residential, day care and community services with the aim of providing better protection for vulnerable people. Policies to raise standards will be supported by 'national service frameworks', originally set out in *A First Class Service* (Department of Health, 1998a). These frameworks will spell out 'service blueprints' and standards that services will have to meet in all parts of the country. These issues about raising standards are also further explored in chapter 10.

The new strategy also calls for health and social services to work more closely together to provide integrated packages of care, and funding will be made available to support partnership activity. In balancing the scales between the freedom of patients and the control of patients for their own and the public's benefit, this new strategy promise to improve services and increase available resources – particularly in terms of risk management practices, earlier intervention, increasing beds and secure places, and 'assertive' outreach. However, support in these areas may make services 'safer and more supportive', but it also increases the likelihood of increased social and medical control. This is a basic 'goals conflict' within mental health services – though, of course, the two sets of goals may overlap, for example, patients may wish to be controlled as they are fearful of the consequences of their illness. The question now is what the 'technologies of control' should be, the extent of user involvement, and how this may impact on the relationship between professionals, and between professionals and their clients. Whatever their humanitarian shortcomings, there is no doubt that the old asylums were effective in terms of control. Is there a way of recapturing that function, while retaining a humanitarian and therapeutic input? It is perhaps not surprising that therapeutic communities are now coming back into favour. For example, the Henderson hospital, the single most celebrated therapeutic community in the UK, has just received substantial funding to expand services through the establishment of two 'clone Hendersons' in Birmingham and Manchester. At the same time, the High Security Psychiatric Commissioning Board, now responsible for the UK Special Hospitals such as Broadmoor and Rampton, and the Home Office, have both commissioned, again with substantial funding, detailed reviews of the research evidence for the use of therapeutic communities in secure settings.

There has been an expansion in mental health services across the population, in the ideas, theories and treatments for and about the more common mental disorders, and in the range of mental health professionals that has been variously termed the 'psychologization' (Kovel, 1981) or 'psychiatrization' of society (Rose, 1990). The growth of the psychiatric society is reflected in the growth of the 'psy' professions (Castel, 1988) or of the 'psychological complex' (Rose, 1985), and as part of 'surveillance medicine' that problematizes the normal and contributes to the reconfiguration of identity (Armstrong, 1995). It can be seen as a component of the development of community care, since it involves services in the community, but it encompasses rather different groups of users.

It is also significant that these recent policy initiatives all call for increased collaboration between health care practitioners to further service goals. However, the emphasis on the 'control' of patients will undoubtedly mean that social work will continue to be a junior partner in the care of the mentally ill.

Moves to develop greater collaboration include moves towards increasing the shared elements of professional training and moves towards the introduction of generic mental health workers. Significantly, the Audit Commission reporting in 1994 suggested shifting responsibility for meeting care needs of those with enduring mental health problems to care assistants. This critique, if implemented, could reverse the growth in community mental health nurses and may impact on the role of social workers. However, whether this would improve patient care is questionable, and it has been viewed as a means of trying to reduce care costs.

Conclusions

The century's end is a time of significant social and political change. The UK is witnessing a transformation of the 'welfare settlement' of the 1940s with heated debates about the ideological and moral underpinnings for these developments. New inequalities have arisen which the new Labour government has committed itself to tackle. Within the mental health services, inequalities have a long history: class, race and gender inequalities have permeated the diagnosis and treatment of mental illness. Caught between the basic concerns to balance social control with care and treatment under conditions of expenditure restraint, these inequalities have often been overlooked, but are nevertheless fundamental features of the mental health services which have significant implications for service quality and effectiveness.

Profound changes are underway in the social and political relationships of care, particularly between people with mental health problems and the caring professions, leading to a questioning of the nature of expertise. This is not confined to the UK; there is, in many countries, a renewed commitment to address issues of maintaining high-quality care, alongside growing public and political concerns about the 'risks' attaching to community mental health care. These trends have significant implications for the future of policy and practice in mental health and the nature of the task which services will have to address.

Chapter 7

Social Services and Social Security

Michael Hill

Introduction

At various points in other chapters, attention is drawn to issues about poverty and about means testing. Yet, as indicated in chapters 1 and 2, an important characteristic of the British personal social services system is that it has been, since 1948, entirely separate from the social security (or income maintenance) system. In this respect, it differs from many other countries in which the last resort income maintenance system (often called social assistance), available to those without adequate support from social insurance or any other sources, is linked with social care in various ways. The implications of separation in the British case are that there are ways in which policies for social services have had to be designed to take into account social security policies (or vice versa), and in which decisions makers in the local authorities take account of – or even perhaps try to influence – social security ones.

Before proceeding to more detailed matters, it is appropriate to set out the main reasons why social security matters are likely to be relevant for the work of social services authorities. First, local authority social services clients often have low incomes, as is indicated elsewhere in this book, and particularly emphasized as an issue for child care in chapter 4. Hence, social services workers need to take into account social security policies – particularly where there are rights to benefits that have not been claimed, or errors that have been made in assessing benefits, or where it may be possible to seek the use of the discretionary powers given to social security agencies to enable additional help to be given.

Second, any distinction between income maintenance policies and social care policies will be difficult to draw in practice. This will be partly because policy processes – and particularly the motivations of politicians – do not necessarily channel policies into logical divisions. In other words, there have been both situations in which service delivery agencies have acquired cash-giving powers and in which cash-delivery agencies have seen it as necessary to include services to accompany benefits. However, there is a more fundamental issue that that to be taken into account: there are many situations in which cash benefits or services in kind represent alternative, and therefore inevitably overlapping, ways of solving social problems. This is most evident where residential services are involved, that is, where there is an obvious choice to be made between the supply of accommodation and a grant to enable people to pay residential charges.

Third, social services authorities apply means-testing procedures to ration access to, or assess contributions towards, many of the services that they provide. Since the social security system means tests many of its benefits, there is a need for its decisions to be taken into account when social services use means tests. For example, if a social security means test has been used to determine a minimum income appropriate for a family's survival, it will not normally be desirable for another organization – such as a local authority – to impose charges for its services that further reduce disposable income. Similarly, peculiar anomalies arise when separate agencies apply means tests without regard to those used by others, for example the 'poverty trap' in which a rise in gross income produces little or no rise in disposable income because of adjustments to benefits or the charges for services.

In the discussion to follow, these three issues will be found, mixed together in various ways, but before proceeding to that discussion, a brief comment is appropriate on the organization of the British social security system.

The foundations for the modern British social security system are often seen as having been laid down in the legislation based on the Beveridge Report in the 1940s. In many ways, that is misleading for a description of the system applying at the end of the twentieth century. The effort to make social insurance the backbone of the social security system has largely failed, though some insurance benefits (particularly pensions) are still significant ingredients of many people's incomes. Mostly, however, for those without work, either private provisions or means-tested benefits supplement basic insurance benefits. Crucially, then, means tests function to minimize state benefits to those who have private pensions or sick pay, with related assets tests having a similar impact on those with substantial levels of savings. For those in work, but with low incomes, there are also means-tested benefits. One additional important means-tested benefit for low-income people, both in and out of work, is housing benefit. There is also one group of benefits, most of which are not means tested, which are important for many social services clients: specific benefits to provide additional support for disabled people.

Terminology may cause some problems for some readers, particularly as this chapter goes back a little in time. In Britain, the expression social security is applied indiscriminately to all forms of state income maintenance, whether insurance based or not, in line with the modern name for the responsible ministry. The main social assistance scheme has been restructured and the benefits renamed several times. It was national assistance between 1948 and 1966 – with a semi-independent body the National Assistance Board (NAB) responsible for it. Between 1966 and 1986, it was called supplementary benefit – with a body called the Supplementary Benefits Commission (SBC) to provide advice to the government on the scheme between 1966 and 1980). Since 1987, it has been called income support.

The benefits system is the responsibility at national level of the Department of Social Security. At the local level, benefit delivery is through a national agency, with local offices, the Benefits Agency. Housing benefit, however, is administered by the lower tier level of local government – in other words, by the same authority as social services where there is a one-tier system, and by district councils where county councils are the social services authorities. The rules for the housing benefit system, and most of the money for housing benefits, are under the control of the Department of Social Security.

To explore the issues about social services/social security relationships in detail, it is necessary to recap and supplement here the historical account of chapter 2. While, between 1948 and 1986, the main preoccupation was with the relationship between social workers and the means-tested benefit system, and readers will find this reflected in the available literature, events in the 1980s and early 1990s have shifted the emphasis to a series of complications about community care. The older issues are still relevant, but they have assumed a lower salience. Their past history merits attention because they may yet again 'burst' through into greater prominence.

Cash and Care in the Years after the End of the Poor Law: An Evolving Relationship

The elimination of the Poor Law involved a sequence of legislation between 1929 and 1948. No sooner had local government taken over the cash-assistance powers of the Poor Law in 1929 than the government began to prepare legislation to take all means-tested support for unemployed people under its own direct control. This was a period of high unemployment and there were wide divergences between local authorities in the provisions they were prepared to make for assistance to unemployed people. Central government regarded some local authorities, largely ones under strong Labour Party control, as too generous. Legislation passed in 1934 took all responsibility for relief for unemployed people away from local government and brought it under a national body, the Unemployment Assistance Board.

In 1940, the Unemployment Assistance Board was renamed the Assistance Board and took over from the local public assistance committees responsibility for means-tested benefits for elderly people. This process of 'nationalizing' poor relief was completed by the 1948 National Assistance Act, which added 'National' to the name of the Assistance Board, and shifted away from local government all remaining powers to give cash grants to poor people.

As has been noted above, this nationalization or centralization of social assistance took the British system in a direction taken by few other countries. In most other European countries, it remained a local responsibility. This shift was influenced by popular hatred of the old Poor Law. It was seen as possible to develop services for all freed from the stigma of the means test and the workhouse because the 1948 National Assistance Act gave all income maintenance responsibilities to a national body and the duty to provide residential and domiciliary care to the local authorities. One of the implications of the National Assistance Act was that people with low incomes, and thus entitled to payments from the National Assistance Board (NAB), who needed residential care would become residents of local authority maintained care homes. The Act enabled central government to develop a framework of assessment rules in these circumstances that left no room for ambiguity about the respective responsibilities of the NAB and the local authorities. There were also rules that enabled the NAB to give limited financial support to people in private care homes and nursing homes. However, until the 1980s, the numbers of these homes were small and the rules that the NAB, and its successor organizations operated, severely limited the amount of help available in this way.

At the time of the National Assistance Act, as explained in chapter 2, local authority domiciliary care services were limited. As they began to grow, however, an issue emerged that, by the 1990s loomed large on the agenda of issues about social services/social security relationships: Should means tests apply to these services, and if so, how? There have been varied solutions to these issues. Some authorities simply do not charge for some services. At the other extreme, some impose charges regardless of the income of recipients. Between these two extremes are various approaches to means testing. We will return to this issue in the section on Disability, Community Care and Local Authority Means Testing (on pages 132–5).

Cash Benefits and Welfare Rights

More complex issues about benefits for families also emerged. The services for children were given a quite distinct identity by the 1948 Children Act, and developed their own special approach to community care within the children's departments of the local authorities. A concept of social work was able to develop, very different from that within the US welfare departments where income maintenance and social work are closely linked (Stevenson, 1973). Social workers, regardless of their political persuasion, came to see it as very important that they were able to give aid, advice and support to their clients without, at the same time, having responsibility for their incomes. What this implied was that, whereas personal social services under the Poor Law were essentially for the poor, and were involved in the control of the lives of the poor, it was possible to conceive of the new children's services as available to all without discrimination.

That, then, was the ideal; the reality was – and still is – a little different (Jordan, 1974; Hill and Laing, 1979). It is clearly the case that very high proportions of the users of the personal social services are low-income people. It is quite hard to envisage a situation in which it could be otherwise. As shown in chapter 1, the peculiarity of the personal social services is that they are concerned with a range of benefits that is also provided in other different ways, by both commercial enterprises and voluntary activities.

As also indicated in the discussions in chapters 1 and 3, there is a correlation between the forms of pathology that come to the attention of social workers – delinquency, child abuse, even publicly threaten-ing mental illness – and poverty (Holman, 1978). This fact has led to considerable controversy about the social work task. Some observers of trends in social work philosophy in the 1960s criticized a tendency to give attention to family pathology without regard to family poverty (Sinfield, 1969). Stevenson, in a measured exploration of these issues, argued that 'reaction against the psycho-analytic orientation of some social work has pointed up, quite properly, the importance of material need but one must avoid the oversimplification of implying that cli-ents "live by bread alone"' (Stevenson, 1973, p. 30). As the debate developed, it shifted from an either/or argument to one about appro-priate roles for social workers. Jordan, for example, a writer with evid-ent concerns about poverty and rights to benefits wanted to see social workers freed from concerns about their clients' incomes (Jordan, 1974). Others continued to see the need for social workers to deal with the cash problems of clients as a necessary prelude to other kinds of work; a discussion of alternative perspectives is given in Hill and Laing (1979, ch. 4).

The question, then, is: How is this to be achieved? Clearly, there are several options. One is to ensure that social workers are benefits ex-perts, with skills at helping clients to obtain benefits. Another is to make available, in social services authorities, good advisory support to social workers. A third is to set up an alternative 'welfare rights' service within authorities to whose 'case-workers' benefits problems may be referred. These three options may be combined in various ways, and there are others, outside social services. It may be argued that the best place for welfare rights advice is outside the rather specific con-cerns of a social services department, in another department within local government (consumer advice, for example), or in an independ-ent agency like the Citizens Advice Bureaux. Finally, there is an ideal-istic argument, if you believe that 'poachers' and 'gamekeepers' can work side by side, that the best place for welfare rights advice is in the benefit providing organizations.

In fact, since the emergence of these concerns in the 1960s, all of the options discussed above have been tried, in various places and in vari-ous forms (Fimister, 1986). There has even, in fact, been an advice line within the Benefits Agency, until it fell foul of the quest for staff cuts in 1997. Such is the volume of need for advice on social security issues, and aid in correcting errors and contesting appeals, that, despite a multiplicity of welfare rights initiatives, there is still a substantial unmet need for work of this kind. Within social services authorities them-selves, the typical model involves a combination of an information service and training programme for field workers with specialists to whom particularly intractable problems (where debt advice, or assistance with an appeal, for example) may be referred.

In the introduction, reference was made to the way the model of a clear cash/care split might be undermined by specific policy responses. One such which was to cause considerable complications for social services/social security relationships arose in the 1960s out of what Packman (1975, p. 60) called 'the frustration of recognizing many family situations where cash or help in kind would greatly assist preventative and rehabilitative efforts, yet there were no funds for them to use'. In response to lobbying to remedy this situation, a power given by the 1963 Children and Young Persons Act in England and Wales (now in the 1989 Children Act) and – rather more emphatically by the 1968 Social Work (Scotland) Act, enabled money payments to be made to help social services clients where these might assist in keeping children out of care. Here, then, was a statutory recognition of a connection between lack of money and social pathology.

There are two problems about these powers. The one which has been the subject of a rather exaggerated polemical literature is the danger that they might be used to reward good behaviour and become a social control device within social work (Handler, 1973; Jordan, 1974). The problem about this argument is that these powers are scanty by comparison with the more general powers social workers have to intervene in families. The argument above makes much more sense in systems where cash and care are much more fully integrated – to be fair, one of the main reasons for warnings about this issue was to discourage moves further down that road.

A much bigger problem is the extent to which power to give money in emergencies overlaps with similar power already held by the social security authorities. The consequence of the new power was shown by a number of studies (Lister and Emmett, 1976; Hill and Laing, 1979) to be, to a very large extent, payments by social services authorities to people who were already in receipt of means-tested benefits which might qualify them for comparable help from the social security system. Of course, that help would depend on the exercise of discretionary powers by social security officers, but at least, in that case, formal decisions would have to be made and appeal rights would have existed, as is not the case with the social services system (Adler, 1974).

The issues discussed here still apply but, since 1986, the social security system has been very different. This is discussed further in the section on the impact of the 1986 Social Security Act (pages 129–32). The other point to make here is that the issues of overlapping cash-giving powers have remained relatively small in scale because of the recognition by the local authorities of the very large door they could be opening to expenditure growth, if they did not keep tight control over the giving of grants.

The Welfare Responsibilities and Concerns of Social Security Agencies

The whole discussion in this section, so far, has been in terms of the issues about cash, in one sense or other, with which social services authorities have had to deal, but some comment is also appropriate about what may be described as the welfare or care responsibilities of the social security authorities. The social security system shifted – between the 1950s and 1980s – from quite high involvement with these issues to very low involvement, but there are currently signs of some turning back on this. It is therefore appropriate to review the history of this a little.

It is interesting to note that *Portrait of Social Work* in a Northern town in the 1950s (Rodgers and Dixon, 1960) – reported in chapter 2 as finding few people in local authority employment who could be described as social workers – discussed the role of the National Assistance Board as a welfare agency. It noted the large size of case loads which made welfare work, in general, limited but also that considerable attention was given to particular 'cases' and that staff derived satisfaction from their 'welfare work' particularly with old people. The author, who was an NAB officer in the early 1960s, certainly saw his role in these terms. The following extract from the NAB's annual report for 1961 sets out the official view of the welfare function of the Board at that time (National Assistance Board, 1962, p. 26):

> The National Assistance Act requires the Board to carry out their duties in such a manner as shall best promote the welfare of the persons concerned. Even if no such statutory obligation existed, the Board's officers who day in day out are visiting the homes of the poorest, and among them the loneliest and least reliable members of the community would inevitably come across problems in plenty which cannot be solved simply by the issue of a regular assistance allowance . . . Help and advice of all kinds may be needed, and although a great part of what the Board's officers can do . . . must consist of putting the people concerned in touch with some specialist service or organization, there are also many opportunities for more direct and personal help.

There were a number of reasons why that particular approach did not survive. During the 1960s and 1970s, the volume of work coming to the NAB/SBC increased rapidly, relative to this staff complements declined and visiting frequencies decreased sharply. The rather benign view of the means-testing system, embodied in the above quotation, became increasingly challenged by welfare rights organizations and claimants' organizations.

When the Supplementary Benefits Commission (SBC) was set up to replace the NAB in 1966, there was a search for new ways to deal with issues of welfare. A temporary social work adviser was hired to make recommendations on this (Stevenson, 1973). She suggested the use of a team of professional social work advisers and the strengthening of arrangements under which local offices developed specialist members of staff (Special Welfare Officers) to work with some of claimants with multiple debt problems. Liaison with local authority social services authorities would be an important element of this work.

However, despite initiatives like this, the SBC gradually backed away from the NAB's view of its concerns with welfare. Statements of their welfare responsibilities changed subtly to ones which merely stressed the need to be courteous, to collaborate with other agencies where appropriate and to remain alert to situations where referral might be appropriate. An SBC chairman (Donnison, 1977) expressed the new philosophy as follows in 1977:

> The administrative procedures and philosophies of the 1960s – which relied on benign discretion and a lot of visiting, often among old ladies whom the staff got to know pretty well – will not do in the harsher world of the 1970s with its staff shortages, sharper class conflicts, a punitive scrounger press, and a range of customers growing more like those of the 1930s than anyone thought possible.

The Special Welfare Officers continued, after 1980, with a new title, Special Case Officers to 'advise and help claimants who have particular difficulty in managing their finances, or otherwise pose especially complex time-consuming problems which are not appropriate for referral to other agencies' (DHSS, 1980). These officers continued this work until the implementation of the 1986 Act, to be discussed below, when they were absorbed into the teams assembled to administer the Social Fund.

Finally, a brief comment is appropriate on three other tasks which the NAB/SBC took on, which may not be seen strictly as 'care' tasks, but which did have significant implications for the social security/social services boundary.

First, the NAB inherited a network of lodging houses for tramps which became regarded as resettlement centres where people with an itinerant way of life might be given assistance to settle down. In the period in which the SBC was re-examining its responsibilities in the late 1970s, it became the official view that neither the 'housing' task performed by these centres nor the 'case work' task of assisting people to settle down were appropriate roles for an organization that was seeking to concentrate on the delivery of benefits alone. The difficulty, however, in offloading these tasks was that neither housing departments trying (in many areas) to cope with homelessness with falling resources nor social services authorities with increasing pressures on more specialized staff wanted to take on this activity. A closure process was initiated, in the mid-1980s, which tended to involve merely pushing people out to cope on their own. As the number of centres declined, the proportion of residents with mental health, alcohol and drug problems increased. At the same time, the incidence of these problems literally 'on the streets' was increasing. Here, then, was an area of policy where the main problem was not, like the other issues discussed in this chapter, overlap between the organizations, but a gap between them!

Another NAB inheritance from the past was centres where people who had had long experience of unemployment might be given some rudimentary training to help them to return to the regular labour market. In the years of very low unemployment, these centres functioned alongside better equipped training centres run by the employment services, largely because those centres did not want to do anything for their 'problematic clientele'. A similar reticence from the employment service's job search advisers led the NAB, in the 1960s, to develop their own special staff of Unemployment Review Officers to try to assist (or coerce?) long-term unemployed people into work. Once unemployment began to rise in the 1970s, all these arrangements came under further consideration and, in the 1980s, as the orientation of the employment services began to change from being a rather discriminating job search and training service to become an adjunct of the benefits system, the case for a special service attached to means-tested benefits disappeared.

Why include mention of 'unemployment review' activities in this discussion of social security/social services relationship? There are two reasons for this. One is that with the rise of unemployment, social services authorities started asking: 'What can we do for the unemployed?' They recognized that, in accordance with the arguments advanced above about seeing human problems in a holistic way, they ought to have an answer. Yet, in practice, they could do little, and some social workers were so bold as to suggest that, in some circumstances, family care resources might increase with father in a stable situation of unemployment!

The provision of cash benefits for unemployed people has become intensively linked with measures which aim to ensure that individuals actively seek work and undergo training, and counselling processes that increase their personal marketability. This change of the name of the cash benefit from 'unemployment benefit' to 'job seeker's allowance' in 1996 underlined this. The Blair government has particularly emphasized its commitment to this approach with measures it describes as 'tackling barriers to work' (Department of Social Security, 1998, para. 24) which apply to single parents and to disabled people as well as to applicants for job seeker's allowance. These measures obviously concentrate mainly on work qualifications, and may have a coercive aspect, but can also involve attention to the wider personal and social problems of the people they target.

The Blair government has stressed the need to tackle problems in an integrated way. This has also involved the setting up of a Social Exclusion Unit to recommend new approaches to social problems like rough sleeping, school dropouts and drug taking. While there are no explicit changes to the way the social security system operates which follow, at the time of writing, from these initiatives, it may be that they will contribute to some reversal of the social security system's retreat from involvement with care issues outlined above.

The Impact of the 1986 Social Security Act

Earlier in this chapter, it was shown how concerns about the resources of social services clients led to the development of what is described as 'welfare rights work'. During the 1980s and 1990s, the character of welfare rights work changed as the social security system changed. Before 1980, the concern was for social assistance officers to exercise their extensive discretionary powers. After 1980, the complex structure of apparent 'rights' in new social assistance legislation required that poor people secured help in finding their way through the regulations, identifying things to which they were entitled and making the increasingly hard-pressed social security administration grind into action.

In the first year or so after the enactment of the 1980 changes, single payments fell sharply; then, claimants and their advisers began to learn the game. They began to recognize which things they should ask for. In some areas, take-up campaigns were mounted publicizing the regulations. While the latter were complicated, and could not regularly be circulated among claimants, it became possible for advisers to identify the issues to raise. In practice, therefore, people began to learn, for example, that they would have to meet clothing needs out of the basic grant, but that there was a wide range of circumstances in which they could ask for grants for furniture replacements, and so on. The managerial aim to curb single payments had not been achieved. The expenditure growth trajectory went on upwards. Single payments rose from just over 1 million in 1981–2 to 4 million in 1984–5 and 5.5 million in 1985–6. At this stage, the cost of single payments had reached over £300 million a year, and the government took steps (as a preliminary to more radical changes planned for the 1986 Act) to limit payments by altering the regulations on eligibility.

Hence, the Department of Health and Social Security, not to be so easily defeated by the welfare rights movement, and under great pressure from the Treasury to cut public expenditure, decided to have another go at the problem. Its response was the 1986 Act which, effectively, abolished additions and rights to single payments. In place of the latter, the Social Fund was set up. With this scheme, which remains in operation, there are no rights to single payments, the budget is cash limited and 70 per cent of that budget is for loans rather than grants.

Grants from the Social Fund are described as Community Care Grants, and what is emphasized, in the guidance manual for decision makers, is their provision to assist individuals moving out of institutional care into the community. There are powers for grants to be given to help people to be maintained within the community, but the manual generally places these as of lower priority and requires officers to be very reluctant to give them. Loans are not merely limited, inasmuch as there are elaborate instructions in the Social Fund manual about circumstances in which officers may or may not give loans, but also their very character as loans tends to limit the demand for them. They are interest free loans repayable out of individual benefits. There are strict rules about the amount of an individual's benefit that may be deducted for loan repayment in this way. Accordingly, there are situations in which individuals are refused loans on the grounds either that they are already overcommitted by the repayment of previous loans or that they have other kinds of debt commitments which would make it impossible for them to repay loans. Hence, while the introduction of the Social Fund involved a distinct return to discretion, this phenomenon is very different in kind to that which operated in the 1970s. Cash limiting and the loan concept provide a means for the Department of Social Security to control severely the impact the welfare rights movement can have on this area of social security expenditure.

The system established by the 1986 Act raised difficulties both for local authority welfare rights activities and for their own cash-granting powers. The Department of Social Security embodied in the Social Fund guidelines for their own staff an expectation that social workers would co-operate in the assessment of need for Social Fund help, and, in particular, in sorting out cases where Community Care Grants would help people to leave or remain out of institutional care. The local authority associations, the main social workers' organization (British Association of Social Workers) and the main local government trade union (NALGO) all refused to accept the role the Department of Social Security identified for social workers. Instead, a complicated policy of 'determined advocacy' was adopted, in essence involving agreeing to help clients to fight the Social Fund for the best possible deal (Community Care Grants being the ideal) while not co-operating with the Social Fund staff to vet claims, sort out budgeting problems or cool out 'undeserving' claimants. This proved to be a difficult stance to put into practice. The efforts to undermine the new system by pressing clients to demand loans failed, leaving advocates with a dilemma that they did not necessarily want to argue their clients into loan debts. Advocacy in a structure without rights is problematical!

In the years since the enactment of the Social Fund, welfare rights systems have been under considerable resource pressure as local authorities have been forced to cut budgets. Attention has shifted to other issues (discussed on pages 132–5) rather than fighting the Social Fund. The non-cooperation stance offers social workers a way to deal with the new situation, but it also provides an encouragement to the view that social workers must treat the material circumstances of their clients as something they can do nothing about. Some would call that a return to 'real social work'; for others, it is the ultimate encouragement to 'cop out' and forget the extent to which poverty is a cause of other social problems (Wilson and Hill, 1988; Becker and McPherson, 1988).

There was another possible response to the Social Fund, however: to substantially increase the availability of cash payments from local authorities, possible under the child care legislation. Not surprisingly, at a time of considerable conflict between central and local government particularly focused on the curbing of local expenditure the local authorities were unwilling to take over an expensive responsibility from central government. They responded by maintaining a tight control over this expenditure (Jones, 1989).

To sum up this section, the social security changes brought in by the 1986 Act threw social workers and welfare rights specialists into turmoil. Rights to single payments more or less disappeared. Instead, restricted discretionary payments were available in exceptional circumstances, but generally only as loans. This new Social Fund scheme seemed to require social services personnel to replace the conflictual pattern of behaviour required to secure rights by collaboration with social security officers to determine needs for help. The loans rules suggested a need for a different approach to obtaining resources for clients, since successful 'advocacy' might bring with it heavy indebtedness to the system. The position was further complicated by the fact that social services authorities retain their power to make grants. In practice, this power is little used, and most departmental budgets for this item are limited. When the Social Fund was introduced, there was a fear that, if social workers were co-opted into helping to determine needs for grants and loans, they could be back to money rationing responsibilities in a big way. In practice, social workers seem to have coped with the conflict, very often by turning a deaf ear to material needs. Meanwhile, as shown in the next section, local authorities and particularly their welfare rights staff have found that they have other social security/social services interfaces to deal with.

Disability, Community Care and Local Authority Means Testing

While the establishment of the Social Fund was a set-back for one of the major concerns of welfare rights activities, the single payments, hitherto available under the Supplementary Benefits scheme, were by no means the only welfare rights issues to concern social services authorities. The following is a list, by no means exhaustive, of other issues:

- The need, in the light of the complexity of the social security system, to check benefit entitlements. Severe reductions in social security staff mean that error rates are high, face-to-face contacts are low and very little advice on entitlements is given by officials.
- High levels of indebtedness, consequent on benefit cuts and other economic pressures make debt advice important.
- The complexity of the additional benefits available to assist sick and disabled people (Attendance Allowance, Invalid Care Allowance, Disability Living Allowance and Disabled Person's Tax Credit) makes advice on benefit availability, and help with claiming benefits and appealing against decisions, important. In this area of social security, principally, it is issues about the disability tests, rather than means tests, that need attention.

- The development of housing benefit and community charge benefit (council tax benefit after 1992) in the 1980s, and efforts by the government to reduce access to these benefits in the 1990s, brought a new field of activity, where the target for attention might be administrators in the same local authority as the social services department.
- Efforts by the government to cut benefits to unemployed people involve stricter tests of entitlement, longer periods of disqualification and limited benefits for young people. In this case, a special issue for social services authorities arises in respect of youngsters who have recently left local authority care and who cannot readily fall back on family networks for support; special rules offer partial protection for this group, the problem lies in securing their operation.
- Legislation in 1995 replacing Invalidity Benefit by Incapacity Benefit made it much harder for long-term sick people below pension age to receive benefits, applying a test that they must be unfit for *any* work. Here then is another decision-making process that may yield problems for which advice is needed, including help with appeals.

Two items in that list – additional benefits for disabled people and housing benefit – merit particular attention because of the way they interact with the implementation of the 1990 National Health Service and Community Care Act. That Act (as shown in chapters 2 and 5) is, in many respects, a response to a boundary problem between social services and social security – the relatively uncontrolled subsidy of private residential care by the income support system which developed in the mid-1980s. It might be thought, therefore, that the new legislation eliminated that problem. Of course, in many respects, that was the case, but some problems remain.

The main issue about benefits for disabled people raises an important issue of principle about the most appropriate way to support care. On grounds of individual rights to self-determination, it may be argued that the best way to assist people who need care is to ensure that they have the cash to purchase that care. They can then be consumers making their own choices. Attendance Allowance and Disability Living Allowance function in this way. People obtain them by proving that they have disabilities for which extra care is necessary. They do not have to show that they are paying for that care, or even, for that matter, receiving it. Fimister shows how important welfare rights activities have been in helping the many people who do not know about, or understand these benefits, to obtain extra cash. He quotes six reported projects in the 1990s and comments that these are just 'some of many examples of take-up initiatives which are supporting community care objectives and seeking to compensate for the failure of the benefit system to deliver entitlements to large numbers of very vulnerable people' (Fimister, 1995, p. 96).

Fimister (1995, p. 96) goes on to argue from the above experience for the 'incorporation of benefit checks into community care assessments', but that is where we encounter a complication. If those benefits are claimed, they may be regarded as enhancing the capacity of their claimants to pay local authority charges for residential or domiciliary services. In this case, the ultimate consequence of the welfare rights activity is not to benefit claimants but to effect a transfer of money from national to local exchequers. This was the case with the statutory residential care means test, until the government spotted the issue and amended the rules so that attendance allowance could not be claimed by people receiving local authority support in care or nursing homes. The only beneficiaries from attendance allowance in residential care are people whose incomes or capital are at levels that disqualify them for local authority help. However, issues about this remain in some local authorities where this benefit is taken into account in the assessment of charges for domiciliary care.

The means testing of domiciliary and day care remains a matter for decision by individual local authorities. There is great variation in practice from authority to authority. Some approaches to means testing will interact with social security or housing benefit means tests in ways which disadvantage people close to an income threshold, making them *de facto* worse off than people whose original incomes appear to be lower. This implies a 'trap' effect, similar to the poverty trap for people who have a combination of low earnings and benefits. If, for example, a social services authority refuses to rebate charges for services (such as home help) where people have an income above the income support level, the impact of having to make payments upon people whose incomes are only just above that level may be to reduce their actual disposable resources to below income support level (Alcock and Pearson, 1999).

Similar effects will apply with rules that apply cut-offs to entitlements because of assets in excess of a specific amount (Alcock and Pearson, 1999). The capital issue is also important for payments for residential care; see also chapter 5. At the time of writing, people with £16,000 can be given no help with the costs of residential care. This implies that someone with only very slightly above that figure and an income sufficiently low that they would otherwise qualify for help will be likely to be making heavy inroads into their assets. The moment their assets fall below the threshold (assuming they know their rights) they will be able to apply for a significant amount of help. They will still have their assets taken into account, with the use of a statutory formula, until they have less than £10,000. This much criticized situation (Royal Commission on Long-Term Care, 1999) is of course a social services, not a social security, policy issue, but it parallels similar processes applied to means testing for both income support and housing benefit.

Housing benefit is not available to people who receive support for their residential care costs from a local authority, but there is a range of what Fimister calls 'middle ground' forms of accommodation arranged along a 'continuum' between straightforward residential care and independent living arrangements 'supported lodgings; "adult placement" or "adult fostering" schemes; group homes and hostels' (Fimister, 1995, p. 20). These are important for many social services clients, particularly mentally ill people, individuals with learning difficulties and young people who have recently left care. The rules about the respective contributions to these schemes from local authorities, income support and housing benefit are very complex (Fimister, 1995, p. 56):

> The benefit and charging systems do not reflect the gradual nature of this continuum: they leap dramatically from one regime to another, amongst residents whose circumstances are often quite similar. Service users, their relatives and carers are of course frequently baffled by this, as are the staff of social services, health and housing agencies, which do not necessarily have ready access to specialist interpretation of these strange goings on.

It is not appropriate for any more detailed discussion of these issues here. In any case, there was, during the 1990s, a continuing struggle to make the rules clearer so anything detailed that might be said here could be out of date by the time this book is in the hands of readers. It is sufficient to say that here are some complex and only partially resolved boundary issues and that social services staff and other advisers need to be vigilant to spot, as Fimister outlines: 'exceptions to rules', 'transitional arrangements', 'local variations in rule interpretation' and 'administrative error' (Fimister, 1995, pp. 56–7).

Conclusions

This chapter suggests that social security and social services policy need to be seen as two closely related policy streams. That closeness come not merely from their common roots in the Poor Law, but also from the fact that, as Olive Stevenson (1973) argued, human needs cannot be neatly parcelled out into administrative categories such as cash and care.

The issues in this chapter have been handled in a more or less historical sequence, because it is important to see how boundary problems have evolved over time. It may be argued that policy makers have had some success in eliminating some boundary issues. This success has partly depended on a willingness of policy makers to draw firm lines, not worrying too much about anomalies that follow from them, as in the case of the Social Fund rules and the shift of the subsidy of residential care to local authorities. These still have 'knock on' consequences for individual welfare. In the case of the Social Fund, these leave in their wake a host of problems about debts or about the provision of household necessities which social services staff may have to try to solve on behalf of their clients. In the case of community care, the issue may be that social services authorities cannot afford to support arrangements that hitherto the open-ended income support budget subsidized. There is also a range of special complex anomalies associated with the various alternative ways of supporting care.

Part 3

Organization: Present and Future

Chapter 8

The Central and Local Government Framework

Michael Hill

- Introduction
- The Role of the Department of Health
- The Audit Commission
- The Local Government Context
- The Collective Representation of Local Authorities
- Local Government Finance and the Social Services Function
- Policy Making in Local Government
- Organizational Issues about Health Service Collaboration
- Conclusions

Introduction

As shown in chapter 1, the formal legal responsibilities of local authorities as the providers of social services can be put quite simply. They have the responsibility to implement a body of laws enacted by Parliament to provide personal social services in the community. The context in which this is done is similarly legally structured by a body of Parliamentary legislation defining the arrangements for local authorities. In England, a central government department – at the time of writing and for some time past – the Department of Health – exercises a general surveillance over their social services activities and has a responsibility to draft further legislation when appropriate. In addition, another central department – the Department of the Environment, Transport and the Regions (DETR) – has a general responsibility for local government. In Wales, the Welsh Office exercises both of those functions, in close collaboration with the English Departments but, in this case, the setting up in 1999 of a Welsh Assembly with devolved powers may eventually lead to changes in the formal arrangements there.

The Role of the Department of Health

In a document published to inform local authority councillors about the personal social services, the Department of Health (1996b) states that its 'role is essentially strategic – it is not involved in the day-to-day delivery of social services'. Some of the comments below about the limitations on local authority autonomy may lead readers to consider that the expression 'only strategic' rather understates the position.

The local authority social services system in England is part of the responsibilities of the Secretary of State for Health. The Secretary of State is a political appointee, and is almost certain to be a member of the Cabinet. The combination of health and social services under one Secretary of State involves a putting together of a service that is directly accountable to the government, the National Health Service, with one which comes under local government. In terms of public expenditure, the National Health Service is a much larger element in the Secretary of State's responsibilities. The local authority personal social services expenditure represents about 20 per cent of the total expenditure for which the Secretary of State is responsible. The combination of this with the more direct accountability and the politically sensitive nature of many health policy issues inevitably means that there is a risk that social services will be neglected by the Secretary of State. He or she will, however, be assisted by several junior ministers, and it will be the case that one or more of these will be required to take a particular interest in the personal social services. At the time of writing, the Secretary of State is assisted by two Ministers of State and three Parliamentary Under-Secretaries. One of these has been allocated lead responsibility for general social services matters including all aspects of policy on local authority social services.

Within the Department of Health, the team of civil servants who are responsible for the local authority social services are organized within the Social Care Group, one of three business groups in the department as a whole. That group has joint heads. One of these is the Head of Social Care Policy; the other is the Chief Social Services Inspector, appointed with a dual role as a policy adviser and as the professional head of a team of inspectors. At the time of writing, the Chief Inspector is a former local authority Director of Social Services; so was her predecessor.

Within the social care group, there are five policy branches with responsibilities for the development of government policy for the personal social services. There is also the Social Services Inspectorate, described (Department of Health, 1999f, p. 81) as:

> the professional part of the Social Care Group ... The Inspectorate brings professional and management expertise to: inspect the quality of social care services, manage the department's links with social services departments and other social care agencies; provide policy advice.

The Inspectorate, through its Inspection Divisions, conducts a programme of joint reviews of social service authorities with the Audit Commission, over a five-year cycle. These 'provide an independent assessment of the effectiveness of each ... authority' (Department of Health, 1999f, p. 82). Between these reviews, a range of other service inspections are carried out.

The Chief Inspector is also responsible for four regional offices, charged with managing the links with the local authorities, monitoring policy implementation and promoting good practice. These are separate from the Inspection Division to draw a distinction between inspection as a formal process and the overall management of the personal social services policy development, daily monitoring and support.

The organization of the Social Care Policy branches as a combination of professional staff (most of whom are qualified social workers) and generalist administrators is designed to ensure that the Secretary of State has expert policy advice available when drafting new legislation or providing guidance on existing legislation. These also give the Department the capacity to run significant initiatives and funding programmes. This mixed structure is replicated elsewhere in the Department of Health to provide inputs from medicine, nursing and other health service professionals. There is a regular flow of information and advice to local authorities from the Social Care Group.

The citing of the central government responsibility for the local authority social services within the Department of Health, while having the disadvantage that, if the Secretary of State becomes preoccupied with health issues, social services issues may be relatively neglected, has the advantage that the close connections between health care and social care policies may be readily identified. Among the duties of the Social Care Group staff is the responsibility to work closely with those responsible for the National Health Service on all aspects of interconnected health and social care policy.

The Audit Commission

Reference has been made above to the role of the Audit Commission as a participant in the social services inspection process. It is appropriate to include here, therefore, a brief note on that body. The Audit Commission was set up in 1982 to bring the supervision of local authority auditing in England and Wales under a single body. Auditing of local government activities has a long history. Its primary purpose is to ensure that public funds are only spent for statutorily legally approved purposes. The Audit Commission's powers were subsequently extended both to the auditing of some other public bodies, such as the National Health Service, but also, more importantly, for the personal social services, to responsibility to carry out national studies to promote 'economy, efficiency and effectiveness in the provision of local authority and National Health Service services' and to 'define comparative indicators of local authority performance that are published annually' (Audit Commission, 1999). The programme of joint reviews of local authority social services with the Social Services Inspectorate was set up in 1996.

The Local Government Context

The 1970 Local Authority Social Services Act applies to 'specified' local authorities. These are the top-tier authorities in those parts of the country with a dual system of counties and districts. Where there is no dual system – as in many of the more urbanized areas – the system is unitary, and thus the single authority is also the social services authority. The structure of local government has been subject to a regular process of review over the past thirty or so years, but the general principle operating, except where there is a separate regional authority (as there will be in London from 2000 and may be elsewhere subsequently), has been that social services are located in the top-tier or unitary authorities.

Parliamentary legislation defines the powers of local authorities, and may set limits to those powers. It also imposes on local government a range of duties. The relationship between central and local government in Britain is a complex one. Local government is not autonomous, but neither is it merely local administration. Some statutes impose fairly clear tasks for local authorities while others give powers, and indicate ways in which those powers should be used, without undermining the scope for local initiative. Other Acts of Parliament merely grant local authorities powers, which they may choose whether to use. Local authorities are therefore to some degree able to make or elaborate policies and are not merely implementing agencies. In the account of recent developments below, this issue is relevant. Readers may consider from what they will read below, and in subsequent chapters, that local authority policy initiating powers have been substantially undermined.

The Collective Representation of Local Authorities

Before proceeding to more detailed issues about local government, it is appropriate to interpose a brief section on the ways in which the local authorities interface collectively with central government. The Local Government Association, represents all local authorities in England and Wales and was launched in 1997; previously, there had been separate associations for the different types of local authorities. It is financed by the local authorities collectively, has an annual assembly and does its day-to-day work through a network of committees and panels. It has its own staff, including a Head of Social Affairs, Health and Housing, who services a committee of the same name chaired by a local councillor from one of its member authorities. There is also an Association of Directors of Social Services, which holds an annual conference and has sub-committees and local meetings.

There are other independent bodies which local authorities support, and from which they receive advice. The key examples are the Employers' Association for Local Government and the Improvement and Development Agency for Local Government, an association of local authority chief executives (the Society of Local Authority Chief Executives – SOLACE) and the Chartered Institute of Public Finance and Accountancy, an organization to which many of the financial staff of local authorities belong.

Local Government Finance and the Social Services Function

Local authorities have three major sources of income: local taxes, payments for the provisions of services, and government grants. The first of these, the council tax, levied on all domestic households, forms only about a quarter of the revenue of the average English local authority and only about 17 per cent of the average Welsh one (Office for National Statistics, 1999a, table 17.15, p. 220). Local authorities receive grants from central government, designed to return a share of the centrally determined business rates to local authorities and to supplement local revenues in a way which takes into account local needs. These grants constitute 74 per cent of the income of English authorities and 84 per cent of Welsh ones (Office for National Statistics, 1999a, table 17.15 p. 220). Those figures do not take into account income from direct charges for services, of which rent payments constitute the major element. Other charges do not contribute a large proportion of the general revenues of local authorities. However, they are important for many community care services.

Local government finance has gone through a period of dramatic change during the 1980s and 1990s. There was, until the mid-1980s, a system of rates on property, both domestic and business, collected by local authorities. Then, the government replaced domestic rates by a tax on individuals – the community charge or 'poll tax' – and centralized control over business rates. The poll tax was met by a popular reaction which contributed to the end of Margaret Thatcher's career as Prime Minister (Butler et al., 1994). After her fall, her successor, John Major, sharply increased the central government grant to soften the impact of the poll tax, financing this out of an increase in value added tax. He then, in 1993, replaced the poll tax by the council tax. The latter is a simplified form of the former domestic rates, with the number of adult occupants of the property partly taken into account.

All these changes to local taxation involved a sharp reduction in the independence of local government. Even before the poll tax, the Conservative government had given itself powers to prevent local authorities from raising local taxation over centrally prescribed limits. This 'capping' practice was continued. The Labour government elected in 1997 has ended what it described as 'crude' council tax capping, but it retains a 'reserve power to control excessive council tax increases' (DETR, 1998, para 5.7, p. 34). It is certainly not increasing the central funds going to local government.

The centralization of the commercial rating system had the effect of bringing a high proportion of local revenue under direct central control; and the panic reaction to reduce the impact of the poll tax, after Margaret Thatcher's fall, had the effect of pushing up the centrally controlled proportion to the levels reported above. The Labour government has made clear that it intends to retain the proceeds of the business rate, but it may allow authorities the opportunity to levy supplementary rates and to give rebates (DETR, 1998, para 10.8, p. 77).

The income for social services is a share of the total revenue available to the local authority, together with a number of specific grants; see pages 147–8. It may seem contradictory that, while central government can and does specify the duties of the local authorities in relation to social services, the funding of this activity depends mainly on claims that have to be made on a general local authority budget. It may, therefore, be the case that those responsible for social services regard their financial allocation as insufficient to fulfil their duties.

In fact, of course, it may be quite difficult to reach a clear view on what a necessary financial allocation will be. In practice, however, those responsible for social services will be aided, as they engage in the internal politics of making claims on the local budget, by various things. Traditionally, their main weapon has been the capacity of the central surveilling department – the Department of Health – to make comments on the adequacy of services. Hence, they will be able to argue with the benefit of (or expectation of) such evidence that they will be in default of their duties if not adequately funded; which means, in the last resort, that the local authority as a whole, as the legally responsible entity, will be in default of its duties. There are then powers available both to citizens – through the courts – and to central government to force the fulfilment of the legal responsibilities to provide these services. The 1970 Local Authority Social Services Act gives the Secretary of State the power to issue directions to local authorities, with which they must comply. Similarly Section 7 of that Act enables the Secretary of State to issue general guidance. Disregard of that guidance, when it cannot be justified, may result in legal action.

Of course, these last resort powers are rarely invoked – the threat of their use is sufficient. Nowadays, though, there is something else, as well as that very blunt legal weapon: central government, in calculating its grant to local government and in scrutinizing a local authority's taxation plans, uses a formula which indicates what it thinks each local authority needs to carry out its main functions. This is a very complex computer formula which uses a variety of demographic and geographical data to calculate for each service a 'standard spending assessment' (SSA). A handbook produced by the Department of Health for elected members of local authorities (Department of Health, 1996b, p. 43) describes this as follows:

> The total SSA for social services is calculated for children's services, residential services for elderly people, domiciliary services for elderly people, and all other services. . . . SSAs are based on factors that have been shown to be related to the demand for, or cost of, a particular social service.

Hence, if those responsible for social services consider that they are being starved of funds in favour of other services, they may be able to point to this data to make their case.

Central government justifies its interventions in local government in terms of its concern with national economic management. It is its financial control over local government that tends to weaken its claim that the central–local relationship is a partnership. The problem is compounded by the lack of a satisfactorily independent way for local government to raise its own revenue, but then the whole issue is further confused by concerns about 'territorial justice' – that citizens should expect reasonably comparable treatment, wherever they live.

Clearly, a local authority is in a peculiar position in our centralized state. On the one hand, its services (and particularly its duties in respect of those services) are defined in centrally determined statutes and it has, at national level, a department which watches over its actions. That situation may be defended in terms of principles of central government accountability and of territorial justice. On the other hand, it is a democratically elected authority, which might expect to determine its own priorities. The contradiction is handled through some complex central–local government politics. At the national level, in England, there are separate service ministries. The role, for social services, of the Department of Health has already been identified. The Department for Education and Employment (DfEE) is its most significant 'rival' in bids to influence local government. These departments have to make a case for the services for which they are responsible and impress it on the DETR, the ministry which presides over local government and allocates and regulates its funds. The service ministries then indicate to those responsible for the relevant local authority services their views of their needs but the latter have to fight among themselves for the resources available to the local authority as a whole. In the counties and unitary authorities in which social services operate, they stand second only to education as a charge on the budget.

Table 8.1 gives some idea of the level of social services expenditure in English local authorities in relation both to total local authority expenditure and to the biggest call on local authorities' budgets (education). This shows that the proportional growth discussed in chapter 2 seems still to be occurring. However, caution is needed over these figures, because they represent a period when the gradual take-over of community care expenditure from the social security budget was still occurring; see pages 36–7 and 87.

The whole budgeting 'game' has been much changed in recent years – through the struggle by the centre to control local authority expenditure during the late 1970s and the 1980s and the peculiar political events surrounding the poll tax. The DETR has become so much more precise about the money available, and its appropriate use, as governments have concluded that they do not want local authorities to have

Table 8.1 Net local authority personal social services expenditure in England relative to education expenditure and total expenditure (£ million) with percentages of the totals in brackets

	1995–96	1996–97	1997–98[a]	1998–99[b]
Personal social services expenditure	7,324 (15%)	7,943 (16%)	8,461 (16%)	8,940 (17%)
Education expenditure	18,438 (38%)	18,691 (37%)	19,127 (37%)	20,168 (37%)
Total local authority expenditure	48,154	50,002	51,757	53,953

[a] Provisional out-turn when the statistics were compiled
[b] Budgeted amounts
Source: Office for National Statistics (1999a, table 7.14, p. 288)

open-ended budgets and uncontrollable tax raising powers. There is a widespread view that the system should move from that described above to one in which there are specific central allocations for each main local government function.

In fact, at the time of writing, there are signs of changes in the direction of the view set out in the last sentence. In the White Paper *Modernising Social Services*, the creation of a 'Social Services Modernization Fund' was announced to 'deliver over £1.3 billion of new money targeted at . . . key areas' (Department of Health, 1998e, para 1.16). Table 8.2 provides a picture of the specific social services grants to English local authorities in the financial year 1999–2000, with the extra items coming from the 'modernization fund' identified in the last column. These specific grants are only a small percentage of overall expenditure, but the new items from the modernization fund have pushed it up significantly. Without them, the grants would only be 1.5 per cent of the total to be spent. While the budgeting 'game' played within local authorities, described above, may have some impact on the eventual outcomes, it is clearly the government's intention to ensure that this 'new money' is effectively used to benefit social services.

The bulk of local authority capital expenditure is funded by borrowing. Central government also maintains control over local authority borrowing. The trend, in recent years, has been away from a system of controls requiring proposals for specific purposes ('supplementary credit approvals') to broad limitations ('basic credit approvals') on total borrowing by the local authority as a whole, with each local social services authority being given an indicative figure as an 'annual capital guideline'. The system is currently a complex combination of

Table 8.2   Special and specific grants to local authorities 1999–2000 (£ million)

	Grant	Extra from the modernisation fund
Childrens services grant	75.0	75.0
Mental health grant	116.5	46.4
Partnership grant	253.0	253.0
Carers grant	20.0	–
Prevention grant	20.0	20.0
Training support programme	39.0	3.6
Aids support grant	15.5	–
Drug and alcohol misuers grant	4.8	–
Total grant	543.8	398.0
Grants as a percentage of total budgeted expenditure	5.6	4.1

Sources: Department of Health (1999f, tables 1 and 2, pp. 88 and 89) together with Department of Health (1998d, para 1.16) for the figures used in the last column (actual figures may differ very slightly from those promised)

these two approaches to control. However, capital expenditure may also be funded out of revenue. Thus, in 1997–8, English local authorities spent £160m on capital projects; £28m of this came from specific 'supplementary credit approvals', £53m from 'basic credit approvals' and the remainder from revenue (Department of Health, 1999b). Capital spending by local authorities has been comparatively low in the 1990s, under the influence of policies which encourage local authorities to contract out services, particularly the capital intensive residential care.

Policy Making in Local Government

Policy making in local government is the responsibility of elected members who represent districts, or wards, within each authority in much the same way as MPs represent constituencies. Today, a great deal of local politics is arranged along party lines, and most councillors represent the political parties that are also found at Westminster.

As shown in chapter 1, the legislation giving local authorities the responsibility for the personal social services requires them to appoint a director and to set up a committee, but even those prescriptions may be interpreted in a variety of ways. The traditional pattern of British local authority organization involves organizing functions by departments and organizing political responsibility through committees ultimately accountable to the whole council.

The latter principle should be noted as involving a contrast with the political accountability structure used for central government inasmuch as, formally speaking, there is no political separation between legislature and executive, but rather the separation of the legislature (the council) into committees with functional responsibilities. In addition, many local authorities operate 'policy committees' which aim to coordinate the activities of the authority as a whole. In most authorities, the parties are represented on the committees in proportion to their distribution on the whole council. Generally, the majority party will assume the chairmanship of each of the committees. The committee chair becomes, therefore, in a sense the functional 'minister' for that authority and will be likely to work very closely with the director.

Directors of social services are appointed, on a permanent and full-time basis, by the local politicians. Clearly, therefore, political considerations may enter into the original choice of director, and a change of party control could lead to a situation in which he or she may be felt to be incompatible with the political leadership. This is not a point which should be exaggerated here. Local government officers see themselves, like civil servants, as the impartial servants of the authority. Similarly, most appointing committees try to avoid overt political bias. Hence, the general expectation is that a change of power in a local authority will not render the positions of its permanent staff untenable.

There is also embedded, in the distinction between the roles of the politicians and the committee and the roles of chief officers, some issues about accountability. Many years ago, a local government official put the most important point about this in the following, rather colourful, way (Darlow, 1965, p. 276):

> The leader of the party who were in control of the council walked into my office and said 'Oh, Mr Town Clerk, we have decided to do so and so.' I said 'Oh have you? Well I am going to play golf.' He looked at me somewhat flabbergasted and asked what I meant. I said 'Well, if you are going to decide important matters of that description without a word of advice, then you do not want me or any of my colleagues: you want an army of "yes-men"!'

Since that time, there have been many local politicians who will have been eager to behave in the same way as the leader of that council. Many of their officials will not respond to them in that direct way, but still the response is legitimate. However clear politicians may be about their mandate or their ideology in an area like the personal social services (among many others in local government), it is important that they recognize that they have hired their senior management staff for their service specific expertise. It is also the case that they have a full-time involvement with the affairs of the department, while councillors (normally) are only part-timers. Local government law in Britain goes even further in that officials have a duty to give advice to politicians and that, in the event of a breach of the law, they may be held responsible alongside the councillors. That responsibility hangs essentially on the advice they give. If they advise against an action, they will want to ensure that this is on the record. Then, if councillors disregard the advice, the officers will not be held responsible. Similarly, if the officers fail to give advice, they may be deemed to have failed in their duties.

There are some complex conventions about the roles of councillors in respect of matters of detail, the general expectation is that they will be responsible for overall service arrangements and that, while they may make representations to staff about individual cases, they will not expect to make decisions about individuals in committee. This is not always honoured. There are, however, some situations in which the law makes it clear that individual decisions are the responsibility of particular members of the local authority staff. In the case of detention decisions under the Mental Health Act, the responsible individual is explicitly the relevant 'approved social worker'. In the field of child care, it is the courts which must make the ultimate decisions to take children into care but, again, the relevant staff have obligations to take emergency action and to provide evidence to the courts. Here, then, are two situations in which neither the elected members nor, in theory if not in practice, senior management staff (including the Director) are the responsible decision makers. In addition, there is a variety of complex ways in which staff have duties to exercise care and take responsibilities in their work, and their managers have responsibilities to supervise and support them. There are some complex issues here, which tend to be explored (painfully for those concerned) when investigations are necessary into service failures, such as lapses in child protection.

In the everyday world of local government administration, officers and councillors do not spend time reminding each other of their rights and duties, let alone the letter of the law. Rather, we find that efforts are made to achieve a division of labour between them which takes into account political responsibilities, official expertise and the inevitable differences of perspective between full-time officials and part-time politicians.

There has been a long-standing concern in the study of the policy process to draw distinctions between politics and administration, or between policy making and implementation (Hill, 1997). Conventionally, the former in these pairs of words are seen to be the sphere of the politician and the latter the sphere of the official. Efforts to make these terms more specific see policy making as the setting of general directions for activities and the resolution of key value questions (particularly those over which there is general public concern or debate), implementation as the translation of those 'directives' into practice. However, these distinctions are hard to draw in practice. On one side, the politicians will want to argue that anything they are interested in, or being lobbied about, is their concern. On the other side, officials will argue that general policy directions need to take into account practical considerations only apparent to implementing staff. Furthermore, politicians will be eager to influence detailed decisions; after all, it is they who are regularly lobbied about specific issues – why has Mrs X no home help, why are the children of family Y neglected and so on. In practice, too, they may find it much easier to work on these day-to-day matters than to consider abstruse issues about the way funds are allocated or the department organized. It is these last issues on which the expertise of senior staff is particularly needed. On top of all this, 'value questions' are likely to concern staff as much as they concern politicians and, in social services, the staff are likely to have professional identifications in which value concerns are of importance.

All this adds up to saying that, while broad efforts are made in local authorities to establish a notion of broad general accountability to the committees and the council which leaves detailed matters to be handled outside the political arena, this is a complex and inevitably often contested matter. Certainly, the director and senior officers expect to be advisers to the committee, along the lines set out in the quotation above. On the other hand, politicians have to be seen as a key 'channel' for representations about detailed decisions. In the well run authority, there are accepted conventions on how officers 'advise' politicians and about how politicians separate the raising of detailed matters from the general run of (public) committee activity.

However, this 'traditional' approach to the organization of local authorities is under review. It has been noted that changes to the financing of local government during the 1980s and 1990s severely curbed its autonomy. That curbing was accompanied by a much more directive approach to many policy issues. Another related development was pressure on local authorities to contract out the provision of services. In some areas of local government work, a procedure to ensure the consideration of competitive tenders was made compulsory. As far as social services functions were concerned, the pressure was less direct, in particular the requirement to spend 85 per cent of the 'new' money coming over as a result of the ending of the social security funding of residential care on services from the private or voluntary sector. One Conservative minister, Nicholas Ridley (1988), championed the idea that local authorities should become 'enabling authorities' planning services and then letting contracts to private and voluntary sector service providers. The new Labour government has some sympathy with this perspective. In his introduction to a White Paper *Modern Local Government in Touch with the People* (DETR, 1998, p. 2), the Secretary of State, John Prescott, says:

> There is no future in the old model of councils trying to plan and run most services. It does not provide the services which people want, and cannot do so in today's world. Equally there is no future for councils which are inward looking – more concerned to maintain their structures and protect their vested interests than listening to their local people and leading their communities.
> ... our modernising agenda is seeking nothing less than a radical refocusing of councils' traditional roles. A fundamental shift of culture throughout local government is essential ... So we have a demanding agenda for change, which we in central government will take forward in partnership with local government.

The government has replaced the Conservative Compulsory Competitive Tendering legislation by a wide requirement for councils to seek 'best value' in the design of all their services and the central surveillance system has been strengthened, giving central government powers to intervene if they think this requirement has not been satisfactorily met.

Taken together, all these developments are changing the role of local authorities, and of elected members in particular. Ridley argued that the 'enabling authority' would just meet occasionally, say once a year, to let all the contracts. While that view would not be shared by most people, there are questions to be raised about what the large number of local councillors do with their time. A consultative document produced by the DETR, foreshadowing new legislation, makes a distinction between the policy work of councillors and the 'representative' work. It suggests that most councillors' time is 'spent in largely unproductive committee meetings' while 'they have on the other hand little time for their vital representative work' (DETR, 1999a, para 1.16). This leads therefore to a recommendation that local authorities should set up small streamlined executives to take the key policy decisions, with the remainder of the councillors concentrating on representative roles. The government proposes to enact legislation which will encourage local authorities to move in this direction.

Among the ideas for stronger 'executives' within local authorities, one controversial suggestion is that authorities should have directly elected mayors, who will then appoint cabinets to assist them. The idea of the directly elected mayor comes from cities in the USA and elsewhere. The traditional approach in Britain has been to elect a mayor from the council members annually, probably on the basis of seniority, to chair council meetings and perform ceremonial functions. With this arrangement, the most powerful councillor is normally, therefore, the leader of the largest political group on the council, and many of these have become *de facto* local 'Prime Ministers'. At the time of writing, the lukewarm response around the local authorities to the elected mayor idea suggests that the government will have difficulty in pushing that idea forward on a voluntary basis. However, the general idea that local authority policy-making procedures should be streamlined may be accepted. If that is the case, functional committees are likely to disappear in favour of executive committees operating as local 'cabinets'.

Some local authorities have moved forward on these issues in advance of legislation. The London Borough of Lewisham, set up an investigatory committee and consulted the public. Their approach is commended by the DETR (1999a, para 2.4). They want to have an elected mayor, who will appoint a cabinet of eight members from an elected assembly. The latter body would be a representative and policy scrutiny body, which could only overturn a recommendation from the mayor with a two-thirds majority. Since all this cannot be achieved before legislation, they are meanwhile abolishing all traditional committees, 'except those required for quasi-judicial functions', replacing them with an 'executive cabinet committee', 'scrutiny panels' and committees to perform investigatory functions ('select committees') (London Borough of Lewisham, 1999). Barnsley has adopted a more complex design involving a nine-member cabinet, scrutiny commissions, regulatory boards for statutory functions and eight area forums (with relevant ward councillors and co-opted members to keep in touch with specific parts of the authority) (Barnsley Metropolitan Borough Council, 1999). Other councils are moving more cautiously in the same direction. East Sussex is abolishing committees and setting up a 'cabinet' with a leader and five other councillors, with each of the latter responsible for one of the main services (social services, education, etc.). Under their proposal, the absence of committees means that the full council will have to meet more often to approve 'cabinet' decisions (East Sussex County Council, 1999).

These developments obviously have implications for the management of social services. It is not clear how authorities like those described above will deal with the statutory requirement to appoint a 'social services committee'. Authorities are already allowed to interpret that in a relatively flexible way, and the government has indicated that it will probably abolish that requirement in its planned legislation. Changes of arrangements at councillor level may, but do not necessarily, imply the restructuring of local government departments. However, there is also rethinking occurring about this subject. This is discussed further in chapters 9 and 10.

Organizational Issues about Health Service Collaboration

Chapter 1 explores the many links between the personal social services and other services (both inside and outside local government) and emphasizes the importance of the links with the National Health Service; chapters 1 and 2 suggest that, from time to time, a case is made for integration of these two services. Chapters 4–7 of part 2 demonstrate the links in practice, so a few further comments are therefore appropriate here, on the organizational issues about the interface between personal social services and health.

Immediately after the setting up of the unified social services system, the health service was also restructured. This involved the creation of Area Health Authorities to play the lead executive role at local level, with district management teams below them. With only minor exceptions, these new Authorities were given areas that were coterminous with those covered by the local authorities responsible for the personal social services.

The 1973 legislation that established Area Health Authorities (AHAs) required the setting up of Joint Consultative Committees between those Authorities and their corresponding local authorities. While this extended beyond the social services function, it was the collaboration between those responsible for this and the health authorities which was seen to be particularly important. The Committees were to be composed of appointed AHA members and local councillors, backed by a joint group of officers. The legislation also indicated how the government expected them to engage in joint planning activities and to share resources; see Webb and Wistow (1986), particularly chapter 10, and Challis et al. (1988) for a discussion of the activities that developed between 1974 and the mid-1980s.

A number of government initiatives in the 1970s reinforced this initiative. The government itself engaged in national joint planning for health and social services, emphasizing the need for the development of community services and for more attention to the needs of groups such as chronically sick people and people with learning disabilities (DHSS, 1976; 1977). When doing this, it recognized that something more than a planning system and exhortation from the centre was needed. In 1976, it developed a system of joint finance 'to encourage collaborative planning by making available earmarked National Health Service development moneys for social services projects which would relieve pressure on health services' (Webb and Wistow, 1986, p. 141).

This joint finance system grew initially, but was then set back by financial constraints on both 'sides of the fence'. Local decision makers grew cautious about 'new money' available only for a fixed period of time. In general, the commitment to joint working cooled a little in the 1980s. Further organizational changes for the health service, implemented in 1982, broke up the neat geographical equation between administrative areas for the health service and local authorities that had been regarded as so important in the 1970s.

However, the restructuring of arrangements for the delivery of both health services and local authority social services at the end of the 1980s brought issues about collaboration back into focus. The 1989 White Paper on community care (Department of Health, 1989a, p. 49), which preceded the 1990 legislation, devoted a chapter to 'collaborative working', and it was argued:

> For the past 15 years policies designed to promote effective collaboration between health and local authorities have focussed mainly on the mechanics of joint planning and joint finance. Significant progress has been made but this approach no longer fits well with the Government's aims for the NHS. . . . nor with its proposals for community care.

The document went on to stress the government's concerns to have 'strengthened incentives and clearer responsibilities' (Department of Health, 1989a, p. 49). It emphasized the need for social services care assessments before discharge from hospital, a topic discussed on pages 91–2. It argued that the development of purchaser–provider arrangements by both types of authorities should be co-ordinated, and asserted that joint planning would, in future, have to involve the making of planning agreements. It promised a reassessment of the working of joint finance.

There were aspects of those parts of the 1990 Act that were particularly concerned with health service organization which may have made collaboration more difficult. Overall, the Act may be seen as imposing tighter forms of budgetary control over the health service as a whole. One of the main implications of these is that they have increased the propensity of health authorities, at the margin, to try to pass on responsibilities to other agencies. The purchaser–provider split also complicates the relationship between service planning and service delivery. One other aspect of the reforms which may also have worked against collaboration – and which certainly raises questions for the future – is that it ended local authority representation on health authorities of all kinds.

On the other hand, with the increased emphasis on *community* as opposed to *institutional* care, the relationship between the role of the National Health Service and the role of the local government managed social care services has become more complex. What this implies, in practice, is a combination of medical care from GPs and community-based nursing staff, on the one hand, and social care, from home helps, social workers and so on, on the other. Deficiencies on either side may have to be made up by extra services on the other. Both are, in many respects, supplementing the care responsibilities assumed by families. Gaps between the contributions from either side have implications for individuals and their carers.

Hence, in the ferment after the 1990 Act, collaboration between the health service and the local authority social services was given a new impetus. The importance of that impetus was acknowledged by the incoming Labour government. Its White Paper *The New NHS* (Department of Health, 1997h) speaks of a requirement for National Health Service Executive Regional Offices to 'take a stronger role in ensuring local partnerships are developed between the NHS and Local Authorities' (p. 23) and it claims that 'patients with continuing health and social care needs will get access to more integrated services through the joint investment plans for continuing and community care services which all Health Authorities are being asked to produce with partner agencies' (p. 27). The local authorities are to be involved in the new health policy initiatives – experimental 'health action zones' and 'general practitioner commissioning'.

Primary Care Groups have been set up to commission – as opposed to 'purchase', as was the case before – health services for their area. These groups are expected to take responsibility for ensuring that there is an integrated system of primary care in their area, as well as commission secondary care. Eventually they are expected to become 'trusts'. They are required (Department of Health, 1997h, para 5.15):

- to be representative of all GP practices in the Group
- to have a governing body which includes community nursing and

social services [author's emphasis] as well as GPs
- to take account of social services as well as Health Authority boundaries, to help to promote integration in service planning and provision
- to have clear arrangements for public involvement.

At the time of writing, it is much too early for any judgements to be passed on the extent to which these new arrangements will lead to more effective co-ordination of health and personal social services, but it must be noted that they could transform the relationship between the two services, at least in respect of some groups of social services clients, to the extent that it would become appropriate to look again at the overall framework for the provision of personal social services.

Conclusions

This chapter sets out the general legal, political, financial and organizational framework within which local authority social services are embedded. It suggests that it is important to see that social services work has to be carried out in a complex, and in some respects, controversial context of local government law and central–local government relations. It suggests that local authorities have been, and are still, going through a dramatic period of change. It draws attention to the implications of that change for the roles of councillors. Chapter 9 looks, in more detail, at the internal organization of social services work. In doing so, it similarly suggests that a general model was set up in the years since the Local Authority Social Services Act which is now coming under further review. That model involved the concentration of social services in a single department, albeit organized in a variety of ways; but now the unitary departmental model is coming under challenge.

Chapter 9

Organization within Local Authorities

Michael Hill

- Introduction
- The Organization of Social Services: The Model after Seebohm
- Elaborating the Model: Preoccupations in the 1970s and 1980s
- The 'Big Bang' of the 1990s – Community Care and the Children Act
- Contemporary Models of Social Services Organization
- Staffing of Social Services Authorities
- Conclusions

Introduction

In the book as a whole, the expression 'social services departments' is largely avoided on the grounds that not all local authorities organize social services in single exclusive departments and that there is, at the time of writing, an increasing interest in the use of alternative organizational models. However, in the overwhelming majority of authorities in fact there are unitary social services departments. Hence, much of this chapter examines patterns of organization within departments, with discussion of alternative models to come at the end.

The Organization of Social Services: The Model after Seebohm

The Seebohm committee (Seebohm, 1968, Cmnd. 3703), whose report recommended the passing of the 1970 Act, clearly saw a need for a single specific local authority department but noted: 'There is no such thing as a statutory *department* in English local government at present' (para 632, p. 193). In the 1970 Local Authority Social Services Act, the government referred to the 'social services function' and required local authorities to have a 'director of social services'; it did not refer to a need to have a 'social services department', but, in the context of the functional department model prevalent in local authorities and the concern of this legislation, and of the Seebohm committee, with social services integration, this was generally interpreted as requiring the setting up of social services departments in each responsible authority.

There is a classical dilemma about the organization of large-scale activities, which has been widely discussed in management and organizational studies literature, which may be tersely described as 'the problem of bureaucracy'. The conventional design for a large, multi-activity organization involves a multi-layered hierarchy, a pyramid with the director at the top, a series of management layers and the 'street-level' or 'coal-face' staff at the bottom. Such a design is seen as facilitating hierarchical accountability but imposing distance both between hierarchical levels and between operational staff at different parts of the base of the pyramid (who are required to relate to each other through their first common manager in the structure). This has been described as the 'Fordist' model of organization, better (perhaps) for the manufacture of a uniform product like a standard car than for more diverse and changing activities. Not surprisingly, it is a design that is particularly challenged by those concerned with human services and with professional activities for which a great deal of expertise is concentrated at the bottom (Pollitt, 1990). However, to move away from the pyramid design seems to pose some dilemmas about control and co-ordination, and, in the last resort, requires some alternative thinking about accountability. Not surprisingly, there is a quest for a model which uses the pyramid ideal but does not carry it to extremes – in other words, the ideal is a relatively flat hierarchy with specialist expertise coming in 'sideways' as advice to managers.

Those designing departments after 1970 had to devise ways to integrate the comparatively small children departments with larger welfare departments. The former operated with flat hierarchies; basically, a team of child care workers and children's home managers directly responsible to a children's officer. The latter tended to accord more closely with the Fordist model inasmuch as their main concerns were with the delivery across a geographical area of a range of comparatively routine services. The Seebohm Report's emphasis on the need to co-ordinate personal social services seemed to involve an expectation that there would be some integration of the different kinds of activities. The local authorities implementing the new Act saw it as inappropriate to simply maintain the two kinds of organizational structures side by side, only co-ordinated at directorial or senior management level.

The alternative view clearly presupposed some kind of 'team' approach in which the different social services were the common responsibility of a number of 'generic' managers, but that minimalist interpretation of the new ideal was rare. Many aimed to go further to create generic social work practice in which different 'street-level' staff themselves related to a mixed group of clients; or, if that was a step too far, at least they tried to engender a situation in which a street-level 'team' contained workers with different kinds of clients working together collaboratively.

This 'team' ideal was easier to realize for a group of social workers than it was between social workers and those delivering specific practical services – like domestic work or meals. Above all, it was difficult to integrate into this new model the residential care homes, a much more salient feature of the welfare departments than they had been of the children's departments.

Handling ways to integrate these different aspects of social services work without elaborating a 'Fordist' design was further complicated by geography. Many of the new social services authorities, particularly those in the counties, had to deliver services across a wide geographical area. Furthermore, while a new department might be able to make choices about ways individual teams of workers might be distributed across its area, it would have much less discretion about institutional facilities. These would be fixed entities, probably unevenly distributed across the authority. In other words, while the best way to maintain a flat hierarchy for an integrated approach to social casework might be to set up a geographical network of teams, arguments for central control over the management of institutions and the allocation of places in them might be quite compelling. Given that, then, middle management arrangements might be important to facilitate the linking of these rather different concerns. If the area covered by the authority, as a whole, was then particularly large, at least a three-level structure of the centre, intervening 'districts' and local 'area' teams was likely to be the pattern of organization chosen.

However, the move towards the generic ideal was complicated by another consideration. The integration of very different activities – with different legal frameworks, organizational concerns and probably (though this is to challenge the generic ideal so dominant in social work at that time) skills – brought with it dilemmas about how best to use specialist advice within the department. This was not a problem peculiar to social services departments, most complex organizations need expert advisers (sometimes called 'staff' as opposed to 'line' members of hierarchies). These advisers may be located at various points in the structure: advising 'up' to senior managers making strategic organizational and policy decisions; advising 'down' to field level officials faced with problems which go beyond their basic experience; or indeed advising 'across' to generic middle managers on a mix of policy and operational issues. In local authority social services, these people were particularly important – to assist the transition to genericism with appropriate support and training. Furthermore, there was a view that these experts might need to be themselves 'case-load' carriers inasmuch as there were specific client groups whom it was particularly difficult to serve in the new system.

On top of all these complications, there were other organizational issues to be handled. The new complex departments needed accountancy expertise: should this come from a central finance department, or should there be one or more accountants answerable to the director? The same was true of legal expertise. The Seebohm report also indicated a need for strategic planning in the new departments. Was that something to be done by line managers, or was it a specialist function? There was similarly a call for the development of a research capacity. Finally, as already indicated with regard to the roles of specialists, there was a need for a heavy investment in training. Was this to be another specialist activity, or something managers and expert advisers did as a 'side line'? Could it be something that a generalist local authority personnel office looked after?

All of these considerations led to three kinds of elaborations to structures.

- The development at the top of the organization of a managerial system of one or more tiers in addition to the director: sometimes a deputy director, generally a team of assistant directors with specific specialized functions and, often, a further tier of senior management staff (often called 'principal officers' in local government jargon).
- One or more of the assistant directors might head a team of workers, all of whom stood outside the main 'line' service delivery structure, with responsibilities for training, research, monitoring, planning, etc.
- The development of specialist advisory roles at middle management and team levels to handle particular kinds of problems.

This discussion will go on later to more recent elaborations to social services structures and to look at some actual contemporary structures. The key issue being emphasized here is that all social services authorities developed, and still retain, structures which aim to offer localized services while recognizing the need to integrate varied activities and different specialisms, and to ensure that specialist services are available to assist at all levels. Accordingly, the most strenuous efforts to try to keep the hierarchy flat nevertheless produced structures with at least four levels. Size, particularly the geographical area to be covered, had a significant impact on this. Broadly, the larger the authority, the more the levels at the outset. Later, authorities began to experiment with ways to minimize hierarchy through decentralization. This is discussed in the next section.

Elaborating the Model: Preoccupations in the 1970s and 1980s

It is not proposed to offer readers an elaborate discussion of issues and concerns that have rapidly become *passé*, but before going on to the strong forces which have influenced the structure of the contemporary social services authority it is important to consider some ideas which have both influenced social services' organization and prepared the foundations for more radical recent changes.

The discussion above has endeavoured to highlight the extent to which social services authorities struggled initially with two ideas – the desirability of minimizing the pyramidal 'Fordist' hierarchy and the ideal of integration along 'generic' lines – but these by no means exhaust the considerations that have been introduced into the debate about the ideal structure. Four others will be given attention here:

- Decentralization, as a concern about direct access and responsiveness to the consumer
- Decentralization as an issue about political accountability
- Integration with other related social services
- Roles in relation to other providers of personal social services

The Seebohm Committee was concerned that the accessibility of the personal social services to the public should be enhanced. The development of the local social services team as the agency of service delivery seemed to be a development in the right direction, particularly if genericism enabled there to be people in the small teams, necessary to achieve a local service, who could respond effectively to demand. As suggested above, though, localism in a large local authority might imply a rather long chain of command. What was necessary if such localism was really to be meaningful was the delegation of responsibility to local team members so that they had the authority to respond to needs and would not have to refer back up the chain of command for authorization of actions. The ideal of the 'patch team' was developed with high levels of discretion to respond to local problems in a flexible way (Hadley and Young, 1990). Ideally, the patch team would have a delegated budget and the power to make rationing decisions and to draw in resources from voluntary and other agencies.

Also, part of the 'patch' philosophy was the idea that there should be consultation of user and carer groups at the local level. Such consultation, however, could be seen to be in conflict with local democracy. After all, the local political decision maker for the social services team is the central social services committee. Hence, another variant on the notion of decentralization involved the moving of local authority decision making to local committees composed of the elected members from each ward or district.

This form of decentralization was not, of course, applied to social services alone, but also to other local services. Hence, some local authorities developed neighbourhood offices (Hambleton et al., 1989; Hambleton, 1992) where citizens might make contact with all, or most, of their local authority service providers. Some reinforced this localism with local committees of councillors. These neighbourhood offices offered the potential for another problem to be addressed: that of the links between personal social services and other services. The most obvious connection that could be made was that between social services and housing.

Unfortunately, however, the neighbourhood approach provided little scope for attention to the most important of the connections with other services – that between social services and health. While it may have been to some extent the case that decentralization facilitated links with primary health care delivery systems – GPs, health visitors and district nurses – other links with the health delivery system depended more on authority co-terminosity and tended, therefore, to contribute to the identification of liaison with the health service as a central, rather than a local, issue within local authorities. In fact, as noted in chapter 8, the issue of co-terminosity has proved to be a difficult one for local authorities because of a succession of authority boundary changes on both sides.

The literature on 'patch teams' was inspired to some extent by a rather different concern evident in the Seebohm Report. This was the idea that local authority social services should become more than simply emergency services for exceptional social casualties and should become recognized as having a role in support of the wide range of family, neighbourhood and voluntary agency care activities in the community. Whether that was ever a realizable ideal is questionable. The point here is that writers like Hadley and Young (1990) suggested that the patch team should take on a role as the facilitator of a wide range of community and voluntary effort. In the later 1980s, that perspective began to become linked with a related, but rather different, perspective – that local authorities should abandon their roles as the providers of services for an 'enabling' one in which they supported and co-ordinated private and voluntary effort (Ridley, 1988); see the discussion in chapter 8. The development of this role entails a very different set of organizational arrangements at the local level.

The 'Big Bang' of the 1990s – Community Care and the Children Act

The account of social services history in chapter 2 notes that the 1989 Children Act and the 1990 National Health Services and Community Care Act produced a substantial rethink of local authority social services. Aspects of the latter Act particularly contributed to reorganization.

The implication of the community care legislation for the organization of social services which has received the most attention was the government's expectation that there should be an organizational split between its role as the purchaser of services and its role as provider. This was further emphasized by the expectation that local authorities should become to some extent 'enabling authorities', not directly providing themselves but purchasing from private and voluntary organizations. That aspect of the change was emphasized through the fact that the government required 85 per cent of the new money – coming to local authorities as a result of the phasing out of the social security funding of residential care – to be spent on the external purchase of services.

However, the purchasing–providing distinction is too simple. An official summary of the guidance to local authorities on this theme (Department of Health, 1996b, p. 13) indicates that:

> [a]uthorities will need to consider . . . whether the purchasing, commissioning and providing roles of the social services department should be separated and, if so, at what level.

That statement recognizes that the general task of arranging contracts is a rather different one from making specific arrangements within that contractual context for assistance to particular individuals, and that there are issues about the appropriate level for each of these activities.

On the other hand, in the White Paper which preceded the legislation, the government made it clear that it looked with favour on those experiments in the provision of care packages to individuals which delegated specific purchasing activities to as low a level as possible (Department of Health, 1989a, p. 21):

> Care management provides an effective method of targeting resources and planning services to meet specific needs of individual clients. The approach has been successfully employed in a number of schemes and projects, some of the best known of which are in Kent, Gateshead and Durham.

It went on (p. 22):

> The Government also sees advantage in linking case management with delegated responsibility for budgetary management. This need not be pursued down to the level of each individual client in all cases, but – used flexibly – is an important way of enabling those closest to the identification of client needs to make the best possible use of the resources available.

This may be seen as a general endorsement of the 'patch' approach discussed above, perhaps with systems to facilitate participation by the consumer and/or carer.

At the other end of departments, the community care legislation also required local authorities to look again at their overall management of services. The White Paper said (p. 18):

> [a]ll social services authorities will be expected to discharge these responsibilities effectively and efficiently. In order to do so, authorities may need to strengthen their existing management arrangements. In particular, they will need to give attention to the adequacy of systems for planning, accountability, financial control, purchasing and quality control. Support services, like training of staff at all levels, will also need early attention.

Another specific requirement of the new policies was that, given that external providers were to increase in importance, local authorities were to look again at the way in which they carried out their responsibilities to inspect independent sector residential care homes under earlier legislation (a 1984 Act updating previous legislation).

They were to ensure that this activity was clearly separated from their roles as purchasers and providers of care. Finally, as noted in chapter 8, the government expected local authorities to look again at the organizational arrangements for effective joint working and liaison with other services, in particular the National Health Service.

Clearly, here was a series of issues, some of which were almost certain to produce the reorganization of internal authority structures. At the start of this discussion, another Act was also highlighted – the 1989 Children Act – which did not have overt organizational implications but certainly required local authorities to look again at the ways in which they were providing services for children. However, the crucial point is that, facing two important pieces of legislation, local authorities could go in one of two ways, with very different organizational implications. They could conclude that there was no need to relate the changes to each other, but this would mean that, since the community care legislation required substantial organizational changes, they would then be starting to turn their backs on the big preoccupation of the 1970s – the creation of integrated 'generic' departments, teams and (perhaps) workers. They would have to separate the way they organized work with children and work under the community care legislation, simply because very different arrangements were required. The other way they could go was to try to relate the changes to each other, reproducing for their child care work some of the organizational arrangements for the community care work – the separation of commissioning, purchasing and providing. The more detailed discussion of organizational arrangements, below, throws more light on this theme. There are grounds for the view that the first option, rather than the second, has been selected by many authorities. Child care work needs to be well integrated, and explicit purchasing of services is not a particularly frequent necessity. Therefore, inasmuch as child care work has gone a different way, in organizational terms, a process was started which could fragment social services authorities. This view is confirmed by Lewis and Glennerster's (1996, p. 201) study of the implementation of the community care legislation:

> There have been problems in treating children within the framework of the purchaser–provider split. Indeed, work with children has tended to remain separate. To some extent this reflects the different preoccupations of the Children Act (with partnership and prevention) from those of the community care legislation. ... While it seems that the community care legislation has raised the profile of work with adults, some bifurcation of departments along lines more familiar after 1948 than after Seebohm seem likely.

There is a related issue here about the extent to which the Children Act (and, in fact, the earlier mental health legislation) called for an increased emphasis on professional social work skills while the community care legislation envisaged the development of a 'care management' function which did not necessarily entail the use of social work skills as traditionally conceived. This, too, may contribute to the structural splitting of departments.

Lewis and Glennerster looked at the implementation of the new legislation in a county and four London boroughs. They paid particular attention to organization changes, which occurred in all the authorities, with varying degrees of radicalism and at varying speeds. All involved ways of introducing splits between purchasing and providing, but an emphasis on separating the overall contracting process from day-to-day case decision making was more evident than a split between the assembling of care packages and the delivery of those packages. Many resisted the 'arms-length' concept implied by some of the recommendations for the latter, arguing for the need for a continuing process of adjustment between the translation of need into a purchase and the providers' interpretation of that. None of the authorities 'found it possible or desirable to devolve budgets to those closest to the users, that is, the care managers' (Lewis and Glennerster, 1996, p. 203).

Overall, apart from the developing child care/community care split, perhaps, therefore, we can speak of change as more evident at the top of authorities, and in their basic structures, than at the street-level.

Contemporary Models of Social Services Organization

The remainder of this chapter illustrates the ways social services are organized using information secured on the organization of 12 different authorities. Those authorities are not named, not because the information is secret but because the material is only used to give more concrete form to the general argument. Organizations change so regularly that it is likely that named authorities would be organized rather differently by the time this book is read, and it would be most inappropriate that readers should be misled by dated information on how any specific authority is organized.

The authorities divide into five groups:

1   Three counties (top-tier authorities set up by the 1972 Local Government Act), referred to as Counties 1, 2, and 3
2   Two unitary Metropolitan authorities set up by the same Act, referred to as Metropolitan Districts 1 and 2

3 One London borough

4 One new unitary authority established in 1997, when a large urban district was allowed to take on the social services (and other) functions previously carried out by a county council

5 Five authorities, all discussed together in a separate section (pages 173–5) because they have social services functions combined with other services in various ways: two new unitary authorities, two metropolitan districts and one London borough

Single department systems

Most departments have a management team at the top consisting of a director and a number of assistant directors. County 3 is typical, with the structure set out in figure 9.1.

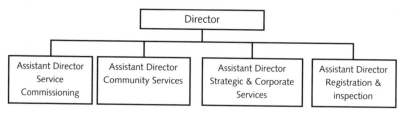

Figure 9.1 Top-level management in County 3

The top-level team in County 3 contains a mixture of an assistant director concerned with commissioning, one for directly managed services, one for support services and a separate assistant director for registration and inspection, presumably to try to keep that function independent. There is no sign of either a geographical split or a client group split at that level. However, the service commissioning assistant director is the responsible manager for children's services. In contrasting, County 2 has assistant directors for children and families and community care, but no sign of a commissioning/provider split at that level. A combination of the two approaches is provided by Metropolitan District 1; it has an 'arms' length' registration and inspection unit without an assistant director but reporting directly to the director as shown in figure 9.2. Here, also, there is an explicit separation of all children's services under an assistant director.

Metropolitan District 2 effects a compromise between the two approaches by separating commissioning and providing, but having two assistant directors for the former – an adult commissioning one and a

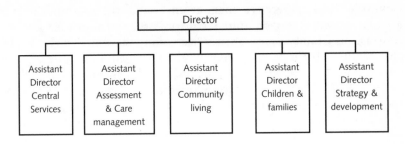

Figure 9.2 Top-level management in Metropolitan District 1

child commissioning one – but with apparently shared responsibility for the lower parts of the commissioning structure.

The new unitary authority has gone even further than any of the authorities examined in basing its top-level organization on a client group division (figure 9.3), but with an alternative approach to the titles given to the managers. Here, inspection and registration comes under the head of services for older people.

None of the authorities examined has a geographical split at top level. A study of social services organization in the 1970s found some authorities with assistant directors with separate territorial responsibilities (Department of Health and Social Security, 1978). It is suspected that the reorganizations to deal with the new community care legislation in the 1990s will have extinguished the last examples of this. Certainly, Lewis and Glennerster (1996, p. 50) report an example of a county which rid itself of an organizational arrangement involving a director and a deputy director with six divisional directors below them in favour of a three-way split between purchasing, providing and quality assurance.

All of the counties split into territorial divisions at the next level. Interestingly, there are different approaches to relating the client group divisions and purchaser–provider divisions to the territorial one. In

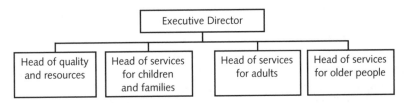

Figure 9.3 Top-level management in the New Unitary District

Counties 1 and 2, there is a client group split at the assistant director level, and accordingly separate territorial organizations for these. By contrast, in County 3, it is the service commissioning division which has a territorial split. In this authority, child protection, adoption, youth justice and the emergency duty teams are all centrally managed. In County 1, there are two separate 'operations' assistant directors responsible for both 'district' managers and 'service' managers. These assistant directors combine particular functional responsibilities with presumably 'generic' territorial oversight.

These examples illustrate how geographical divisions are very much affected by service divisions. This issue becomes more complicated further 'down' their hierarchies. What has been established so far?

(a)   Varying approaches to top-level divisions between direct provision of services and commissioning/purchasing/quality control/inspection on the one hand and client group divisions on the other
(b)   An absence of territorial divisions until either one or both of the two kinds of divisions set out under point (a) have been made

As well as having to find ways to combine these divisions, social services authorities have to place a range of support services, specialized services that need to be centralized and services that are highly concentrated in one or a few locations.

The rather complicated points in that last paragraph can be best illustrated by looking at the way in which the new unitary authority, which has opted for a client group split at the first level below the director, handles some of the middle management issues in each client group divisions. Figure 9.4 does this, adding (to complete the picture for the authority as a whole) the management staff for quality and resources.

The question is: To what extent can this 'relatively' simple structure be regarded as typical? It is not appropriate to burden readers with endless details of the organizational arrangements in other authorities. Instead, a few comparative comments are offered. The new unitary authority described above is relatively small. It has opted for a structure with a strong client group split running all through. Indeed, it is quite difficult to spot the purchaser–provider splits in figure 9.4. Broadly, they would seem to be between one and four for children's services (bearing in mind that this split is not so important as in community care. In the two community care parts of the department, manager 3 in the services for older people group has purchasing responsibilities and manager 2 has provider ones. As far as adult services, the split is at a lower level. This can most clearly be seen in the

Head of Services for Children and Families with four subordinates	Head of Services for Older People with four subordinates	Head of Services for Older People with three subordinates	Head of Quality and Resources with five subordinates
1 Service Manager Assessment supervising team managers responsible for child protection enquiries, assessment, child disability and emergencies 2 Service Manager Quality supervising child protection co-ordinators, reviewing officers, the family group conference manager and the children's rights officer 3 Policy Development Officer (children and families) 4 Service Manager Family Support supervising residential homes, family support, child protection support, the family placement officer and the after care unit manager	1 Service Manager Physical Disabilities supervising three team managers for physical disability services, the occupational therapy team manager and the manager of the joint equipment store 2 Service Manager Learning Disabilities supervising two team managers and two unit managers 3 Policy Development Officer (services for adults) 4 Service Manager Mental Health/Substance Abuse supervising two unit managers and three team managers	1 Service Manager (Provider Services) supervising managers of residential homes, home care services and day centres 2 Policy Development Officer (older people) 3 Service Manager (Care Management) supervising six team managers	1 Policy Development Manager, supervising two health development officers 2 Human Resources Manager supervising a personnel manager and a staff development manager 3 Contracts, Premises and Projects Manager supervising a contracts officer, a business support manager and a partnership funding manager 4 Finance Manager supervising two accountants 5 Performance and Development Manager supervising a service quality (complaints) officer, a performance review officer, a research and management information officer, a planning co-ordinator and an information services officer

Figure 9.4 Middle management arrangements in the New Unitary District

responsibilities of the service manager for learning disability who supervises two teams (in effect, purchasers) and two units (providers). Some of the other authorities make the purchaser–provider split much clearer in their structures.

The new unitary authority's quality and resources 'division' has equivalents in most of the other authorities, though varied terminology is used – central services, support services, etc. There are functions that may be attached to the organization in various ways, as separate services, or advice services to main 'line' staff, or advisory services to the top management team, or some combination of these. Included in this mixed bag of activities, in some authorities, there is money advice, gypsy services, anti-poverty projects, minority communities, welfare rights and equal opportunities.

Earlier in this chapter, it was emphasized that social services were bound to have to struggle with what was called 'the problem of bureaucracy'. Note, for example, in figure 9.4, the various places where the third-tier managers identified have responsibilities for teams or units. These – field services teams, care institutions, domiciliary services – will have their own managers, perhaps under-managers and, of course, staff. A 'street-level' worker in a social services authority will sit at the bottom of a structure with at least the four levels above him or her, as shown in figure 9.5 and, in many services, there will be a fifth 'area' level.

It is appropriate to interpose here some indication of the overall size of the social services departments. The new unitary authority that has been examined in some detail, and probably the smallest of the authorities considered here, has a 1999–2000 budget of £43 million and 1101 employees. That is a substantial enterprise. However, County 1, certainly the largest authority discussed here, had a budget of £143 million and had nearly 4,000 staff in 1997–8.

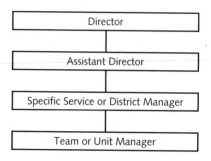

Figure 9.5   Minimal hierarchical levels

Models that combine social services with other functions

The discussion in this section is mainly based on information from reports by the Social Services Inspectorate on 'local authorities where social services are combined with other functions'. While, as in the previous section the present tense is used, the reports were from various dates and the structures may well be rather different by the time of writing, let alone by the time they are read. This does not matter; what is being illustrated are various alternative models for social services delivery.

There has been quite a long history of combinations between social services and housing. If this simply means that they are united at committee or director level, this is unremarkable as far as the subject matter of this chapter is concerned. The statutory requirement for there to be a 'director' of social services may be fulfilled in that situation by the designation of either the overall director or the next-tier figure, who has explicit social services responsibilities, as 'director'. However, some authorities have mixed the social services and housing functions in more complex ways. Of the five examples examined, two involved a social services and housing combination. The simplest one came from an authority where, below the director, there are three assistant directors for 'quality assurance', 'operations' and 'strategic commissioning'. In this situation, both purchasing and providing for social services are placed under an operations assistant director. The areas of work where social services and housing responsibilities were more explicitly merged were those less concerned with the delivery of services. The other authority had run the management of the two services together very much more, as part of its aspiration to decentralize services delivery. It organizes all its activities through five 'service clusters' each headed by a 'corporate board director' and a team of seven 'general and service managers', four of whom have social services responsibilities. These four managers have responsibilities for 'social work services', 'service provision', 'strategic planning and employee support' and 'quality assurance'. The 'director of social services' role is given to the manager for 'social work services'. In many respects, this case would appear to be one where there is simply a social services hierarchy and a housing one. However, much actual service delivery is the responsibility of neighbourhood organizations with their own lead officers. In that sense, there appears to be a dual hierarchy as far as 'street-level' workers are concerned.

The other three authorities have departed much more radically from the traditional organizational form. The first, a new unitary authority, is best described through the use of a simplified organization chart for the whole authority (figure 9.6).

The interesting feature of this model is the inclusion of children's services within a 'strategic directorate' that includes education. The rest of social services are within the neighbourhood services strategic directorate, and that director is the designated 'director of social services'. The consequence is that the head of children's services is partly responsible to that individual.

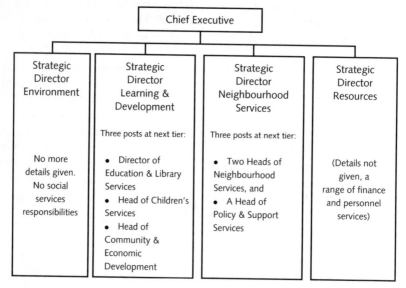

Figure 9.6　Organization chart for one of the authorities combining social services with other functions

The second authority, another new unitary one, is organized into six business units each headed by a policy director who is a member, under the chief executive, of a corporate directorate. These are the relevant units for this discussion:

- One with financial services, marketing and tourism, leisure contract services and adult social services providers
- One with revenue and benefits, legal services, highways and transport, children and family services, and adult social services commissioning – the head of this unit being the designated 'director of social services'.

Here, we have an interesting combination of a purchaser–provider split for adult services and integration of children and family services, but both are linked with services with which they have little in common. In this case, both education and housing, the two activities which might have most in common with social services are outside the two business units, and are, in fact, themselves split between units. There is a deliberate policy of giving 'policy directors' a mixed portfolio of 'business units' and they do not have day-to-day responsibility for the management of those units. Hence, at a working level, the model has a more 'normal' appearance, with three business units for social services: adult provision, adult commissioning, and children and family services.

The last authority in the group examined, a metropolitan district, describes itself as having 13 grouped functions rather than departments. Social services are identifiable in two of the functional groups: care in the community and children's services. These functional groups have 'heads', but above them there are 'executive directors' with lead responsibilities that do not link up in any simple hierarchical way with the functional groups. Thus the executive director designated 'director of social services' does not have either community or children's services among his or her functional responsibilities.

As the law stands at the moment, these five authorities are required to have a social services committee. Since joint committees with other activities are not ruled out, this requirement is satisfied through a joint social services and housing committee in the first two authorities. In the second two, on the other hand, there is a single social services committee despite the managerial splits for social services activities. In the last case, information is not available on the committee structure.

Staffing of Social Services Authorities

In the discussion above, much has been made of the extent to which social services authorities since 1971 have had to deal with organizational issues affecting large numbers of staff. While managerial arrangements have been emphasized, it has been recognized that there is an extensive staff at 'street level' in every authority. In this section, a little more is done to give a picture of social services staffing as a whole using data, not from a sample of authorities but from English local authorities as a whole. The Department of Health compiles data on this from annual returns from local authorities. This data is published in a bulletin on 'staff of social services departments' (reflecting that even the Department of Health still categorizes social services as belonging to distinct 'departments'!). The return for September 1998 indicates a national social services staffing of a whole time equivalent of 223,500 people divided between 150 local authorities (Department of Health, 1999j): an average of 1,490 persons per authority.

The dispersion of staff in settings away from central management is clear from the fact that only 9 per cent are classified as in central, strategic or headquarters roles; 50 per cent are in area offices or field work tasks, 28 per cent are working in residential care; and 14 per cent in day care (Department of Health, 1999j). Bear in mind that the existence of contracts with private and voluntary providers, particularly in relation to residential care means that these figures substantially understate the total numbers in services *which* social services authorities have commissioned.

Tables 9.1 gives some idea of the dispersion of area office staff between various tasks, and table 9.2 shows how social workers are used.

Some rough generalizations may be arrived at by comparing these tables, with caution since they classify staff in rather different ways.

Table 9.1   Local authority area office staff 1998 by tasks[a]

	Numbers (and % of total)
Domiciliary provision	50,500 (45%)
Services for children	19,400 (17%)
Services for adults	11,600 (10%)
Specialist teams (physical disability, mental health etc.)	7,700 (7%)
Support services (clerical, drivers etc.)	12,900 (12%)
Management staff	1,700 (2%)
Others	8,100 (7%)

[a] Figures are 'whole time equivalents'
Source: Calculated from Department of Health (1999j, table 3)

Table 9.2   Local authority social work staff 1998[a]

	Numbers (and % of total)
Children's work	14,300 (43%)
Health setting/specialist teams	9,200 (28%)
Adults/elderly	7,300 (22%)
Generic	1,700 (5%)
Day centres	900 (3%)

[a] Figures are 'whole time equivalents'
Source: Calculated from Department of Health (1999j, table 4)

Around 74 per cent of the staff working with children are social workers. It may also be noted that, while there are 7,300 social workers working with adults (including elderly people), 62,100 of the total area based staff work either with adults or in domiciliary settings. Hence, in this case, the social worker percentage is only 12 per cent.

All the figures quoted so far use 'whole time equivalents'. In fact, nearly half of social services staff (44 per cent) work part-time (Department of Health, 1999j, table 8). A study of social services staff carried out in the early 1990s indicated that around two-thirds of social services staff in England are female (Balloch et al., 1999, p. 18).

Conclusions

This chapter conveys some idea of how social services are organized within local authorities. It shows how the pioneers in local authorities after the 1970 Act saw themselves as creating unified organizations, so much so that it became taken for granted that the Act created social services *departments* and required them to be generic. However, tensions were built into the idea of unification. There were very different requirements for the different services. This is most evident in the sharp differences between the difficult child protection task and the much more straightforward, and relatively large-scale, task involved in delivering care to frail elderly people. However, the other adult clients of social services also have diverse needs for activities distinguishable from either of these tasks. There was conflict also between the organization building task that occurred in the 1970s, creating multi-layered bureaucracies, and the aspiration that social services (and other local government services) should be responsive and, therefore, managed close to the people at 'street level'.

Then, separate demands from new legislation and from critics of weaknesses in local authority social services increased the tendency to see the management of child protection and mental health work as requiring different organizational arrangements from that for other work. However, it was the introduction of the idea of the purchaser–provider split in the community care legislation that proved to be the greatest challenge to the earlier integrated model.

Of course, in a real organization, it is not just a matter of choosing between alternative principles – genericism or specialization, centralism or localism, a bureaucracy or an internal market. Rather, there is likely to be an attempt to effect a compromise that recognizes the strengths and weaknesses of each principle. In any case, any modern organization is – notwithstanding its managers' enthusiasm for reform – partly a product of its history. Hence, as the arrangements for different authorities discussed in this chapter show, the modern arrangements for the management of local authority social services are complex and diverse.

Organizational change has gone on incessantly throughout the period since 1970. It is therefore rash to say that this book has been written at a time when such change is particularly dramatic. Nevertheless, the last part of this chapter, if read in conjunction with the discussion of local government change and the changing relationship between health authorities and local authorities in chapter 8, does offer evidence for that contention. Issues about where that change may be leading the personal social services are explored further in chapter 10.

Chapter 10

Modernizing Social Services: The Management Challenge of the 1998 Social Services White Paper

Stephen Mitchell

- Introduction
- Background: The 1997 Inheritance
- Why Modernize?
- Modernizing Adult Services
- Modernizing Children's Services
- Strengthening Regulation of Services and the Work-force
- Improving Performance
- Conclusion: The Key Challenges

Introduction

The Labour government was elected in May 1997 with a manifesto commitment that 'we will help build strong families and strong communities, and lay the foundations of a modern welfare state in pensions and community care' (Labour Party, 1997). The manifesto contained only two specific commitments in the personal social services field:

- To introduce a 'long-term care charter' defining the standard of services which people are entitled to expect from health, housing and social services
- To establish an independent inspection and registration service for residential homes and domiciliary care

The manifesto also stated that a Royal Commission would be established 'to work out a fair system for funding long-term care for the elderly', the recommendations of which were likely to have significant implications for the responsibilities and resourcing of local social services authorities, assuming they were accepted and implemented by the government.

It soon became clear that the government desired a radical transformation of the management and delivery of social services by local authorities, as part of a broader programme of 'modernization' of public services encompassing both the National Health Service and local government. There are three core imperatives of this programme of reform:

1   To ensure that policy is made strategically, for the long term, linking up across government to tackle problems in a 'joined-up' way
2   To make public services more responsive to users
3   To achieve higher quality and efficiency in public services

White Papers on the modernization of the National Health Service and local government were published in December 1997 and July 1998. Taken together, they provided an important backcloth to the modernization agenda for social services which was published in a White Paper *Modernising Social Services* (Department of Health, 1998e) in November 1998. The overall canvass on which modernization is being painted was subsequently laid out in the *Modernising Government* White Paper in March 1999 (Cabinet Office, 1999). This defined the seven principles of modernization

1   Focusing on results
2   Rewarding success and not tolerating mediocrity
3   Working in partnership with the private and voluntary sectors
4   Organizing services around the convenience of people using them
5   Harnessing new information technology in the delivery of services
6   Re-valuing services
7   Making policy strategically for the long term in a joined-up way

This chapter describes the main changes proposed in the Social Services White Paper, indicates how their implementation is being taken forward and identifies the challenges which will have to be faced if 'modernization' of the personal social services is to be achieved.

Background: The 1997 Inheritance

It is important to locate the Labour government's modernization programme for social services in an understanding of what has gone before, particularly by way of the stance of central government in relation to a significant policy and expenditure programme. As described elsewhere in this book, the social services functions of local authorities were first drawn together in the 1970 Local Authority Social Services Act, following the Seebohm Report on Local Authority and Allied Personal Social Services in 1968 which recommended that a more coherent and integrated approach be taken to the management and delivery of personal social services in and for local communities. The 1970 Local Authority Social Services Act not only defined and delineated the social services functions in a schedule, but provided the basis for the establishment by most local authorities of social services departments to discharge them, led by a statutory director of social services, accountable to a social services committee also required by statute. Although there have been significant policy shifts during the three decades since the Local Authority Social Services Act was passed, and the list of social services functions has been subject to change, the basic statutory framework has endured largely intact while patterns of service management and delivery have evolved. The 1998 White Paper, and accompanying changes in local government and the National Health Service, seem likely to presage a more radical change in the framework of responsibilities and accountabilities, with a far more prominent role being played by central government in the shaping of service management and delivery than hitherto has been usually the case.

There have been a number of distinct phases in the evolution of the central–local relationship in social services. During the first decade of their existence, directors of social services faced the challenge of creating local authority departments during a period of growth in the resources available for the discharge of social services functions, which was matched, if not exceeded, by a growth in the expectations of them. This was also a period of national policy development, particularly for the 'priority' service groups: people with mental illnesses and people with learning disabilities (mental handicap as it was then called). These were the subjects of two White Papers in 1971 and 1975 setting out major service development agendas; they required joint planning and collaboration structures to be established between local authorities and the National Health Service, including the introduction of joint finance arrangements under the auspices of Joint Consultative

Committees which also included representatives of the voluntary sector. The stance of central government during this period was essentially facilitative.

The second phase was a period of retrenchment following the public expenditure crisis of the late 1970s, and the election of a Conservative government in 1979. The 1980s was a decade in which the relationship between central and local government was characterized by mutual distrust and, sometimes, open conflict, particularly regarding the extent to which local authorities should be able to fund local services through local taxation at levels which were not in line with the government's public expenditure plans. Constituting some of the major functions of local authorities, social services were inevitably caught up in these battles. With the formation of the Social Services Inspectorate in 1995, through a reorganization and re-focusing of the existing professional division concerned with social work within the Department of Health, central government moved into a closer relationship with social services management and performance issues, while continuing to emphasize that social services were primarily the responsibility of local government.

The third phase, in the 1990s, saw the implementation of the community care changes, proposed in the White Paper *Caring for People* (Department of Health, 1989a) and legislated for in the 1990 National Health Service and Community Care Act, which entailed a very substantial transfer to local authorities of resources from the social security expenditure programme. In parallel, a new statutory framework was implemented for children's services following the 1989 Children Act. The Department of Health played a major, active role in prescribing, monitoring and supporting the implementation of both these programmes of change.

The formidable policy implementation challenges of the 1990s were, in large measure, successfully tackled. However, the Conservative governments of the 1980s and 1990s never really succeeded in providing an overall policy and strategy for the personal social services, in which the role of local authorities could be clearly, and positively, located. This lack of a clear strategy with which all concerned in central and local government could identify, was compounded by continuing evidence (not least from Social Services Inspectorate reports) of serious deficiencies in the quality, effectiveness and efficiency of social services. This led to some questioning as to whether the local authority environment was the appropriate location for these complex functions.

In response to these problems, the Conservative government published an overarching White Paper, *Social Services: Achievement and Challenge* (Department of Health, 1997g) in March 1997. Interestingly given what was shortly to follow, this set out an intention to 'modernize' the statutory framework, with a view to ensuring stronger accountability of local authority councillors and managers for the quality, suitability and efficiency of social services, and a commitment to establish a new regulatory framework for social care in close conjunction with the regulation of directly related health care. Similar proposals were to feature strongly in the successor Labour government's subsequent modernization plans. However, these were also to represent a radical departure from the Conservative government's stance of a largely residualist role for social services, which made clear that 'the principal responsibility for social care rests on individual members of society and society's own networks for mutual support', with the role of statutory social services being to support these networks, and to commission care 'to support those for whom these networks fail'.

'Modernization' for the in-coming Labour government meant a much more socially inclusive approach, on the basis that 'social services are for all of us' (Department of Health, 1998e, para 1.1). Rather than policy being framed on the basis of social services supporting a small number of social casualties, social services were to be seen as 'an important part of the future of a caring society'.

The next section of this chapter sets out why the Labour government thought that social services needed modernizing, and what this led to in terms of specific proposals in the Social Services White Paper. Taking forward these proposals will, in many cases, require primary legislation, followed by, in some cases, lengthy periods of implementation, so it is by no means certain what the timetable will be for the major changes which are envisaged. The state of progress on the key elements of the change programme at the time of writing (autumn 1999) is then described. Central government seems likely to adopt a directive and interventionist stance in this programme.

The conclusion to the chapter identifies the key dimensions of the challenge for local authority social services, which will confront both elected members and senior managers in taking forward the modernization agenda. Although these will appear in new guises in the first decade of the new millennium, they have all been present to some degree in the previous three decades of 'post Local Authority Social Services Act' social services.

Why Modernize?

It is important to recognize that modernization of social services is part of an overall social services policy thrust towards tackling social exclusion – the process through which individuals or groups are wholly or partially excluded from full participation in the society in which they live. Social exclusion results in individuals or areas suffering from a combination of linked problems, such as unemployment, poor skills, low income, poor housing, high crime environment, bad health and family breakdown.

In this context, government ministers and their policy advisers concerned with social services, including those in the 'centre' of government, particularly the Prime Minister's policy unit which played an active role in policy formulation, were faced with two questions:

> How do we provide vulnerable and needy people with the support they need while promoting independence, inclusion and self-reliance? How do we harness economic and social regeneration in communities to the benefit of the most marginalized and dependent members of communities?

Ministers were concerned that social services did not generally respond to people's needs in ways which enabled those receiving social care to act themselves to reduce or even cease dependency. In common with other social policy ministers dealing with welfare reform, employment and community safety, they wanted an approach to reform which made local organizations think creatively in partnership, try new approaches and structures, and innovate, but *all* within a clear government defined framework of goals and objectives. More specifically, there were a number of concerns about the management and delivery of social services which policy makers identified as needing to be tackled

- The lack of effective safeguards to secure *protection* of children and vulnerable adults, given particular prominence by failures in the statutory child care system, and highlighted by the Utting report of a review of safeguards for children, *People Like Us* (Department of Health, 1997e)
- Continuing problems in the *co-ordination* of social services with housing and health services
- An absence of clear statements about *objectives* for social services, combined with a lack of *standards* for what users could reasonably expect, and *measures* for judging the effectiveness or success of social services interventions
- Too much *inconsistency* in the availability of social services both between different parts of the country and within individual local authorities, with a particular lack of clarity in eligibility criteria

- *Problems of efficiency*, exemplified by inexplicable variations in unit costs – the White Paper referred to the costs of services differing by 30 per cent for similar services in similar and neighbouring local authorities

To tackle these problems, the White Paper identifies a set of key principles which are defined as constituting a 'third way' between a perceived trend in the 1980s and 1990s towards privatization of care provision, and a previously established pattern of near-monopoly local authority provision. Perhaps the most important of these principles is that 'people should be able to receive the care they need without their life having to be taken over by the social services system', and that 'care services should be organized, accessed, provided and financed in a fair and open and consistent way in every part of the country'. The intention is to move the focus away from identifying responsibility for the provision of care, and on to issues about the quality of services and the outcomes achieved for people using them.

Modernising Social Services goes far beyond being a declamatory statement of principles and intentions. This is not a White Paper which only, or mainly, defined a stance; rather, it sets out a whole range of measures and initiatives which are seen as necessary for the 'third way' vision to be accomplished through 'promoting independence, improving protection and raising standards'. This is very much an agenda for *action*, an aspect which was emphasized by the publication in April 1999 of the *Modernising Social Services: Implementation Diary* (Department of Health, 1999g), which disaggregates the White Paper into 26 separate policy initiatives for which time-scales and milestones are mapped out. These include the development of a national training strategy for all staff in social services at one extreme, and the revision of the existing inter-agency guidance on child protection at the other. This is an extremely prescriptive approach to policy making and implementation in the social services field, which has not been attempted on such a wide scale hitherto, and it remains to be seen how successfully this can be carried through.

Space does not permit an elaboration of all these measures, but a number of the 26 initiatives can be seen as of touchstone quality, illuminating both the thrust and the implications of the overall approach being taken by the government to modernizing social services. The following sections of this chapter identify and describe particularly important initiatives in the areas of adult services, children services, regulation of services and the work-force, and arrangements for assessing and intervening in performance.

Modernizing Adult Services

The Social Services White Paper was prepared and published during the period (summer and autumn 1998) in which the Royal Commission on Long-Term Care was meeting, and considering fundamental issues about the relative responsibilities of the state and the individual for purchase of nursing and personal care for adults. The White Paper is not therefore concerned with these fundamental issues about the financial responsibilities and flows, but with how to give better direction to social services so that they could serve adults better. The starting point is the legacy of the community care reforms implemented in April 1993, which gave social services the responsibility to assess the care needs of individuals, to provide or fund the care identified as needed (within available resources), and to ensure that the care given was what the person concerned needed.

The 1998 proposals build on the framework established earlier in the 1990s, with a view to promoting people's independence while ensuring their protection, providing services more consistently across the country, and making service systems more centred on service users and their families. A whole raft of measures is proposed in the White Paper, some of them extremely wide ranging including the development of a prevention strategy, within which local authorities will be required to establish an approach to target services that helps people to do things for themselves for as long as possible in their own homes, and helps people with social care needs of working age to take up, remain or return to work for as long as possible. The development of these local strategies is to be supported by a specific grant, part of the overall Social Services Modernization Fund described in chapter 9, which provides £100m to local authorities over the three years 1999/2000 to 2001/02. As a condition of the grant in the first year, local authorities were required to develop preventative strategies with local agencies and to produce plans with relevant health authorities by early autumn 1999 setting out key objectives and how they intended to implement them. At late-1999, it is envisaged that the subsequent years of the grant will see the Department of Health making conditions for the grant more specific, with greater clarity as to what local authorities are expected to do and achieve.

Other initiatives are more specifically focused: for example, the *Fair Access to Care Services* initiative. The White Paper includes a statement of national objectives for social services, one of which is 'to identify individuals with social care needs who are eligible for public support, to assess those needs accurately and consistently, and to review care packages as necessary to ensure that they continue to be appropriate and effective'. This objective provides the basis for a drive towards greater consistency in the systems for deciding who qualifies for services, and the White Paper indicates that guidance will be developed which sets out the principles local authorities should follow when devising and applying eligibility criteria, including the need for compatibility with National Health Service criteria for access to continuing care. The guidance is expected to give due weight to the importance of regular reviews of people in receipt of services to ensure that needs remain within eligibility criteria and that services continue to match needs. Since the publication of the White Paper, developmental work on these issues has been taken forward with seven local authorities and in consultation with a wide range of relevant interests. At the time of writing, it is anticipated that this will provide the basis for Department of Health publishing draft policy and practice guidance for consultation in early 2000, and that all local authorities will be required to operate within the guidance by April 2001.

Perhaps the touchstone initiative of the proposals for modernization of social services for adults is the proposal to develop a 'long-term care charter', linked to a range of measures to improve commissioning of services by local authorities on the basis that 'better commissioning will help to ensure that services meet people's specific individual needs and that groups with particular needs, such as people from ethnic minorities, are better served'. The intention of the charter is to set out more clearly at national level what people – both users and carers – can expect if they require support from social services (as well as health and housing) but also what individuals' own responsibilities are in their dealings with these providers of statutory services. The purposes of the charter are defined as: empowering users and carers by promoting awareness of local services and making it clear how agencies are expected to respond to their needs; and, to give local authorities a tool against which they can set their local standards as one basis for monitoring their overall performance.

Work on the long-term care charter proceeded during the preparation of the White Paper with consultation with a wide range of stakeholders. A draft charter *You and Your Services: A Charter to Improve Services for People Needing Ongoing Support or Care* was published for consultation in May 1999, as a joint publication by the Department of Health and the DETR which has responsibility for government policy on housing services. At the time of writing, the intention is to revise the draft national charter in the autumn of 1999, with a view to its publication as the basis of a requirement for local authorities to introduce local charters in April 2000. Local housing, health and social services authorities will be required to co-operate in drawing up these joint local charters, using the framework provided by the national charter, and linking in to local joint planning mechanisms for producing health improvement plans and community care plans and housing investment plans. The national charter was developed on the basis of the principles of public service produced by the Service First Unit of the Cabinet Office, and was drawn up following a period of consultation including 15 regional focus groups. The guidance makes clear that social services authorities will lead the process of developing local charters and will be expected to bring together multi-agency project groups to work through the key stages of producing and implementing these charters. Once local charters are in place, local authorities will be required to put in place a developmental strategy to support the charter, covering training and support for staff, protocols for sharing information across agencies, mechanisms for integrating standards into contracts with independent providers, and dealing with complaints. Monitoring of performance against the charter is expected to become part of routine management in social services authorities, which will be expected to publish progress against the charter areas of performance in an annual joint report for the local community.

The long-term care charter has been selected here as a particularly illuminating initiative of the overall modernization policy because of a number of its key characteristics. These include the premise that local action should be taken within a nationally established framework, the highly inclusive and consultative approach to taking forward all aspects of the initiative, the focus on outcomes for service users, and the requirement for clear action within fairly tightly defined time-scales. Another particularly characteristic feature of this initiative is the emphasis on partnership between the different public sector organizations involved in ensuring a high quality and consistent response to the needs of services users whose various requirements for assistance and support cannot often easily be compartmentalized.

This emphasis on breaking down barriers between public sector organizations is a central component of the modernization agenda generally, and has been given particular prominence in taking forward health and social services policy.

In the White Paper *The New NHS: Modern, Dependable* (Department of Health, 1997h), the government made a commitment to consulting on ways to encourage further joint working between health and social services. This commitment subsequently bore fruit in a consultative document published in September 1998, *Partnership in Action* (Department of Health, 1998g) which started from the premise, expressed in the ministerial foreword, that 'all too often when people have complex needs spanning both health and social care good quality services are sacrificed for sterile arguments about boundaries'. The consultative document sets out the government's plans 'to make partnership a reality throughout England by removing barriers in the existing system, introducing new incentives for joint working and achieving better monitoring of progress towards joint objectives'.

The document identifies joint working as being required at three levels: strategic planning, service commissioning, and service provision. The consultative document makes clear that major structural change is not seen as the answer to the boundary problems identified, and that there is no intention to set up a new statutory structure of single purpose health and social services authorities. Rather, the intention is to legislate to make joint working easier through arrangements whereby health and social services authorities can:

- operate 'pooled budgets' (putting a proportion of their funds into a mutually accessible joint budget to enable more integrated care)
- lead commissioning arrangements with one authority transferring funds to the other, which can then take responsibility for purchasing both health and social care
- integrate provision so that one service providing organization can provide both health and social care.

This flexibility will allow National Health Service organizations greater freedom to provide social care and allow social services authorities to provide some community health services on behalf of the National Health Service. All these new measures will be accompanied by a new statutory duty of partnership on all local bodies in the health service, and on local authorities to work together to promote the wellbeing of their local communities.

To pave the way for the introduction of these flexibilities and the stimulation of partnership, a new specific grant providing nearly £650m over three years was introduced, with a particular emphasis on improving rehabilitation services, avoiding unnecessary admissions to hospital and institutional care, and improving hospital discharge arrangements. The requisite legislation changes were enacted in the Health Act 1999, which also abolished the requirement to establish a Joint Consultative Committee at the apex of the joint planning structures between local authorities and health authorities. Implementation is now being planned, but this requires regulations governing the new operational flexibilities to be laid before Parliament in autumn 1999. At the time of writing, it is anticipated that local authorities and health authorities will be invited to register (with the Department of Health and NHS Executive Regions) their interest in using these operational flexibilities in autumn 1999, with a view to some use of the flexibilities commencing in April 2000. Although these flexibilities will be, in principle, available across the whole of the shared areas of responsibilities between health and local authorities, it is anticipated that they will, initially, be tested out in the areas of commissioning and providing community care services for adults.

Modernizing Children's Services

The White Paper sets out a prospectus for a thoroughgoing and comprehensive programme of improvements in children's services. Three priority aims are defined

1   To ensure that children are protected from sexual, physical and emotional abuse and neglect
2   To raise the quality of care for children in care or 'looked after' by local authorities
3   To improve the life chances of children in care

The starting position is one in which there has been much evidence of failure by local authorities to provide services and protection systems of the requisite quality and rigour. Much of this evidence has been presented in Social Services Inspectorate reports on inspections, alongside evidence of serious abuse in individual cases. In 1997/8, the Department of Health received reports of 91 cases of children dying or suffering serious injury at the hands of adult abusers.

The previous government commissioned in 1996 a *Review of the Safeguards for Children Living Away from Home*, led by a former Chief Inspector of Social Services. This focused on children looked after by local authorities (approximately 55,000 at any one time) but also in boarding schools and penal settings. Sir William Utting's report *People Like Us* (Department of Health, 1997e) was published a year before the White Paper, and presented a trenchant critique of the established state of affairs as the basis for over 150 recommendations.

The government's response to this report (Department of Health, 1998) made a number of commitments to action, including ensuring that proper complaints procedures existed in all residential care settings, and publishing national standards for foster care. However, the Utting report and Social Services Inspectorate's work had revealed deep-seated and serious problems in the system of public care for children, including a lack of clear eligibility criteria for children, an insufficient range of placement options, particularly for children with highly specialized needs, and a tendency to regard adoption as an option of last resort. Underlying these particular deficiencies were fundamental problems in management, strategic planning and financial and other information systems.

Consequently, a major initiative was launched in the run-up to publication of the White Paper, termed the 'Quality Protects' initiative. Its distinctive features include a detailed statement of national objectives for children's services, broken down into those which are child or family outcome related (e.g. 'to ensure that children in need gain maximum life chance benefits from educational opportunities, health care and social care'), and those which are service related (e.g. 'to ensure that referral and assessment processes discriminate effectively between different types and levels of need and produce a timely service response'). Local authorities were required to produce Quality Protects Action Plans by early 1999 addressing these objectives and 15 'key tasks', including establishing clear financial and human resource strategies, and making sure that 'political structures help members and officers to work together to provide quality care for children'. The implementation of these plans was fuelled by a specific grant totalling £375m over the three years 1999/2000 to 2001/02, for which six priority targets were defined:

1   Increasing placement choice for looked after children
2   Increasing support for children leaving public care
3   Developing management information systems
4   Improving assessment, care planning and record keeping
5   Developing effective quality assurance systems
6   Establishing or improving arrangements for 'listening to children and young people'

By mid-1999, all 150 local authorities had produced the required action plans, providing the Department of Health with 'the richest array of information about the position of children's services we have ever had' (Department of Health, 1999m). On this basis, and an evaluation of their contents (Department of Health, 1999d) which not surprisingly found that 'some of the fundamental building blocks of successful local strategies were not in place', a national 'work programme' was developed to take forward work in 16 specified areas. This programme is to be progressed jointly by central and local government, positioning the Department of Health squarely at the head of a programme of social services reform with clearly defined intended outcomes in an almost unprecedented way.

The Quality Protects initiative is characteristic of the overall modernization agenda in its emphasis on inter-agency collaboration, particularly between the public authorities responsible for education and housing. Indeed, one of the outcome objectives defined in the White Paper is that 'the proportion of children leaving care at 16 or later with a GCSE qualification or GNVQ qualification will increase to at least 50 per cent by 2001 and to at least 75 per cent by 2003'. Although this target is arguably at least as much the responsibility of the education system as the social services system, it was included in the Department of Health's 'Public Service Agreement' contract with the Treasury concluded following the 1998 comprehensive spending review. Its achievement will require active collaboration between local social services and education authorities.

The White Paper proposals for improvements in children's services encompass much more than the Quality Protects initiative, including legislating to strengthen arrangements for preventing unsuitable people from working with children (the 1999 Protection of Children Act, which resulted from a government supported private member's Bill), and planning to legislate to create new and stronger duties on councils to support care leavers up to at least age 18, while developing new arrangements for each 16–18-year-old leaving care to have a clear plan setting out a 'pathway to independence' (Department of Health, 1999c). Nevertheless, Quality Protects has so many of the quintessential features of 'modernization' as defined by the government – an overall vision and clear objectives, national framework accompanied by a requirement for local plans, inter-agency working and partnerships, commitment to involvement of service users, ring-fenced and targeted funding, specific performance targets for outcomes for service users and clear accountabilities for success or failure – that it can, in many respects, be seen as a microcosm of the Social Services White Paper reform programme as a whole.

Part of the analysis of previous failure at the heart of the initiative concerns gaps in the regulatory regime, in particular the fact that small private children's homes are excluded from regulation, and that no regulatory safeguards apply to the increasing number of independent fostering agencies. These deficiencies are to be tackled through a comprehensive reform of the overall regulatory regime for social services, which will entail the removal of regulatory responsibilities from local social services authorities and the creation of a new system of independent regulation which will inspect and register children's services in all sectors (statutory, private and voluntary).

Strengthening Regulation of Services and the Work-force

As well as being commissioners and providers of social services, local social services authorities also have significant statutory responsibilities for regulation of services provided by the private and voluntary sectors, and for inspection of services in all sectors. A consultation document published in September 1995 by the Department of Health and the Welsh Office on the registration and inspection of social services, *Moving Forward* (Department of Health, 1995b), defines these terms as follows:

> *Regulation* means setting acceptable standards for services, and enforcing those standards by registering, issuing licences to or otherwise formally recognizing service providers who meet them and taking action against those who do not. *Inspection* means supporting the regulatory function by monitoring the initial and continued compliance by service providers with the standards set and identifying areas where the quality of care received by the user is inadequate.

The consultation document set out, in an appendix ,the established structures for the regulation and inspection of social services, which derived from the 1984 Registered Homes Act (the registration and inspection of private and voluntary residential care homes for adults), and the 1989 Children Act (the regulation and inspection of private children's homes and day care for children under eight). A number of other regulatory responsibilities (e.g. for voluntary children's homes and voluntary adoption agencies) are the responsibility of the Secretary of State for Health. Local authorities' own services, whether residential homes for adults or community homes for children, or adoption services are not currently subject to regulation, but they are subject to inspection. This structure of regulation had evolved over a long period, with the 1984 Registered Homes Act and the 1989 Children Act consolidating and reinforcing and, in some respects, extending established arrangements. However, it was perceived as having major deficiencies in terms of lack of comprehensiveness of coverage (e.g. it excluded domiciliary care and day care) and inconsistency in application of regulatory regimes by 150 separate local authority regulators, working in tandem with approximately 100 health authority regulators responsible for the registration and inspection of nursing homes. There were also significant problems about the lack of independence of regulatory functions of local authorities from their other functions for commissioning and providing services. Although regis-tration and inspection functions had been required to be established on an 'arm's length' basis from the management of other social ser-vices respons-ibilities from 1991 onwards, concerns remained that regulatory responsibilities should not be exercised over an independ-ent sector of service provision by a statutory body which was also responsible for service provision of a similar kind, and which was purchasing services from the providers which it regulated.

The responses to the *Moving Forward* consultation document were reviewed in a detailed report by Tom Burgner on *The Regula-tion and Inspection of Social Services* published in Autumn 1996 (Department of Health, 1996c). Burgner concluded that a system of statutory regulation for the social services would be necessary for the foreseeable future, and he made some fundamental and far-reaching recommendations about issues concerning the structure and scope of regulation, and the standards to underpin regulatory activity.

The Burgner review had been commissioned by a Conservative gov-ernment which indicated in its Social Services White Paper in March 1997, that it intended to legislate to implement the principal Burgner recommendations as soon as parliamentary time allowed. Similarly, the Labour Party in opposition lined up behind the principal Burgner recommendations, hence the manifesto commitment referred to earl-ier. Not surprisingly, therefore, the Social Services White Paper con-tains, at its heart, some detailed proposals for thoroughgoing reform of regulatory arrangements.

Starting from the analysis that existing arrangements for regulating care services have developed in a piecemeal fashion over time, and that there are problems of lack of independence, lack of coherence (with responsibilities split between different authorities and different professional disciplines) and lack of consistency, the White Paper set out proposals to transfer the regulatory responsibilities of local social services authorities and health authorities to a new statutory system altogether. It indicated the government's intention to create eight Com-missions for Care Standards, on a regional basis aligned with the Na-tional Health Service regions at 1999, which would be responsible for regulation of all social services subject to regulation and for the regu-lation of nursing homes. The government has subsequently decided to create a single national statutory body (the Care Commission for Eng-land) to undertake these and some related responsibilities in the field of health care regulation. However, this single organization will oper-ate through a regional structure. The scope of statutory regulation is to be extended to a range of services not currently included, most notably domiciliary care and small children's homes. Of particular significance for the continuing work of social services authorities is the intention to bring local authority directly managed care homes, and local authority home care services within the scope of registration, inspection and enforcement action in the same way as independent providers. Similarly, it is the government's intention that local authority fostering services and adoption services should also be brought within the formal scope of statutory regulation.

The White Paper is at pains to emphasize that, while tightening control of the safety and quality of social services through an enhanced independent system of social services regulation, the government has no intention to ossify patterns of service provision. The diversification of social service provision, particularly the development of sheltered housing schemes incorporating significant amounts of care, continues to pose difficult questions as to what services should be regulated and how this should be done. Thus, the White Paper recognizes that 'in due time, as patterns of services change, there may be a need for changes in the range of services subject to regulation'. It is, therefore, intended that the legislative framework for the new regulation system should allow for flexibility and adaptation in response to such changes, although the extent to which such flexibility can be achieved in legislation remains to be seen.

Implementation of a new regulatory regime, and the transfer of the current regulatory responsibilities of local social services authorities and health authorities to the new Commission for Care Standards, will require primary legislation. This is to take the form of a Care Standards Bill in the 1999/2000 parliamentary session. This legislation will also address the issue of the lack of any formal regulation of those who make up the social services work-force. The existing statutory body, the Central Council for Education and Training in Social Work (CCETSW), derives its statutory remit from the 1983 Health and Social Services and Social Security Adjudications Act, but its functions are restricted to the regulation of training for social workers and other social care staff. There has never been a system for statutory regulation of the social work or broader social services work-force, akin to the professional regulatory bodies and regimes in existence for medical practitioners, nurses and a number of other health professions. The White Paper proposes the strengthening of the regulatory framework for social care by the introduction of, at least some, regulation of social care personnel for the first time, through the creation of a new statutory body called the General Social Care Council (GSCC). This is to take over the current responsibilities of CCETSW (which will be abolished) for the development and regulation of the training system, and link these with arrangements for regulation of staff, possibly through the introduction of registration for key groups of qualified staff. In particular, it is anticipated that the GSCC will establish a register of people with a recognized professional social work qualification early in its life. In due course, the White Paper indicates that consideration will be given to limiting employment in certain positions in the social services work-force to those who have a particular qualification or are registered in the relevant section of the GSCC's Register.

Taken together, all of these changes will establish a radically different regulatory landscape for social services, which will have major implications for the management and delivery of services by local social services authorities, and the recruitment, training and development of their work-force, as well as for their commissioning of services from the private and voluntary sectors. Rather than being the only statutory bodies in the social services field other than CCETSW, local social services authorities will find themselves working with, and subject to, regulation by a national statutory body with a regional organization, which will also work closely on regulatory issues with a new central regulatory body for the social services work-force. This new system is likely to bring into even sharper relief issues about whether the performance of their service delivery functions by social services authorities is of the quality expected by government policy. These issues will also be addressed within the strengthened arrangements for addressing social services performance.

Improving Performance

The determination of the Labour government to achieve improvements in the management, delivery and efficiency of social services is emphasized in the proposals contained in the White Paper for monitoring the performance of social services authorities and intervening in cases of failure. This is in the context of the proposals to establish a 'best value regime' as the key element in the government's agenda to improve the quality of local authority services and the efficiency and economy with which they are delivered. A comprehensive duty of best value – to deliver services to standards covering both cost and quality, by the most effective, economic and efficient means available, is to be supported by a performance management framework for all local authority functions. The best value regime was the subject of the Local Government Bill introduced into Parliament around the time of the publication of the Social Services White Paper in

November 1998, which was passed as the Local Government Act in July 1999 and will be formally implemented with effect from April 2000.

These are the key elements of the best value framework, all of which will be applied to the social services functions of local authorities:

- National best value performance indicators against which local authorities will be required to set targets for improvement
- Fundamental performance reviews by individual local authorities of all their functions over a five-year cycle, in the course of which they will need to decide when to review social services and whether to review social services in one go or as part of a series of smaller reviews of specific aspects of social services, perhaps connected to reviews of other local authority functions
- The preparation of a 'local performance plan' on an annual basis for all of the functions of a local authority, reporting on current performance in comparison with other similar authorities, identifying forward targets for service improvement on an annual and long-term basis, and indicating the intended means by which targets will be achieved
- Independent audit and review of local performance plans by auditors working in tandem with the appropriate inspectorate (in the social services case the Social Services Inspectorate)
- New powers for the relevant government departments to intervene in local authorities where there are serious failures in individual or multiple functions

The Local Authority Social Services Act already provides the Secretary of State for Health with certain powers of direction and intervention in the activities of social services authorities, but the 'best value regime' furnishes the Secretary of State with a more flexible range of powers, including the ability to require an authority to accept external management assistance and, in extreme cases, the power to transfer the responsibility for providing social services functions to another social services authority or another body.

At the time of writing, many aspects of the 'best value regime' which will be applied across local government as a whole are still in the process of development, and the full implications for social services will not be apparent for some time. The DETR, the government department with overall responsibility for the best value regime, published draft guidance on all aspects of it in September 1999 (DETR, 1999b). However, the Department of Health did publish a consultation document in early 1999, *A New Approach to Social Services Performance*

(Department of Health, 1999a), building on the intention stated in the White Paper to 'provide social services authorities with a framework within which to assess their performance, establish standards and set targets for improvement'. A subsequent circular in July1999 (Department of Health, 1999n) reports on the responses to the consultation exercise, in particular those about the proposed performance indicators for social services, organized around the best value conceptual framework for performance indicators of five dimensions:

1 National priorities and strategic objectives
2 Cost and efficiency
3 Effectiveness of service delivery and outcomes
4 Quality of services for users and carers
5 Fair access

The circular confirms a set of fifty performance indicators for social services, mostly derived from existing statistical returns from local social services authorities to the Department of Health, and also indicates that the Department of Health intends to introduce performance indicators on other aspects (including quality of services for users and carers, and fair access) once the necessary developmental work has been done with stakeholders in the social services field. The first full set of social services performance indicators, the *Personal Social Services Performance Assessment Framework* was published in November 1999 (Department of Health, 1999o), giving comparative data for all 150 local authorities. This particularly highlights issues about variations in performance, and urges local authorities to learn from the experiences and good practice of others. It also identifies areas in which vulnerable people were being put at risk through significant numbers of local authorities not fulfilling their statutory duties, for example, inspection of registered homes and review of child protection cases. The publication emphasizes the urgency of making improvements in the management of these functions.

To put the Department of Health in a position to intervene more actively in issues of social services performance, the Social Services Inspectorate of the Department of Health is to develop its capacity to assess the performance of each local authority in delivering the new agenda for social services. This will entail close working with other central government inspectorates as part of the Best Value Inspectorate Forum established in summer1999. It will also entail a stronger role for the Social Services Inspectorate's regional offices, which will be required to build an understanding of local authority performance throughout the year, culminating in an annual review meeting from

2000 onwards which will focus on the social services aspects of the local performance plan and establish how the local authority is responding to the national modernization agenda, objectives and targets. At the same time, the arrangements for joint reviews of social services authorities by a combined unit of the Social Services Inspectorate and the Audit Commission, introduced in the mid-1990s, will be put on to a five-year cycle in line with what is required of local social services authorities themselves under the 'best value regime'. The principal implications of all this for the future role of the Social Services Inspectorate are set out in the *Chief Inspector of Social Services' Annual Report for 1998–99* (Department of Health, 1999f).

Conclusions: The Key Challenges

The conclusion to the White Paper acknowledges that the modernization of social services will be 'a long-term programme'. In line with the general orientation of the government to be concerned with outcomes of public services, seven general dimensions of success are defined, including the aspiration that 'people will be able to have confidence in their local social services'. This reflects the overall ambition that 'public confidence' should be restored in a social services system which is perceived as having lost this confidence. This programme of reform will pose a number of challenges for local social services authorities:

- Policy formulation
- Organizational management
- Resource management
- Policy implementation

Policy formulation

In common with public policy in other areas, social services policy is by no means usually handed down in a fully finished form from Parliament and government to local social services authorities. Rather, there is a major role for local authorities in developing policy through its implementation. This will certainly be as true of the modernizing social services implementation as of the implementation of previous policies, even if the contemporary approach is characterized by a greater level of specificity and prescription by the Department of Health of both the *what* and the *how* than has usually been evident, and a more serious and sustained involvement in monitoring and supporting its implementation.

Organizational management

The management of the delivery of functions as complex as the social services entails major organizational challenges. This is reflected in the general organizational turbulence of local social services authorities. Policy change on the scale required by the modernization programme will compound this. As discussed in chapter 9, a number of local authorities have established arrangements for organizing social services in various patterns of integration with other services, including housing, environmental health and consumer protection. It is anticipated that legislation to reform the political management structures of local authorities will abolish the requirement on local social services authorities to have a 'social services committee', while retaining the requirement to have a director of social services and being more specific (through statutory direction or guidance) about what is expected of a director both in terms of management and professional accountabilities. All this is likely to stimulate further exploration of possibilities regarding the way social services functions are discharged.

Resource management

The management of statutory social services functions will always entail complex resource management issues, both financial and human. The White Paper programme of reform is accompanied by a higher degree of 'hypothecation' or ring-fencing of revenue resources, through specific and special grants, than has ever previously been the case. With this, comes a requirement to demonstrate that funds are being used for the intended purpose, and that the required results are achieved. This more rigorous approach to what has come to be termed 'performance management' will pose particular challenges to local authorities which are perceived to be 'failing', especially if the intervention powers made available to the Secretary of State for Health by the 1999 Local Government Act are used.

Policy implementation

Managing social services functions in a way that maximizes the effective and efficient use of resources will be fundamental to implementation of the new policies. It is readily apparent that the implementation task will be complex, generally requiring social services authorities to operate as commissioners and providers within local inter-agency networks. The emphasis on 'joining-up' the activities of public authorities discharging different but linked functions, and on ensuring positive and stable relationships with the voluntary sector through the newly defined 'compact with the voluntary sector' (Home Office, 1998), will accentuate this.

None of these challenges are entirely new. However, the furtherance of the modernizing social services agenda will certainly require committed and creative management by people accustomed, as in the National Health Service, to 'keeping as many plates as possible spinning, hanging on to a long-term vision while not allowing too many of those plates to crash to the ground' (National Health Service Executive, 1998). In his pamphlet *Managing for Health* (1999), David Hunter criticizes the government for failing to recognize that a new approach to public service management needs to be fashioned if its health policy objectives are to be achieved. Whether or not this critique is relevant to the government's approach to modernizing a social services system which is more at arm's length from the Department of Health than is the National Health Service, implementation of it will certainly test managerial capacity at all levels.

Chapter 11

Conclusions: The Future of Local Authority Social Services

Michael Hill

There were times during the creation of this book when the author wondered if he and his colleagues were writing a book that would turn out to be only a history book, describing and discussing a system of local authority social services which would be no more soon after the book was published. The most extreme version of that fear was that the services would not merely soon be fragmented but that also that local authorities would have lost responsibility for many of them. A more limited fear, which has indeed influenced the way this book has come to be written, was that while local authorities would still be the central actors in the implementation of the personal social services, they would soon be organizing their activities in very different ways to those that had come to be taken for granted in the first twenty-five or so years after the 1970 Local Authority Social Services Act.

Chapter 10, written by a civil servant, Stephen Mitchell, who is closely involved in policy planning in the Department of Health, offers reassurance that the more extreme fear set out above for the fate of this book is not shortly to be realized. Chapter 10 sets out a view of the future that indicates that some of the processes of organizational innovation described in other chapters of the book will continue to be encouraged – even sometimes expected – by central government, but this is contained within a vision that has much in common with the Seebohm Report and the pioneers of social services development in the years after 1971 in its concern with an integrated and consistent strategy.

An examination of any process of policy development over time is likely to show patterns of what is sometimes called 'path dependency' in which new innovations build on and are, therefore, substantially shaped by what had gone before. In the case of the British social ser-

vices, as shown in chapter 2, the radical changes forced by the aboli-
tion of the Poor Law led to the establishment, in the 1940s, of two key
blocks of local authority services – for children and for the welfare of
vulnerable adults – which were brought together in 1971. From then
on, the story is essentially about the alternative ways of trying to ensure that these two blocks are related to each other, while not dis-
regarding the links each has with other services both inside and outside
local government. The movements towards, and then away from, what
is described elsewhere in this book as the 'generic' perspective have
been essentially incremental, taking different forms in different local
authorities.

Hence, from one perspective, there is a need to play down emphases
on those processes which now seem to be fragmenting local authority
social services. An alternative perspective – also extensively explored
in this book – highlights the difficulties in defining what social services
authorities do (pages 4–6), emphasizes the way services overlap with
the concerns of other statutory services (pages 12–19), identifies the
difficulties about distinguishing official responsibilities from personal
and family responsibilities (pages 19–21), and draws attention to the
ways in which only a minority of the population are touched by social
services' activities (pages 38–9). Early in one of these discussions an
analogy was drawn between attempts to define a specific sphere of
personal social services activities and attempts to canalize a river near
to its delta. These considerations suggest that there is no essential logic
to the package of activities seen as belonging to English social services
authorities. When the author wrote a comparative book on social
policy, he found that, while it was relatively easy to bring together a
range of data to compare social security, health, education and social
housing policies across nation states, the diversity of organizational
arrangements made it much more difficult to do this for the personal
social services (Hill, 1996). Indeed, there are even differences between
England and Scotland in what is included in the local authority remit.

If the future of the personal social services is considered with the
considerations set out in the previous paragraph uppermost in the mind,
rather than the continuities emphasized earlier, it is easy to set out
some very different alternative scenarios. In various places in the book,
the twin impacts of the 1989 Children Act and the 1990 National
Health Service and Community Care Act have been stressed. It is not
hard to imagine a reversal of the 1970 Local Authority Social Services
Act to re-establish children's services and adult welfare services as separate activities. Chapter 9 suggests that some local authorities have
moved a long way in that direction. At the same time, the many boundary concerns of both the health service and the local authority educa-

tion services could further that fissile process, and even encourage a new fusion between the health service and social services for adults or between education and children's services. Just before this manuscript went to press, the government's proposal that the inspectorate for the education services (Ofsted) should take on responsibilities for the oversight of day care for pre-school children was greeted with some alarm by the Association of Directors of Social Services. Clearly, what is involved is, in itself, merely a minor boundary adjustment between services (the re-canalization of a small stream) but large changes can develop from small incremental adjustments.

It is by no means irrelevant to this discussion that – as shown in chapter 8 – the local government system is going through extensive changes. The vision of local authorities as small executive organizations meeting once a year to give out contracts as set out by the late Conservative politician, Nicholas Ridley, does not seem likely to be realized, by a new government which – as shown in chapter 10 – has high expectation of local authority performance. However, there is, for the personal social services alongside other local government activities, the expectation that – in the pursuit of 'best value' and of local diversity – many services will be partly, or wholly, contracted out. Furthermore, there is, in the contemporary government's approach to local government, the ultimate threat that underperformance could lead to an authority's replacement by a centrally imposed alternative. On page 197, the relevant powers under the 1999 Local Government Act were described. Evidence that the government will be prepared to carry out that threat is available inasmuch as interventions of this kind are occurring under earlier legislation enabling this line of action to be taking in respect of failing schools and failing education authorities. Hence, when a second edition of this book is prepared, it may be necessary to explain that not every area of England has *local authority* social services.

This discussion has so far contrasted two alternative views of the pattern of personal social services development. One view suggests that there has been a great deal of continuity in the story of the personal social services in England (and Wales), and that there is every reason to expect adjustments to remain incremental. The other has emphasized the fragile nature of the established system, and suggested forces that might lead to dramatic changes. At this stage, we do not want a rather arid discussion about the respective validity of analytical approaches which emphasize continuities and those which emphasize change. In the last resort, a sequence of incremental changes can constitute a revolution.

What has been central to the analysis throughout the book, spelt out extensively in the early chapters and recapitulated above, is that it is impossible to establish a core definition of the personal social services task – distinguishable from other statutory tasks or from the many private concerns of citizens. It is, therefore, not surprising that, over the years, policy makers have worried about boundary issues and experimented with different organizational forms. Paradoxically, this means that there is not *one best way* to organize social services. This puts, as is nicely illustrated in chapter 10, the government of one of the most highly centralized states in the world, controlling a sophisticated apparatus for central surveillance, in a very complex and potentially contradictory situation when it wants (as it does) to have a considerable influence on service delivery. It has to recognize that there are diverse authorities delivering services, using alternative models. Those models may be equally satisfactory, given that there are no simple policy goals but rather a wide range of alternative success criteria; fifty performance indicators have already been identified – see page 198. It wants to encourage good practice and eliminate bad practice, but it has few easy formulae to assist those tasks.

We are in an age that some writers have described as 'post-Fordist'. While that is a formulation this author would not wish to encourage, it does in the present case draw our attention to the fact that there has been a loss of faith in the idea that simple bureaucratic models can be devised to facilitate the efficient accomplishment of tasks (even relatively simple manufacturing ones, let alone complex service delivery ones). The story of the evolution of approaches to local authority social services organization set out in chapter 8 suggests that there was, to some extent, in the early 1970s, a 'Fordist' search for the *one best way* to deliver services. While local authorities' preoccupations with departmental reorganization suggest that this has not been abandoned, a look at the diversity in the real world suggests that this is probably a futile quest. In any case, the development of a distinctly post-Fordist preoccupation with the delegation of tasks to smaller self-managing entities (including, importantly for social services, private and voluntary organizations carrying out contracts) has dramatically increased the number of organizational options.

One of the contradictions that, in the view of this author (who, of course, should not here be taken to be speaking for all the contributors to this book), lies at the heart of the 'political project' of Tony Blair's Labour government is that it passionately wants to exercise central control, but that it recognizes the organizational diversity of the modern administrative system and the problems inherent in trying to establish the best way to perform complex service provision tasks. This means that its change agenda must be, as it is shown to be in chapter 10, elaborate and complex. There will be areas – like inspection – where it will increase uniformity; there will be areas where it can tighten control – through central supervision and the use of performance indicators. However, there will also be areas where, whether it likes it or not, it must launch or encourage experimental projects. Furthermore, there is a need in all this to take into account the impact of surveillance on morale and initiative in a service that crucially depends on the commitments of 'street-level' staff who, to a considerable extent have to be trusted to carry out much of their work out of sight of any supervision system.

What all this means, for the questions posed above about where local authority social services are going, is that it seems most unlikely that the general organizational models established and elaborated in the years after 1971 will be wholly abandoned. It is unlikely therefore that, in the next few years, we will see the wholesale dismantling of the local authority social services systems described in this book, sharing out the pieces, for example, between the National Health Service and education. On the other hand, a fairly extensive review of existing ways of providing the personal social services is under way. As that proceeds, it is far from inconceivable that, as already suggested, local authorities will cease to run some or all the personal social services in some areas. New organizations, such as the Care Commission discussed in chapter 10, will be set up. New organizational forms will also emerge, including important partnerships between the National Health Service and local authorities.

It is to be hoped that these changes will be carefully monitored. The author shares the government's view that, while there may be no *one best way* of delivering services, there are better and worse ways. Embedded in the concern about these, there must be issues about equity and efficiency. It is emphasized at various points in this book that aspirations to make the personal social services more universal in their coverage have not been realized. The resultant services can very easily come to be seen as only for minorities, over which they have little control. Hence, issues about real public accountability need attention. There is a big agenda here, for central–local relations and for the government of local authorities, discussed a little in chapter 8, but going far beyond the concerns of this book.

This book has set out to provide an account of local authority social services, which sets the issues about specific provisions in their wider social, political and institutional contexts. The arrangements for the provision of personal social services have been shown to be complex, ambiguous and sometimes obscure. However, this is necessarily the case, given the real social situations and social problems to which they are a response. The personal social services operate, as has been emphasized, in a complicated position relative to other public services. Hence, while their specific remit to provide care in situations in which other institutions are unable or unwilling to do so puts them in a position in which they have particular responsibilities to combat the sources of social disadvantage, the fact that they are, in many respects, the 'poor relations' of larger and more politically salient services makes this a difficult role to perform. This book has not sought to advocate ways to approach this problem, but, in offering a thorough account of the real world of local authority social services, it provides a realistic foundation for such advocacy.

References

Acheson, D. 1998: *Inequalities and Health*. London: HMSO.

Adler, M. 1974: Financial assistance and the social worker's exercise of discretion. In N. Newman (ed.), *In Cash and in Kind*, Edinburgh: University of Edinburgh.

Alcock, P. and Pearson, S. 1999: Raising the poverty plateau: the impact of means-tested rebates from local authority charges on low income households. *Journal of Social Policy*, 28 (3), 497–516.

Aldgate, J. and Bradley, M. 1999: *Supporting Families through Short Term Fostering*. London: HMSO.

Aldgate, J. and Hill, M. 1996: *Child Welfare Services; Developments in Law, Policy, Practice and Research*. London: Jessica Kingsley.

Aldgate, J. and Tunstill, J. 1995: *Making Sense of Section 17*. London: HMSO.

Armstrong D. 1995: The rise of surveillance medicine. *Sociology of Health and Illness*, 17, 393–404.

Audit Commission 1986: *Making a Reality of Community Care*. London: HMSO.

Audit Commission 1994a: *Finding a Place*. London: HMSO.

Audit Commission 1994b: *Seen but Not Heard: Co-ordinating Community Health and Social Services for Children in Need*. London: HMSO.

Audit Commission 1997: *The Coming of Age: Improving Care Services for Older People*. London: HMSO.

Audit Commission 1999: http://www.audit-commission.gov.uk/ac2/IC

Balloch, S., McLean, J. and Fisher, M. 1999: *Social Services: Working Under Pressure*. Bristol: Policy Press.

Barnes, C. 1990: *Cabbage Syndrome: The Social Construction of Dependence*. London: Falmer Press.

Barnsley Metropolitan Borough Council 1999: (http://www.barnsley.gov.uk/council/modernisation/mod-plans.html)

Beardshaw, V. 1988: *Last on the List: Community Services for People with Physical Disabilities*. London: King's Fund Institute.

Bebbington, A. and Miles, J. 1989: The background of children who enter local authority care. *British Journal of Social Work*, 19 (5), 349–78.

Beck U. 1992: *The Risk Society: Towards a New Modernity*. London: Sage.

Becker, S. and McPherson, S. (eds) 1988: *Private Issues and Public Pain*. London: Social Services Insight Books.

Beveridge, W. 1942: *Social Insurance and Allied Services*, Cmd. 6404. London: HMSO.

Brewer, C. and Lait, J. 1980: *Can Social Work Survive?* London: Temple Smith.

British Deaf Association 1996: *Visible Voices*. York: Joseph Rowntree Foundation.

Brown, H. and Smith, H. (eds) 1992: *Normalisation: A Reader for the Nineties*. London: Tavistock/Routledge.

Bruce, I., McKennell, A. and Walker, E. 1991: *Blind and Partially Sighted Adults in Britain: The RNIB Survey*. London: HMSO.

Butler, D., Adonis, A. and Travers, T. 1994: *Failure in British Government: The Politics of the Poll Tax*. Oxford: Oxford University Press.

Butler-Sloss, Lord Justice E. 1988: *Report of the Inquiry into Child Abuse in Cleveland*. London: HMSO.

Cabinet Office 1999: *Modernising Government*, Cm 4310. London: HMSO.

Castel R. 1988: *The Regulation of Madness: The Origins of Incarceration in France*. Oxford: Blackwell.

Central Statistical Office 1996: *Social Trends 26*. London: HMSO.

Challis, L., Fuller, S., Henwood, M., Klein, R., Plowden, W., Webb, A. Whittingham, P. and Wistow, G. 1988: *Joint Approaches to Social Policy*. Cambridge: Cambridge University Press.

Collins, J. 1992: *When the Eagles Fly*. London: Values Into Action.

Colton, M., Drury, C. and Williams, M. 1995: *Children in Need: Family Support under the Children Act 1989*. Aldershot: Avebury.

Corrigan, P. and Leonard, P. 1978: *Social Work Practice under Capitalism: A Marxist Approach*. London: Macmillan.

Curtis Committee 1946: *Report of the Care of Children Committee*, Cmd. 6922. London: HMSO.

Daniel, P. and Ivatts, J. 1998: *Children and Social Policy*. Basingstoke: Macmillan.

Darlow, G. F. 1965: Who are the policy makers? *Public Administration*, 43, Autumn.

Davies, M. 1986: *The Essential Social Worker*. Aldershot: Gower.

Dear, M. and Taylor, S. M. 1982: *Not on our Street: Community Attitudes to Mental Health Care*. London: Pion.

Denney, D. 1998: *Social Policy and Social Work*. Oxford: Oxford University Press.

Department of Health 1988: *A Wider Vision*. London: HMSO.

Department of Health 1989a: *Caring for People: Community Care in the Next Decade and Beyond*, Cm 849. London: HMSO.

Department of Health 1989b: *Coordinating Services for Visually Handicapped People*. London: HMSO.

Department of Health 1990: *The Care of Children; Principles and Practice in Regulations and Guidance*. London: HMSO.

Department of Health 1991a: *Children Act 1989 Guidance and Regulations*, Vol. 2. London: HMSO.

Department of Health 1991b: *Patterns and Outcomes in Child Placement*. London: HMSO.

Department of Health 1993a: *Children Act Report*. London: Department of Health.

Department of Health 1993b: *Implementing Community Care for Younger People with Physical and Sensory Disabilities*. London: Department of Health.

Department of Health 1994: *Working in Partnership: A Collaborative Approach to Care*. London: Department of Health.

Department of Health 1995a: *Child Protection; Messages from Research*. London: HMSO.

Department of Health 1995b: *Moving Forward: A Consultation Document on the Regulation and Inspection of Social Services*. London: Department of Health.

Department of Health 1995c: *Searching for Service: An Inspection of Service Responses Made to the Needs of Disabled Young Adults and their Carers*. London: Department of Health.

Department of Health 1996a: *Progressing Services With Physically Disabled People*. London: Department of Health.

Department of Health 1996b: *Social Services: Maintaining Standards in a Changing World*, LASSL (96) 9, London: Department of Health.

Department of Health 1996c: *The Regulation and Inspection of Social Services* (the Burgner Report). London: Department of Health.

Department of Health 1997a: *A Service on the Edge: Inspection of Services for Deaf and Hard of Hearing People*. London: Department of Health.

Department of Health 1997b: *Better Services for Vulnerable People*. London: HMSO.

Department of Health 1997c: *Building Bridges: A Guide to the Arrangements for Inter-Agency Working for the Care and Protection of Mentally Ill People*. London: HMSO.

Department of Health 1997d: *Children Looked After by Local Authorities, Year Ending 31st March 1996*. London: Department of Health.

Department of Health 1997e: *People Like Us: The Report of the Review of the Safeguards for Children Living Away from Home*. London: HMSO.

Department of Health 1997f: *Responding to Families in Need; Assessment, Planning and Decision-making in Family Support Services*. London: Department of Health.

Department of Health 1997g: *Social Services: Achievement and Challenge*, Cm 3588. London: HMSO.

Department of Health 1997h: *The New NHS*, Cm 3807. London: HMSO.

Department of Health 1998a: *A First Class Service: Quality in the New NHS*. London: HMSO.

Department of Health 1998b: *Caring for Children away from Home*. London: Department of Health.

Department of Health 1998c: *Health and Personal Social Services Statistics for England*. London: HMSO.

Department of Health 1998d: *Modernising Mental Health Services: Safe, Sound and Supportive*. HMSO, London.

Department of Health 1998e: *Modernising Social Services: Promoting Independence, Improving Protection, Raising Standards*, Cm 4169. London: HMSO.

Department of Health 1998f: *Moving Into The Mainstream: Inspection of Services for Adults With Learning Disabilities*. London: Department of Health.

Department of Health 1998g: *Partnership in Action: New Opportunities for Joint Working between Health and Social Services*. London: Department of Health.

Department of Health 1998h: *Partners in Planning. Approaches to Planning Services for Children and their Families*. London: Department of Health.

Department of Health 1998i: *Quality Protects: Framework for Action and Objectives for Social Services for Children*. London: Department of Health.

Department of Health 1998j: *The Government's Response to the Children's Safeguards Review*, Cm 4105. London: HMSO.

Department of Health 1998k: *Working Together to Safeguard Children: New Proposals for Inter-Agency Co-operation*. London: HMSO.

Department of Health 1999a: *A New Approach to Social Services Performance: Consultation Document*. London: Department of Health.

Department of Health 1999b: *Capital Investment Strategy for the Department of Health*. London: Department of Health.

Department of Health 1999c: *Getting Family Support Right; Inspection of the Delivery of Family Support Services*. London :Department of Health.

Department of Health 1999d: *Mapping Quality in Children's Services*. London: Department of Health.

Department of Health 1999e: *Me Survive Out There?*, consultation document. London: Department of Health.

Department of Health 1999f: *Modern Social Services – A Commitment to Improve: The 8th Annual Report of the Chief Inspector*. London: Department of Health.

Department of Health 1999g: *Modernising Social Services: Implementation Diary*. London: Department of Health.

Department of Health 1999h: *Modernising Social Services, Promoting Independence, Improving Protection, Raising Standards*. London: HMSO.

Department of Health 1999i: *Personal Social Services Current Expenditure in England: 1997–8*. Bulletin 1999/11. London: Department of Health.

Department of Health 1999j: *Personal Social Services Staff of Social Services Departments at 30 September 1998 England*, Bulletin 1999/8. London: Department of Health.

Department of Health 1999k: Press release 36.

Department of Health 1999l: Press release 439.

Department of Health 1999m: *Quality Protects Newsletter, Issue 2, July 1999*. London: Department of Health.

Department of Health 1999n: *The Personal Social Services Performance Assessment Framework*. Local Authority Circular, London: Department of Health. Published with LASSL(99)24.

Department of Health 1999o: *Social Services Performance in 1998/99*. London: Department of Health.

Department of Health and DETR (Department of the Environment, Transport and the Regions) (1999) *You and Your Services*. London: Department of Health.

Department of Social Security 1998: *A New Contract for Welfare*, Green Paper, Cm 3805. London: HMSO.

DETR (Department of the Environment, Transport and the Regions) 1998: *Modern Local Government in Touch with the People*, Cm 4014. London: HMSO.

DETR (Department of the Environment, Transport and the Regions) 1999a: *Local Leadership, Local Choice*, consultative paper. London: DETR.

DETR (Department of the Environment, Transport and the Regions) 1999b: *Implementing Best Value – A Consultation Paper on Draft Guidance*. London: DETR.

DHSS (Department of Health and Social Security) 1971: *Better Services for the Mentally Handicapped*, Cm 4683. London: HMSO.

DHSS (Department of Health and Social Security) 1974: *Social Work Support for the Health Service: Report of a Working Party* (the Otten Report). London: HMSO.

DHSS (Department of Health and Social Security) 1976: *Priorities for Health and Personal Social Services in England*. London: HMSO.

DHSS (Department of Health and Social Security) 1977: *Priorities for Health and Personal Social Services: The Way Forward*. London: HMSO.

DHSS (Department of Health and Social Security) 1978: *Social Services Teams: The Practitioner's View*. London: HMSO.

DHSS (Department of Health and Social Security) 1980: *Reform of the Supplementary Benefits Scheme*, Circular LAC (80) 5. London: DHSS.

DHSS (Department of Health and Social Security) 1985a: *Review of Child Care Law: Report to Ministers of an Inter-Departmental Working Party*. London: HMSO.

DHSS (Department of Health and Social Security) 1985b: *Social Work Decisions in Child Care*. London: HMSO.

Dobson, F., 1998: Frank Dobson outlines the third way for mental health, Department of Health Press Release 311, 29 July.

Donnison, D. V. 1977: Against discretion. *New Society*, September.

East Sussex County Council 1999: (http://www.eastsussexcc.gov.uk/modern/main_page.htm)

Ferlie, E. and Judge, K. 1981: Retrenchment and rationality in personal social services. *Policy and Politics*, 9 (3), 311–30.

Fimister, G. 1986: *Welfare Rights Work in Social Services*. Basingstoke: Macmillan.

Fimister, G. 1995: *Social Security and Community Care in the 1990s*. Sunderland: Business Education Publishers.

Fitzgerald, J. 1998: *Time for Freedom? Services for Older People with Learning Difficulties*. London: Values Into Action/Centre for Policy on Ageing.

Flynn, M., Cotterill, L., Hayes, L. and Sloper, T. 1996: *A Break with Tradition? The Findings of a Survey of Respite Services for Adult Citizens with Learning Disabilities in England*. Manchester: National Development Team.

Fox Harding, L. 1991: *Perspectives in Child Care Policy*. Harlow: Longman.

Garbarino, J. 1982: *Children and Families in the Social Environment*. New York: Aldine.

Gibbons, J. Conroy, S. and Bell, C. 1995: *Operating the Child Protection System*. London: HMSO.

Gilbert, B. B. 1966: *The Evolution of National Insurance in Great Britain*. London: Michael Joseph.

Glennerster, H. and Hills, J. (eds) 1998: *The State of Welfare*. Oxford: Oxford University Press.

Goldberg, D. and Huxley, P. 1980: *Mental Illness in the Community*. London: Tavistock.

Gorrell Barnes, G. 1994: Family therapy. In M. Rutter, E. Taylor and L. Hersov (eds), *Child and Adolescent Psychiatry: Modern Approaches*. Oxford: Blackwell.

Griffith, J. A. G. 1966: *Central Departments and Local Authorities*. London: Allen and Unwin.

Griffiths Report 1988: *Community Care: Agenda for Action*. London: HMSO.

Grimshaw, R. and Sinclair, R. (1997) *Planning to Care: Regulation, Procedure and Practice under the Children Act 1989*. London: National Children's Bureau.

Hadley, R. and Young, K. 1990: *Creating a Responsive Public Service*. Hemel Hempstead: Harvester Wheatsheaf.

Hale, C. 1992: Crime and penal policy. *Social Policy Review 4*, Canterbury: Social Policy Association, 175–99.

Hall, P. 1976: *Reforming the Welfare*. London: Heinemann.

Halsey, A. H.(ed.) 1988: *British Social Trends since 1900*. Basingstoke: Macmillan.

Hambleton, R. 1992: Decentralisation and democracy in UK local government. *Public Money and Management*, 12, 19–20.

Hambleton, R., Hoggett, P. and Tolan, F. 1989: The decentralisation of public services: a research agenda. *Local Government Studies*, 15, 39–56.

Handler, J. 1973: *The Coercive Social Worker*. Chicago: Rand McNally.

Hardy, B. and Wistow, G. 1999: The private sector. In B. Hudson (ed.), *The Changing Role of Social Care*. London: Jessica Kingsley.

Health Advisory Service 1997: *Addressing the Balance: Services for People Who Are Elderly*. London: HMSO.

Health Services Commissioner 1994: *Second Report 1993–4. Failure to Provide Long-Term NHS Care for a Brain-Damaged Patient*. London: HMSO.

Hearn, B. and Sinclair, R. 1998: *Children's Services Plans: Analysing Need; Reallocating Resources. A Report to the Department of Health*. London: National Children's Bureau.

Hendrick, H. 1994: *Child Welfare: England 1872–1989*. London: Routledge.

Hendrick, H. 1997: *Children, Childhood and English Society 1880–1990*. Cambridge: Cambridge University Press.

Heywood, J. 1978: *Children in Care: The Development of the Service for the Deprived Child*. London: Routledge and Kegan Paul.

Hill, M. 1996: *Social Policy: A Comparative Analysis*. Hemel Hempstead: Harvester Wheatsheaf.

Hill, M. 1997: *The Policy Process in the Modern State*. Hemel Hempstead: Harvester Wheatsheaf.

Hill, M. and Laing, P. 1979: *Social Work and Money*. London: Allen and Unwin.

Hill, M. and Tisdall, K. 1997: *Children and Society*. London: Longman.

Hills, J. (ed.) 1990: *The State of Welfare*. Oxford: Oxford University Press.

Hirst, M. 1991: *National Survey of Young People with Disabilities*. University of York: Social Policy Research Unit.

Hirst, M. and Baldwin, S. 1994: *Unequal Opportunities: Growing Up Disabled*. University of York: Social Policy Research Unit.

Holman, B. 1988: *Putting Families First: Prevention and Child Care*. Basingstoke: Macmillan.

Holman, R. 1978: *Poverty*. London: Martin Robertson.

Home Office 1991: *Safer Communities*. London: HMSO.

Home Office 1998: *Compact – getting it right together. Compact on Relations between Government and the Voluntary Sector in England*, Cm 4100, London: The Home Office.

House of Commons Health Committee 1995: *Long-Term Care: NHS Responsibilities for Meeting Continuing Health Care Needs*. London: HMSO.

House of Commons Health Committee 1998a: *Relationship Between Health and Social Services. Minutes of Evidence*. London: HMSO.

House of Commons Health Committee 1998b: *The Relationship Between Health and Social Services, First Report 1998–9*. London: HMSO.

House of Commons Social Services Committee 1985: *Community Care with Special Reference to Adult Mentally Ill and Mentally Handicapped People, Session 1984–5*. London: HMSO.

Hubert, J. 1991: *Home-Bound: Crisis in the Care of Young People with Severe Learning Difficulties*. London: King's Fund Centre.

Hunter, D. J. 1999: *Managing for Health – Implementing the New Health Agenda*. London: IPPR.

Ingleby Committee 1960: *Committee on Children and Young Persons*, Cmnd 1191. London: HMSO.

Jay Report 1979: *Report of the Committee of Inquiry into Mental Handicap Nursing and Care*. London: HMSO.

Johnstone, A. 1999: Fostering changes. *Community Care Supplement: Working with Children in Care*, 27/5/99, 8–9.

Jones, B. 1989: Section one: at the crossroads. *Benefits Research*, 3, 22–5.

Jones, K. 1972: *A History of the Mental Health Services*. London: Routledge.

Jones, K. 1975: *Mental Health and Social Policy*. London: Routledge and Kegan Paul.

Jordan, B. 1974: *Poor Parents*. London: Routledge.

Joseph Rowntree Foundation 1996: *Inquiry Into Meeting The Costs of Continuing Care: Main Report*. York: Joseph Rowntree Foundation.

Kagan, R. 1984: Organisational change and quality assurance in a psychiatric setting. *Quality Review Bulletin*, 9, 269–99.

Kelman S. 1975: The social nature of the definition problem in health. *International Journal of Health Services*, 5, 625–42.

Kirk, H. D. and McDaniel, S. A. 1984: Adoption policy in Great Britain and North America. *Journal of Social Policy* 13 (1), 75–84.

Knapp, M., Hallam, A., Beecham, J. and Baines, B. 1999: Private, voluntary or public?: Comparative cost effectiveness in community mental health care. *Policy and Politics* 27 (1), 25–44.

Korman, N. and Glennerster, H. 1985: *Closing a Hospital: The Darenth Park Project*. Bedford Square Press: London.

Korman, N. and Glennerster, H. 1990: *Hospital Closure*. Milton Keynes: Open University Press.

Kovel, J. 1981: The American mental health industry. In D. Ingleby (ed.), *Critical Psychiatry*, Harmondsworth: Penguin Books.

Labour Party 1997: *New Labour: Because Britain Deserves Better*. London: The Labour Party.

Lewis, J. 1986: *What Price Community Medicine?* Brighton: Wheatsheaf.

Lewis, J. and Glennerster, H. 1996: *Implementing the New Community Care*. Buckingham: Open University Press.

Lishman, J. (ed.) 1991: *Handbook of Theory for Practice Teachers in Social Work*. London: Jessica Kingsley.

Lister, R. and Emmett, T. 1976: *Under the Safety Net*. London: CPAG.

London Borough of Lewisham 1999: (http://www.lewisham.gov.uk/whatsnew/govern/gov.htm).

Lovelock, R. and Powell, J. 1995: *Shared Territory: The Social Support Needs of Visually Impaired People*. York: Joseph Rowntree Foundation.

MacDermott, T. 1999: Poverty: Labour's inheritance., *Poverty*, 102, Spring, 16–19.

Maluccio, A. (ed.) 1981: *Promoting Competence in Clients: a New/Old Approach to Social Work Practice*. New York: The Free Press.

Mansell, J. and Ericsson, K. 1996: *Deinstitutionalisation and Community Living*. London: Chapman and Hall.

Martin, J. P. 1984: *Hospitals In Trouble*. Blackwell: Oxford.

Means, R. and Smith, R. 1985: *The Development of Welfare Services for Elderly People*. Beckenham: Croom Helm.

Means, R. and Smith, R. 1994: *Community Care*. Basingstoke: Macmillan.

Mental Health Foundation 1996: *Building Expectations*. London.

Metzer, H., Gill, B., Petticrew, M. and Hinds, K. 1995: *The Prevalence of Psychiatric Morbidity among Adults Living in Private Households*. London: HMSO.

Middleton, H. and Shaw, I. 1999: Inequalities in mental health: Models & explanations. *Policy and Politics* 27 (1), 43–56.

Monckton Enquiry 1945: *Report on the Circumstances which led to the Boarding Out of Denis and Terence O'Neill at Bank Farm, Minsterley, and the Steps Taken to Supervise their Welfare*, Cmd. 6636. London: HMSO.

Murphy, E. 1993: Mental illness and community care. Paper presented at the conference of the Association of Social Service Directors, Solihull.

National Assistance Board 1962: *Report for 1961*, Cmnd 1730. London: HMSO.

National Audit Office 1992: *Health Services for Physically Disabled People Aged 16 to 64*. London: HMSO.

National Health Service Executive 1998: *Defining the Essential: The Functions, Roles and Costs of Health Authorities and GP Purchases*. London: Department of Health.

National Institute for Social Work 1982: *Social Workers: Their Roles and Tasks*. London: Bedford Square.

Nocon, A. and Qureshi, H. 1996: *Outcomes of Community Care for Users and Carers*. Buckingham: Open University Press.

O'Brien, J. and Tyne, A. 1981: *The Principle of Normalisation: A Foundation for Effective Services*. London: Campaign for Mentally Handicapped People.

OECD 1988: *Ageing Populations*. Paris: OECD.

Office for National Statistics 1998: *Living In Britain: Results from the 1996 General Household Survey*. London: HMSO.

Office for National Statistics 1999a: *Annual Abstract of Statistics 1999 Edition*. London: HMSO.

Office for National Statistics 1999b: *Social Trends 29*. London: HMSO.

Oliver, M. and Barnes, C. 1998: *Disabled People and Social Policy: From Exclusion to Inclusion*. London: Longman.

Onyett, S., Heppleston, T. and Bushnell, D. 1994: Job satisfaction and burnout in community mental health team members, unpublished paper.

OPCS (Office of Population, Censuses and Surveys) 1988: *The Prevalence of Disability amongst Adults*. London: HMSO.

Oppenheim, C. and Harker, L. 1996: *Poverty: The Facts*. London: Child Poverty Action Group.

Packman, J. 1975: *The Child's Generation*. Oxford: Blackwell.

Packman, J. and Jordan, B. 1991: The Children Act; looking forward, looking back. *British Journal of Social Work,* 21, 315–27.

Parker, R., Ward, H., Jackson, S., Aldgate, J. and Wedge, P. 1991: *Assessing Outcomes in Child Care*. London: HMSO.

Parton, N. 1991: *Governing the Family*. London: Macmillan.

Pascall, G. 1986: *Social Policy: A Feminist Analysis*. London: Tavistock.

Philo, G., Secker, J., Platt, S., Henderson, L., McLaughlin, G. and Burnside, J. 1997: Media images of mental distress. In T. Heller, J. Reynolds, R. Gomm, R. Munston and S. Pattison (eds), *Mental Health Matters*, Basingstoke: Macmillan Press.

Piachaud, D. 1999: *Wealth by Stealth in New Economy*. London: Institute of Public Policy Research.

Pilcher, J. and Wagg, S. (eds) 1996: *Thatcher's Children? Politics, Childhood and Society in the 1980s and 1990s.* London: Falmer Press.

Pilgrim, D. and Rogers, A. 1993: *A Sociology of Mental Health & Illness.* Buckingham: OU Press.

Pollitt, C. 1990: *Managerialism and the Public Services.* Oxford: Blackwell.

Prescott-Clarke, P. and Primatesta, P. 1998: *Health Survey for England 1996.* London: HMSO.

Quortrup, J. 1994: *Childhood Matters.* Aldershot: Avebury.

Reid, W. and Epstein, L. (eds) 1977: *Task Centered Practice.* New York: Columbia University Press.

Ridley, N. 1988: *The Local Right: Enabling Not Providing.* London: Institute of Economic Affairs.

Rodgers, B. and Dixon, J. 1960: *Portrait of Social Work.* London: Oxford University Press.

Rogers, A. and Pilgrim, D. 1998: *Mental Health Policy in Britain.* Basingstoke: Macmillan.

Rose N. 1985: *The Psychological Complex: Psychology, Politics and Society in England, 1869–1939.* London: Routledge and Kegan Paul.

Rose N. 1990: *Governing the Soul.* Routledge, London.

Rowlings, C. 1981: *Social Work with Elderly People.* London: Allen and Unwin.

Royal Commission on Long-Term Care 1999: *With Respect to Old Age,* Cm 4192. London: HMSO.

Royal Commission on Mental Illness and Mental Deficiency 1957: *Report,* Cmd 169. London: HMSO.

Ryan, A. 1999: *Able and Willing.* London: Values into Action.

Ryan, M. 1994: *The Children Act 1989: Putting it into Practice.* Aldershot: Arena.

Ryburn, M. 1996: Child welfare services: developments in law, policy, practice and research. In J. Aldgate and M. Hill (eds), *Child Welfare Services; Developments in Law, Policy, Practice and Research*, London: Jessica Kingsley.

Schorr, A. 1995: *The Personal Social Services: An Outside View.* York: Joseph Rowntree Foundation.

Scull, A. T. 1979: *Museums of Madness: The Social Organisation of Insanity in 19th Century England.* London: Allen Lane.

Seebohm Report 1968: *Report of the Committee on Local Authority and Allied Personal Social Services,* Cmnd. 3703. London: HMSO.

Sellick, C. 1996: Short-term foster care. In J. Aldgate and M. Hill (eds), *Child Welfare Services; Developments in Law, Policy, Practice and Research*, London: Jessica Kingsley.

Sheldon, B. 1986: Social work effectiveness and experiments: Review and implications. *British Journal of Social Work*, 16 (2), 223–42.

Sheppard M. 1990: Social work and psychiatric nursing. In P. Abbott and C. Wallace (eds), *The Sociology of the Caring Professions*, Falmer Press, London.

Shore, P. 1985: *Local Authority Social Rehabilitation Services to Visually Handicapped People*. London: Royal National Institute for the Blind.

Simons, K. and Ward, L. 1997: *A Foot In The Door*. Manchester: National Development Group.

Simpson, B. 1994: Bringing the *unclear* family into focus: divorce and remarriage in contemporary Britain. *Man*, 29, 831–51.

Simpson, B. 1999: Nuclear fallout: divorce, kinship and the insecurities of contemporary family life. In J. Vail, J. Wheelock and M. Hill (eds), *Insecure Times*, London: Routledge, 119–36.

Sinfield, A. 1969: *Which Way for Social Work*, Fabian Tract 393. London: Fabian Society.

Sinson, J. 1992: *Group Homes and Community Integration of Developmentally Disabled People: Micro-Institutionalisation?* London: Jessica Kingsley.

Stevenson, O. 1973: *Claimant or Client?* London: Allen and Unwin.

Szasz, T. 1971: *The Manufacture of Madness*. London: Routledge and Kegan Paul.

Thane, P. 1982: *The Foundations of the Welfare State*. Harlow: Longman.

Thoburn, J. 1994: *Child Placement: Principles and Practice*. Aldershot: Wildwood House.

Thoburn, J. 1996: The community child care team. In M. Davies (ed.), *The Companion to Social Work*, Oxford: Blackwell, 290–6.

Todd, C. 1999: Information obtained in interview (manager of Nottingham Social Service Department).

Topliss, E. and Gould, B. 1981: *A Charter for the Disabled*. London: Blackwell and Robertson.

Townsend, P., Whitehead, M. and Davidson, N. (eds) 1992: *Inequalities in Health*. Harmondsworth: Penguin.

Triseliotis, J., Sellick, C., and Short R. 1995: *Foster Care: Theory and Practice*. London: Batsford.

Tunstill, J. 1996: Family support: Past, present and future challenges. *Child and Family Social Work*, 1 (3), 151–8.

Tunstill, J and Aldgate, J. 1999: *Children in Need; From Policy to Practice*. London: HMSO.

Utting, D. (ed.) 1998: *Children's Services Now and in the Future*. London: National Children's Bureau.

Utting, W. 1991: *Children in the Public Care: A Review of Residential Care*. London: HMSO.

Vallender, I. and Warren, C. 1997: *Family Centres; A Planning Guide for Agencies*, Insight No 1. Norwich: University of East Anglia/Family Support Network.

Walker, C. and Ryan, T. 1995: *Fair Shares For All?* Brighton: Pavilion Publishing.

Walker, C. and Walker, A. 1998: *Uncertain Futures: People with Learning Difficulties and Their Ageing Family Carers*. Brighton: Pavilion Publishing.

Ward, H. 1995: *Looking After Children; Research into Practice*. London: HMSO.

Webb, A. and Wistow, G. 1986: *Planning, Need and Scarcity*. London: Allen and Unwin.

Webster, C. 1998: *The National Health Service: A Political History*. Oxford: Oxford University Press.

Wilkinson, R. G. 1996: *Unhealthy Societies*, London: Routledge.

Williams, P. 1995: Residential and day services. In N. Malin (ed.), *Services for People with Learning Disabilities*, London: Routledge.

Willmott, P. 1986: *The Debate About Community*. London: Policy Studies Institute.

Wilson, A. and Hill, M. 1988: Social workers and welfare rights. *Social Services Research*, 5.

Wistow, G. 1987: Increasing private provision of social care: implications for policy. In R. Lewis (ed.), *Care and Control: Personal Social Services and the Private Sector*, London: Policy Studies Institute.

Wood, P. 1980: *International Classification of Impairments, Disabilities and Handicaps*. Geneva: World Health Organisation.

Index